HENRY WILSON:

Practical Radical

A PORTRAIT OF A POLITICIAN

KENNIKAT PRESS

NATIONAL UNIVERSITY PUBLICATIONS

SERIES IN AMERICAN STUDIES

Under the General Editorial Supervision of

JAMES P. SHENTON

Professor of History, Columbia University

Henry Wilson

HENRY WILSON:
Practical Radical
A PORTRAIT OF A POLITICIAN

Ernest McKay

NATIONAL UNIVERSITY PUBLICATIONS
KENNIKAT PRESS
Port Washington, N.Y. // London

Library of Congress Catalog Card No.: 70-139359

ISBN 0-8046-9010-3

Published by

Kennikat Press, Inc.

Port Washington, N.Y./London

For Ellen

Contents

HENRY WILSON:

Practical Radical

A PORTRAIT OF A POLITICIAN

ABBREVIATIONS

HL	Harvard Library
HSP	Historical Society of Pennsylvania
LC	Library of Congress
NYDT	*New York Daily Tribune*
NYT	*New York Times*
RBH	Rutherford B. Hayes Library

Introduction

Many years ago I came across a footnote in Allan Nevins' *Ordeal of the Union* which said that a biography of Henry Wilson was much needed. It intrigued me, but thousands of others had read his comment too, and I supposed that someone must have filled the gap. Still, I looked further and learned to my surprise that little had been done since 1876.

As the years have passed, my astonishment over the lack of attention for Wilson as a topic for historical research has declined. It was not because he was an obscurity, but because his papers were badly scattered. The Wilson Collection in the Library of Congress, as an example, consists of only about a hundred items and few of them shed much light on his life. It makes one suspect that historical fame is sometimes earned by the bulk of papers left behind rather than great achievement. If Wilson had been a diarist, no matter how dreary, he would be far better known today. But he was too much of an activist to be wrapped up in introspection. There were innumerable disappointments in tracking down leads, but gradually many of the pieces fit together. Hopefully, a picture of Henry Wilson, the politician, has emerged. Since life is not endless it seemed best to tell this story with the material now available.

The advancement from indentured servitude and cobbler to United States Senator and Vice President of the United States is a remarkable achievement in itself, and not as much in the American tradition as we like to think. It was a hard struggle and the

3

dominant motivating force throughout Wilson's career was undoubtedly his early exposure to poverty and shame. He never developed an interest in material things, money was unimportant, but he did acquire a thirst for recognition. Apocryphal or not, stories exist today in his birthplace, Farmington, New Hampshire, about his determination to make up for slights from some of his "betters". Somewhere in the recesses of his mind his change of name must have been connected with this attitude too. Complex psychological analyses are not needed to see that he genuinely identified with the underdog. He was one of them. But others, including members of his own family, suffered similar difficulties and did not rise very far. The difference probably lies in his great energy and persistence. After every defeat, and he had many, he found the strength to pull himself together and start all over again.

In Wilson's early political career, the aristocratic members of society recognized his forceful qualities, appreciated his appeal to the lower elements, and saw his usefulness as a lieutenant. When he had the audacity to compete in his own right against these socially and financially entrenched New Englanders, they were quick to suspect his motives.

Historical parallels are dangerous, but there are many startling comparisons between the affairs of today and mid-nineteenth century. They seem particularly pertinent when related to Henry Wilson. Anti-institutionalists were busy then as now. In every movement there is a place for trail blazers who create new public opinion with extreme ideas, but there is also a place for those who do more than make speeches and serve as sacrificial lambs. Talkers and doers are often men of different talents. Wilson did his share of talking, but it was as a doer that he excelled. He had seen the frequent harm that was done by the idealistic thought provokers who had a contempt for reality. In contrast, he was an infighter who was at his best under pressure when others were confused, or marked by their absence in a tense situation. He was also a man of expediency, an opportunist whose methods were not always above reproach. But along the way he developed an understanding of political institutions. He not only accepted the system, he learned how to use the machinery. To the amazement of many, he remained true to the cause of equal rights for everyone, but his career raises the age-old debate between means and ends.

Morality is an open question, and all men's lives are made up of many parts, good and bad. Some men are considered moral, others immoral. The judgments can rarely, if ever, be a matter of fact. More often they are opinions created by an aura that a person radiates. Just as some men are thought of as statesmen, others, in a less reverential way, are thought of as politicians without regard for real accomplishments or careful comparisons. Usually it is what men seem to be, rather than what they are that counts in everyday life. No one can be the final judge. Still, judgments are hastily made and given currency fairly and unfairly.

In his day, the unsanctimonious Henry Wilson frequently horrified people by his insensitivity to morals. Even his supporters hesitated to classify him with such "virtuous" contemporaries as Charles Francis Adams, Charles Sumner, and John Palfrey. But the haunting possibility remains that perhaps Henry Wilson, the callous politician, was judged too quickly. If political morality is related to achieving good for others, his life deserves a closer look and the thread of irony may work in his favor.

Like all historians, I incurred many debts during the years of research. I wish to particularly thank Professor Irwin Unger of New York University for his great kindness and careful criticism of the whole work, Professor Madeleine Hooke Rice of Hunter College for her guidance through the period from 1812 to 1855, and Professor LaWanda Cox of Hunter College for her interest in the chapter on Reconstruction. At the start of this project Professor David Donald, now of Johns Hopkins University, gave me some valuable advice in rapid-fire order at lunch one day. His cordial assistance to a total stranger made a lasting impression upon me. Professor Frank Otto Gatell of the University of California at Los Angeles was also a helpful friend. Responsibility for the failings of the completed book is, of course, mine.

Part of Chapter I appeared in *The New-England Galaxy*. Chapter III, in its essential form, appeared in *The New England Quarterly*. Part of Chapter IV appeared in *Mid-America*. The permission of the editors to reproduce the material, as well as to the Adams Manuscript Trust for permission to cite and quote from the Diary and Papers of Charles Francis Adams is deeply appreciated.

1

The Natick Cobbler

The grinding poverty, the desolate countryside, the hut, the worthless father, the industrious mother—stock ingredients for a tale of triumph over trial—were there from the beginning. Abigail Colbath had her first baby in a hut on the bank of the Cocheco River, about a mile south of the village of Farmington, New Hampshire. It was a boy, and she named him, not too handsomely, Jeremiah Jones. A bitter time of the year, February 16, 1812, and the lonely shack among the hills made a bleak setting for the birth of a child.

The new father, Winthrop Colbath, two years younger than his wife, worked at the sawmill on the river for wages of fifty cents a day.[1] He was no exception to the line of Colbaths that preceded him in New England. Originally from Scotland, the family emigrated to Northern Ireland during the reign of James I, and finally settled in America early in the eighteenth century. They had been a poor lot of farmers and, at twenty-five, it is not likely that Winthrop had any greater expectations for the new arrival than he had for himself. He was a drifter, a Rip Van Winkle sort, with a taste for whiskey, who wanted life to pass by with the barest amount of self exertion. His heritage, established for generations, was indifference and poverty.

Friends said that although the baby looked like his father, he later displayed the mind and character of his mother, perhaps

6

because the father was rarely mentioned approvingly. Abigail's maiden name was Witham, and she, too, came from a poor New England family. She did housework for some of the people in the village, who considered her more sensible and industrious than her husband, and she quickly introduced the child to life's hard realities. Many years later he said, "I know what it is to ask a Mother for bread when she has none to give."[2] But poverty did not halt the expansion of the family. Seven more children rapidly followed each other into the world.

Dreariness and tragedy filled their days. Abigail's anxious life was one of need mixed with the demands of children, sickness, and the curse of an alcoholic husband. Three of the children died young and she saw them buried in a field near their home. The Colbaths, struggling to survive, were members of a class of society to which southern aristocrats were wont to refer as "mudsills", an unskilled class deemed necessary to perform the mean duties of life.

Farmington in the 1820's was a typical New England village with a population of about 1,200, mostly farmers, located thirty-five miles east of Concord. It boasted a meeting house, tavern, general store, and schoolhouse. The white pines, the birches, the clear lakes, and White Mountains in the distance, made a luxuriant view in the summer, but the growing season was short. In the spring the corn around Boston would be well on its way before the Farmington men dug their plows into the stony soil. As a result there was no easy living, and little time to waste, if a farmer intended to provide for his family.

Jeremiah attended a small wooden schoolhouse in the village until he was ten. *Perry's Spelling Book*, Welch and Adam's *Arithmetic*, and *The American Preceptor*, which devoted a chapter to "The Triumph of Virtue", formed the curricular activities under the tutelage of Mistress Guy.

A story is told that at the age of eight Jeremiah got involved in a schoolboy scuffle in a sandbank near the Rochester Road, and that one of the prominent ladies of the village, Mrs. Anstress Eastman, for whom his mother occasionally worked, stopped the fight. As she looked at the ragged and restless ruffians it came into her head to ask if they could read. When the child answered quickly in the affirmative she invited him to her house to use her husband's library.[3] Mrs. Eastman took an interest in the lively little boy, and for a number of years helped him by giving him a Bible, lending him other books, and occasionally passing along "hand me down" clothes for him to wear. She was the sister of Levi Woodbury, later to distinguish himself as Governor of New Hampshire, Secretary of the Treasury under Martin Van Buren, and Associate Justice of the Supreme Court. Her interest in Jeremiah seems to have been important in arousing his interest in American history and government.

When Jeremiah was ten his parents were no longer able to support him at home, so they took the only practical alternative and let him work for his keep at the home of William Knight, a neighboring farmer. The Knights were hard working, highly respected members of the community, and their farm was considered a good place for a boy from a not too respectable family. If he was not treated too kindly, he was also not treated too severely, and for once he had plenty to eat.

In 1828 Winthrop Colbath formally signed an agreement with the farmer committing his son to be "bound out" for a period of four years from his next birthday. The indenture read that he shall:

> well and faithfully serve, demean himself, and be just and true to . . . William Knight . . . as his master, and keep his secrets, and everywhere willingly obey all his lawful commands . . . he shall not play at cards, dice, or any other unlawful games; he shall not haunt or frequent taverns, playhouses, or alehouses . . . he shall not commit fornication; he shall not contract matrimony; he shall not at any time, day or night, depart or absent himself from the service of his said master without his leave.

For services rendered under these restrictions, William Knight agreed to teach his apprentice the occupation of farmer, permit him to attend the District school one month each year, and

> will also find and allow his said apprentice, meat, drink, washing and apparel both linen and woolen, and all necessaries in sickness and in health . . . and, at the expiration of the said term, shall and will give to the said apprentice one yoke of likely working cattle . . . also a surtout for Sabbath Day wear, together with one good suit for everyday wear.[4]

Farmer Knight may have been a man of many virtues, but openhandness was not one of his more noticeable qualities. He

held a deed for the service of Jeremiah Colbath; it was a contract,
and he had every intention of gaining all the benefits that could
accrue to him. In the summer the bound out boy plowed, sowed,
and swung a scythe, and in the winter he cut timber. The one
month of schooling was begrudgingly permitted during slack
periods. That meant that attendance at school was scattered
throughout the year on a "catch as catch can" basis. The first year
Jeremiah went to the opening day of school, and did not show up
again for three weeks. There were always cows to milk, pigs to
feed, water to carry and butter to churn. The chores seemed
endless, and as he grew older they became heavier. He then
chopped chordwood, drove oxen, and worked the bucksaw.[5] In
the eyes of austere William Knight, school was of little consequence, and he and his family were suspicious of anyone interested in too much education. Book learning was no help to a
farmer.

A few small occasions brightened the boy's dreary life. Once
he was given three pennies and walked to and from a muster
seven miles away, managing to spend his entire fortune that gala
day. Another time he earned a penny for digging up a stump of
a tree, a back breaking job, but he was happy with the extra
money.

It was a lonely life for a friendly boy with few opportunities
to make friends. There were no companions, no games, no cherished memories to be recalled as an adult; years later a friend
said that he rarely heard him mention anyone he knew in his
Farmington days, and that he was completely unable to supply
any of the usual sentimental anecdotes of boyish escapades.[6]
Growing up in a land that was ideal for hunting and fishing, he
never even became more than a novice fisherman. Life for the
boy was chiefly made up of long hours of hard labor; to Mr.
Knight idleness was a curse. The young apprentice was a slave,
a restless and ambitious one, but still a slave.

Jeremiah's lack of education galled him so much he determined to teach himself as much as possible at every opportunity.
The opportunities for such learning came only on the Sabbath
or late at night when everyone was in bed. Some nights he would
run home to read *The Dover Gazette* that his mother, still a
loving influence in his life, would borrow from a neighbor; or
other nights he would sit near the kitchen fire in the Knight

farmhouse, and read his latest acquisition from the Eastman library. He burned pine knots for light because the master would not let him waste tallow.[7]

During his time of bondage he read hundreds of books, perhaps more than a thousand.[8] In the nationalistic decades that followed the War of 1812, a new group of American writers appeared on the scene; among them Washington Irving, James Fenimore Cooper, and William Cullen Bryant. The "bound out" boy devoured them all. *The Sketch Book,* and *The Leatherstocking Tales,* were interspersed with biographies, philosophy, history, and occasional issues of *The North American Review.* For all this reading, his was still a spotty education that depended upon a hit or miss selection of accessible books. He learned to appreciate literature, but never to be sure of his grammar or punctuation. He learned much of history, but little of art, something of religion, but nothing of music, a trifle of philosophy, nothing of science.

As the years of labor in the woods and fields passed, the boy developed into a powerful young man, five feet ten in height, with strong chest and arms. He had a high, broad forehead, a round face with wide mouth, and a complexion so dark that in the years ahead it would often be rumored that he was a gypsy. In this stern New England setting he manifested a cheerful nature and a sense of humor. The habit of hard work became a part of his nature, and the strenuous life served to make a strenuous man.

One Saturday, February 16, 1833, Jeremiah reached the end of his service. It was his twenty-first birthday, and in the literal sense he was "free, white, and twenty-one". In the afternoon the master paid his debt of six sheep and a yoke of oxen in accordance with the conditions of the indenture bond. The sheep were sold the same afternoon, but since he was unable to find a buyer for the oxen, he asked his former master if he would keep them for him until Monday. Knight agreed, but charged fifty cents for his trouble.

On Monday the oxen were sold to a man who gave a note for seventy-five dollars. Upon coming of age, Jeremiah had therefore accumulated the equivalent of eighty-four dollars.[9] This was a considerable sum, but still it represented less than seventeen dollars a year for the last five years of his service; meager compensation for the hard labor.

The new freedom of Jeremiah Colbath brought the new responsibility of finding a job, and work in New Hampshire was scarce. His first job was with another Farmington farmer and his daily routine was little changed. The day began, as it had before, in the black of early morning. He fed the stock before breakfast, and after breakfast, as the sun was rising, he would start off for the woods with his team and draw saw logs to the mill until after dark. For his first month's work he received six dollars, and he later said, "when I got the money; those dollars looked as large to me as the moon looks tonight."[10]

Anxious to get ahead, he walked to the neighboring towns looking for more profitable work. He thought he might find something that would pay as much as eight or nine dollars a month, but his visits to Great Falls, Salmon Falls, Dover, and Newmarket turned up nothing. So he was forced to stay a while longer in Farmington.

In June 1833, a Mr. Jones of Farmington presented a petition of Jeremiah Colbath before the New Hampshire House of Representatives for the alteration of his name. The request was grouped with others of a similar nature in a single bill and it was passed and approved by the Governor in July as Chapter 133 of the Laws of 1833.[11] From that date forward Jeremiah Jones Colbath was known as Henry Wilson, but the reason for the change has never been fully explained. Jeremiah Jones Colbath to Henry Wilson; certainly not a pretentious exchange that gained in euphony or camouflaged an unwanted alien strain. It had little to gain except simplicity.

There is one claim that he read the name in a book and that it appealed to him; another states that he was fascinated by a General James Wilson whose fame seems to have diminished as Henry Wilson's grew. A more probable reason for the changed name was that his father was a drunkard. All three stories may be partly true, but none offers a complete explanation. His acquisition of a new name may have been motivated by pride or shame, but Wilson never made the slightest effort to conceal his parentage. He hated alcoholism for he could never remember a time when the tragedy of drink was not present in his home. His earliest memories were filled with the distress that it created, and his reaction made him a teetotaler for life, but whatever his faults, he was never a prig. Speaking of his family he once remarked, "I have abhorred drunkenness while I have loved and pitied its victims."[12] He was always on good terms with both parents and supported them for many years. At the time they appeared to have approved the change of name. At any rate, whatever the cause, it was an unusual thing to do, and may conceal some significant psychological trait. His brothers, John, Charles, Sam and George all retained their original surname.

In December 1833, restlessly looking for wider worlds to conquer, the new Henry Wilson heard that good prices were being paid for making shoes in Massachusetts and he decided to go there to make his living. He packed his belongings in a cotton handkerchief, tied it in a bundle, cut a hickory stick and started on foot for Natick a hundred miles away.

The trip was an arduous one. By the third day his feet were so badly blistered he had to stop at Newburyport to buy a twenty-five cent pair of slippers. One hill seemed to follow another, but he kept moving, and that night reached Lynnfield where he stopped at the home of a Quaker. Before going to bed, Henry insisted upon paying for his room in advance because he wanted to leave early the next morning before the family was up. The Friend accepted, but only reluctantly, since he felt that this implied a distrust of his guest's word.

On the fourth day Henry reached Boston. Weary from the journey, he still took the time to walk over to Breed's Hill to see where the Battle of Bunker Hill had been fought. The corner stone for the monument had been laid a few years before by Lafayette, and one of his heroes, Daniel Webster, had been the orator of the day. From there he wandered downtown to Washington Street to take a look at the office of his old companion, *The North American Review*. Then he made the last lap to nearby Natick. He arrived about midnight and took a room at the Sherman House. The whole trip cost one dollar and twenty-five cents.[13]

He had no job and no knowledge of the shoe industry, but an inherent optimism made him confident that Natick was the place where he could settle down to a prosperous future. Natick—an Indian name meaning "Place of Hills"—was then a pleasant village situated on Pegan Hill in the southern part of Middlesex County, almost half way between Boston and Worcester. The Charles River skirted the south side of town, brooks and woods gave variety to the scenery, and Lake Cochituate, seven miles in length, added to the peacefulness and beauty. Coming into town, one of the first things to attract the eye was a double row of newly planted trees, mostly elms, along West Central Street. The population was barely a thousand, the annual school budget was less than $800, and although shoemaking had gained a foothold, there were no large factories. Farming was still the chief activity.

The shoemaking was done in workshops called "tenfooters" because their cramped dimensions were usually ten feet square. Each shop had four to eight benches, and each bench was placed far enough from the wall, or the next bench, to allow the cobblers' arms to swing out while they sewed with full length thread. The garret, reached by a ladder, was known as a "cockloft" and served as the common receptacle for litter.

The days of mass production were still far in the future. Instead of working on a single part, the workers, who had little skill, made the entire shoe which was called a "brogan". It was a cheap product made for the slave markets in the South and the West Indies, and sold wholesale for about a dollar a pair.[14]

Eager to start work and learn the trade, Henry Wilson rashly hired himself out to a William Legro who had a little shop in the western part of town. Legro agreed to teach him how to make shoes in return for five months labor. It was a foolish deal; in a few days Henry realized that he had been far too impetuous since the trade could be learned fairly easily. There were only four main steps in making a shoe, cutting, fitting, lasting and bottoming. A lapstone and hammer were used for pounding the leather; a knife for cutting the sole and upper leather: an awl to bore holes; and a needle to sew.

At the end of seven weeks Henry bought out his time with Legro for fifteen dollars and went to work on his own account. Fifteen hour days then became routine and often he worked longer. A friend claimed that sometimes Wilson worked all night and two days in succession. His ambition, supported by his physical strength and aversion to inactivity, generated a desire to increase his output. His most remarkable feat of production was the bottoming of fifty-four pairs of shoes without sleep. His landlady thought he was a nice young man, "but keeps us awake by his continued pounding through the night."[15]

In an ordinary week the young shoemaker would make about

five dollars, and of that amount he would pay fifty cents for pegs and two dollars for board.[16] By hard work rather than shrewdness he slowly scraped some money together. His ambition was goaded not simply by the desire to make money, but by the desire to make money to advance his education. Working at his bench, he dreamed that he would go back to school, then to college, and some day become a lawyer. Legend has it that he even announced to a fellow cobbler in a particularly optimistic moment that he intended to be a United States Senator.[17]

Henry became a boarder at the home of Deacon William Coolidge who boasted the largest library in town, a convenience that was certainly not a coincidence. It is variously estimated that the library contained anywhere from fifty to two hundred volumes, but whatever the number, they served a useful purpose. Henry became acquainted with such diverse authors as Voltaire and Oliver Goldsmith, and with more European and American history.

Taking precious time off from his work, he also went to hear Edward Everett speak on the Battle of Lexington. It would have appalled the great orator if he had realized that on that day his rich, musical voice had helped to inspire a young man who in time to come he would regard as a political hoodlum. But the impressionable young man was impressed, as he was on another occasion when he listened to Daniel Webster, a fellow native of New Hampshire.[18]

After three years of overwork, Henry's health broke down. A doctor diagnosed his trouble as a hemorrhage of the lungs and suggested that he go south to recuperate. So in May 1836 he set out for humid Washington, D.C., a strange place for a rest cure. It might seem that his selection of a rehabilitation center was guided by an interest in its political rather than its therapeutic climate. From his window on the train to Washington, Wilson for the first time saw slaves working in the Maryland fields. Touched by the scene, he made some remarks against slavery to the gentleman next to him and was informed that such sentiments were not permitted in the State of Maryland.[19]

In Washington, the convalescent found that the condition of his health did not prevent him from visiting the Congressional galleries and listening to the current debates. He also visited the Williams slave pens at Seventh and B Streets, and saw manacled slaves separated from their families and sold at auction. Not long free from his own bondage, Wilson's sympathy naturally went out to the underdog. He understood the agonies and confinement of the Negroes, and the degradation of the scene made a deep mark upon his mind. From this time on, Wilson was an enemy of slavery.[20]

The Washington atmosphere apparently had a beneficial affect upon the patient because the period of recovery lasted only for the month of June. Refreshed and broadened by his visit to the capital, he returned to New England with a stronger determination than ever to continue his education. Somehow he had managed to accumulate $700, and he felt confident that he could finance himself. On the first of July he started a course at an academy at Stratford, New Hampshire, and in the fall he entered another academy at Wolfeboro for a term. That winter he also taught at a district school in town.

In the spring of 1837, he transferred to still another school at Concord, directed by a Reverend Stone. Here he had a heavy schedule made up of Euclid's "Geometry", Newman's "Rhetoric", "Mental Philosophy", Butler's "Analogy", and "The Geography of the Heavens".[21] While a student at Concord, Henry was selected to serve as a delegate to a state antislavery convention held in that town. It was the first step into the political activity that had long attracted him, but he accepted the appointment with some reservation. Although his sympathies were opposed to slavery, he hesitated to identify himself with a movement that was far from popular, particularly with members of the Whig Party that dominated Massachusetts. Once engaged in the assignment, however, he gave it all his energy and enthusiasm, and was flattered when Wendell Phillips supported some of the views he had expressed.[22]

Happy with school and with prospects for the future, Wilson suddenly found himself penniless once again. The man to whom he had loaned his money for investment while at school had lost everything. All hope for the future was gone. Relaying the news to a classmate, John French, as they took a walk in the woods, Wilson broke into tears. Without his savings he was sure that his chances for a successful career had been blighted. He was now so destitute he could not even pick up a letter at the Post Office without borrowing money to pay for the overdue postage, and he owed two or three weeks board. A Wolfeboro friend came to his rescue by inviting him to board with him, and to pay when he was able. He remained there until the end of the autumn term, and that winter earned enough money teaching school at Natick to repay his benefactor.

When school at Natick was over, Henry had twelve dollars left after paying all his debts. With that amount for a capital invest-ment, he reluctantly went back into the shoe business. It was the panic year of 1837 which had been caused in part, at least, by Andrew Jackson's "wildcat" financing and the blow fell heavily upon farmers and workers. Wilson bought leather to make a case of cheap brogans with his own hands, took them to Jonathan Forbush & Company, wholesale dealers on Blackstone Street, Boston, and exchanged them for more leather and a small amount of cash.[23] Once again there were the long hours at the cobbler's bench, but this time there were fewer bright dreams for the future.

Despite the hard times, Henry compulsively pushed himself ahead. As the year 1838 progressed, conditions in the trade im-proved and he was able to employ additional help. The extra work was often done by young boys and girls, and in keeping with the practice of the times, the pay was frequently collected by the father. There were also "freighters", men who took out work from the shop to do at home. Since Henry Wilson was an experienced shoemaker, he could carefully supervise his employees and de-mand good workmanship. He paid his laborers promptly, and was friendly to them, and was considered a fair, courteous, and honest businessman. At first he occupied space in a shop owned by a David Whitney; later, he bought his own "tenfooter" on Central Street. For the year 1838 his total dollar volume reached the amazing sum of $17,000 and his eighteen employees turned out 18,000 pairs of shoes which were sold as far away as Mont-gomery, Alabama, and New Orleans, Louisiana.[24]

In the next few years Wilson became a typical small entrepre-neur of the shoe industry, but in spite of his rapid progress, he was not well adapted to the role of shoe manufacturer. He had no real business acumen, and little natural inclination to make money. His gains were the result of the forced application of his energy, not the expression of native commercial ability. It was a way to make a living, but he thought that it was a dull way to live. The accumulation of money held no fascination and gave him no satisfaction. Wilson was ambitious; ambitious to the mar-

row of his bones, but the goal in the back of his mind was the
power and glory of politics; politics meant adventure and excitement.

One of the few people to extend a friendly hand to Wilson in
the early days was Erasmus Moore, minister of the Natick Congregational Church. It was a kindness that he never forgot for
Moore was a man of influence in the community when Henry
was a nonentity.[25] One service that the minister performed was to
organize a debating club for the young men of the town. It was
a pleasant pastime in the simple life of the village that broadened
the horizon of the participants and developed their skill in argument. Once or twice a week they would meet in the old schoolhouse. Henry, frightened at first, tired from a hard day's work,
learned to do battle and to think on his feet. He could be quick
with a historical reference, and he had determination and natural
force. The value of the opportunity was clear; he knew that politics demanded the ability to defend as well as to propound, to
create confidence as well as to be confident. Henry also became
acquainted with some of his more intellectually inclined neighbors, and established himself as a citizen of Natick. Erasmus
Moore had brought a stray sheep into the fold. It seemed a matter of little consequence and yet it was a major step in Henry
Wilson's education as a man and politician. From the Natick
Debating Society, he moved into the world he wanted, politics.

Henry Wilson attracted sufficient attention in Natick to be a
candidate for the General Court on a temperance ticket in 1837.
He failed of election, but the attempt publicized his name and
strengthened his acquaintance with local politicians. His life
broadened, and Natick became for him a comfortable place to
live. He even found time for some social life, a phase of living
that had been almost unknown to him. Deacon Coolidge, his
landlord, proved to be a good counsellor, and the First Congregational Church was the center of many pleasant associations.
The friendless boy from Farmington now found that he had many
friends. They liked him, and he liked them; in fact, he seemed to
like everybody, and as time progressed he seemed to know everybody in town. By nature he was an enthusiast and the trait developed an open personality that attracted people to him. Then too,
he was blessed with an aversion to pettiness, a unique asset for
someone living in a small town. Early in his career he learned

that differing opinions were never a reason for personal animosity, and he retained that insight throughout his life.

In the spring of 1840 Wilson challenged the local Democrats to a debate on national issues. The contest caused considerable notoriety in the vicinity since three meetings were required before there was any semblance of a discussion. Wilson confronted his first opponent, Charles Herring, a Natick man, with eighteen or twenty charges against the national administration. The Democrat failed to answer the charges because he had been under the impression that the debate would be confined to the currency question. A second meeting was arranged, but the Democratic opponent fared no better when Wilson, well fortified with reference material, arrived to discuss general currency principles. His startled adversary, who this time had been brought from Framingham, immediately advised the audience of farmers and workers that he was prepared only to handle the Sub-Treasury question. After some private negotiation between the parties, the Democrat agreed that he would try to reply if Wilson would present his argument.

Wilson then expounded the view that the government was duty bound to establish a sound and uniform currency. He said that the Bank of the United States furnished such a currency and that the Democratic sponsored Deposit Banks caused an overissue of bank paper and stimulated speculation. The administration brought forward the Sub-Treasury as their great financial measure, but, Wilson argued, it tended to crush the banks, destroy the credit system, and reduce wages and the value of property. In rebuttal his opponent rose, noted the late hour, and stated that he was not opposed to banks, credit or the laboring man.

The unsatisfactory conclusion to the second engagement called for a third meeting. For this encounter the Democrats imported a rising young politician from Boston, Amasa Walker, to handle the situation. The third debate had greater balance, but the results were indefinite since Walker also agreed that labor would be benefited by a sound currency. Amidst the claims and counter claims over the meetings which appeared in the Whig *Atlas* and the Democratic Boston *Morning Post*, Wilson gained by the attention that he received and by the public impression that he was prepared to take on all comers in debate.[26]

Jonathan Mann, a Natick Whig, later said that Wilson's nickname, "Natick Cobbler", was first used derisively against him at this time by the Democratic *Post,* but that was not the case. Correspondents to the paper respectfully referred to Wilson as a shoe manufacturer whom Whigs styled a "Natick Cobbler". The *Atlas,* on the other hand, frequently mentioned the "Natick Cobbler" and appeared to enjoy creating the image of a laborer speaking for the Whig cause. Sobriquets were popular in the politics of 1840, and Wilson was not the only politician with a handy title to give him identity. In Illinois there was a young railsplitter coming into prominence; in Ohio there was Tom Corwin, the "Wagon Boy", and elsewhere the Whig Party abounded with blacksmiths, cobblers, and other struggling workingmen.

Later that Spring the Whigs heralded Wilson as "a cobbler from the country" at a great gathering at Charlestown. Despite an uncandid claim that he had not expected to be called upon, Wilson made an effective speech that went back to the election of Andrew Jackson who, he claimed, substituted the spoils system for his campaign promises of retrenchment and reform. He also denounced the Customs Houses, Land Offices and Post Offices as "sinks of corruption," and again defended the Bank of the United States. Obviously impressed, a Democratic correspondent for the *Post* wrote that the speech was far superior to Whig speeches generally and that in due time Wilson would be convinced of the error of his ways and "renounce the counter jumpers and bank clerks, with whom he is now associated, and come out manfully for mechanics and laborers."[27]

In 1840 the Whigs nominated William Henry Harrison, the hero of Tippecanoe, to oppose Martin Van Buren for the presidency. It was a rowdy campaign which lacked principles, though it made much of the common man. Some Whig orators painted President Van Buren as an effete aristocrat who put cologne in his whiskers. There were mass meetings, processions, banners, and torchlights galore, and the western custom of stump speaking became popular in New England. The new political technique created an opportunity for a number of novices, Henry Wilson among them, to emerge from obscurity. Young Democrats in Massachusetts also appeared initially at this time, politicos like Nathaniel Banks and George Boutwell, who paralleled Wilson's career for many years.[28]

There were practical reasons for the Whigs to feature Wilson as a stump speaker. They had learned from sad experience with the Jacksonians that polite oratory to limited audiences was not the way to win elections. Now they knew that the times required vigorous, bombastic speech which would appeal to the masses, many of them newly enfranchised or drawn to the polls for the first time. Even though the laboring class of the country was suffering from hard times under a Democratic administration, the Whigs still were handicapped by their aristocratic reputation. The proper antidote to the claim that they were the representatives of northeastern financial power was to create the illusion that the Whigs were pro-labor. Actually, the Party represented a combination of widely varying political elements. Included were Masons and Anti-Masons, tariff men and anti-tariff men, proslavery and antislavery, and advocates and opponents of the Bank and internal improvements who shared a common opposition to Jackson and Jacksonism.[29] It helped to have a mechanic rail against the Democrats and place the blame for reduced wages at Van Buren's door. Moreover, the shoe industry was growing in importance in the state. It was a very useful tactic to give distinction to a member of the craft.[30] Another reason, and most important, was Henry Wilson's personal magnetism. He spoke plainly but effectively at a time when other young Whigs were busy imitating the polished elocution of the popular orator Edward Everett who was considered a model of platform perfection.

Although there would always be some who thought Wilson's method of speaking was heavy and unattractive, his confidence grew and he could sway an audience. His listeners liked his total lack of affectation, his simplicity, inexhaustible good nature, and kindliness. His spirit matched that of the noisy campaign. He easily identified himself with the poor and lowly, yet he could be forcible too. His poverty had given him an unquenchable drive. Although he spent hours in preparation, he would bend over the podium to make close contact with the audience and give the impression that he was making an impromptu speech. Few knew that his effort represented hours of rehearsal in Deacon Coolidge's old oak grove. Log cabins, hard cider, "Tippecanoe and Tyler too," blended perfectly with the style of the "Natick Cobbler" who became known as an interesting campaign personality. He found himself in demand at Whig gatherings where he was then proudly announced under his new nickname. Stumping the surrounding countryside, Charlestown, Cambridge, Roxbury, Lowell, Lynn, Taunton, the canvass received all his natural energy and enthusiasm.[31]

But for all his frenzied activity, Henry was not too busy to take notice of Harriet Malvina Howe, the sixteen year old daughter of Amasa and Mary Howe of Natick. Gentle and refined, she was described as "a lady of education". Little is known of their courtship, but mingled with the hectic campaign, it should have been a warning to the innocent Harriet for the years ahead. Politics was now the dominating influence in Wilson's life, and a successful wife for this restless man would require much patience. They were married on October 28, 1840 by the Reverend Samuel Hunt, the new minister at the Natick Congregational Church. On Election Day Harrison won the Presidency and Henry Wilson gave his bride the good news of his own election as representative from Natick to the General Court of Massachusetts.

The new legislature convened the following January. The lower house had some able members that year, particularly among the Whigs, but many of the places were handed to retired merchants, lawyers, or mechanics, as a compliment for services rendered to the party. Attendance of members was irregular; a full House consisted of about three hundred and fifty, but sixty made a quorum. It was a common practice for merchants or lawyers to casually visit the House, look over the orders of the day, and then go on to their personal business. If an emergency arose, a call would be sent out for them and they would drift back when needed.[32]

In each corner of the attractive but chilly chamber there was a wood fire that radiated little heat. In the winter months, when they usually met, the representatives sat uncomfortably in their overcoats and hats on long seats that had no cushions; when one of them rose to speak he would take off his hat and address the Speaker. On the back of the seat in front of each member was a narrow shelf upon which a book might be placed or a memorandum written, and under the seat was a drawer for documents.[33]

Henry Wilson was one member who had no intention of missing the business of the day. When he entered the House for the first time he noticed that an old farmer had drawn one of the better seats; so he quickly offered him three dollars to exchange places. The farmer accepted the money just as quickly as it was offered and Wilson happily sat in a strategic location where he could get down to work.[34]

Not many days of the session passed before Wilson attracted controversy with his first speech. His maiden effort, presumably as a spokesman for the workingman, must have filled more than one of his impoverished constituents with misgivings. He opposed a bill to exempt laborers' wages from attachment because he felt that it would encourage dishonesty among the working classes. In his opinion it was time to legislate for the poor creditor as well as the poor debtor.

After a lapse of a few days, Ichabod Lindsey, a bold speaker from Charlestown, replied that during the last campaign he heard a cobbler from Natick tell the laboring men of his town that the laws, made by the Democrats, allowed the last dollar of the poor man to be taken from him, and that the speech was so persuasive he almost became a Whig himself. Now he could not believe that any man could be so hypocritically inconsistent.

But the new member from Natick was neither subdued nor embarrassed, and he responded with the assurance of a veteran legislator. He regretted to take the time to reply to the "gentleman", he begged pardon, "the member", from Charlestown who belatedly attacked him. His campaign speech, he claimed, dealt with general politics, not state events, and he never uttered the sentiments about the last dollar of the laborer's wages. He did not seek popularity, but merely acted in accordance with his conscience and hoped that the bill would be recommitted. And it was.[35] His line of reasoning may not have been consistent with his campaign image, but he carried off his argument and at the same time remained a friend in the minds of workingmen. The characterization as the "Natick cobbler" was too well impressed upon his public to shake their faith. Also, it was still possible to speak as a small businessman and have good relations with labor. Conflicts between capital and labor were not always sharp because most workingmen hoped to move up in society and frequently succeeded. Wilson was an example of that upward mobility, and since he had been both a laborer and a capitalist he could speak genuinely about both. Throughout his career he would be identified with workingmen while maintaining a pro-business attitude.

Wilson also spoke in favor of a bill repealing a lingering old slave code which forbade intermarriage of whites and Negroes because it was founded on inequality and caste. Thus in his first session he exhibited the two dominant strains of his political philosophy; he was liberal in social affairs, conservative in economic matters. Personally and as a politician, he combined resentment of social inequality with a New Englander's esteem for the right of property.[36]

He was already fretting about the equivocation of the Whig Party on the slavery issue. He had not forgotten the manacled slaves that he had seen in Washington seven years before. Now he wanted to do something politically to help their cause, and he saw party politics as the most effective means. The election of 1840 resulted in the triumph of the Whigs, but Wilson was aware that little had been done for the cause of free men, and with the accession of John Tyler to the presidency, it appeared that the Slave Power was still in control of the Federal government. Abolition remained a despised cause. It was only a few years before that Whittier had said that to advocate emancipation, or to defend those who did so "was like preaching democracy in Constantinople, or religious toleration in Paris on the eve of St. Bartholomew".[37] Slavery was not a respectable topic of conversation for respectable people. More than one well-to-do Boston family owed its comfortable existence to commercial ties with the cotton interests and consequently thought it best not to magnify the issue. While they may not have been for slavery, they were certainly not for abolition. New England aristocrats like Wendell Phillips and Thomas Higginson, who dared to speak for abolition had automatically become social outcasts. Social ostracism was hardly a problem for Henry Wilson. His New England world was far from the life of the rich, respectable Winthrops, Lowells, or Ticknors. In their circles such people were as much alarmed about mechanics taking an interest in politics as they were about people who talked too much about the evils of slavery.

But the antislavery movement, especially in its political phase, was on the rise. Many of the "best people" might ignore it, they could oppose it, but they could not stop it. Here and there men and women broke away from the docile crowd to form the core of a formidable minority. In the small villages and rural areas there were mechanics, farmers, and small businessmen who pressed forward with the unpopular cause. Henry Wilson was one of these. Wilson was not afraid to speak up about slavery in unfriendly quarters. But by 1840, it was no longer an heroic thing to do since his constituency in Middlesex County was already a stronghold of abolition principles.[38]

By 1841 Wilson was expressing grave doubts about the Whig victory of the year before. The party leaders disappointed him and he feared that defeat and disgrace awaited them. Although he was busy selling shoes, six thousand pairs in three weeks, he breathlessly wrote to William Schouler, a Whig editor, "For one I had much rather be in the minority than abandon our principles." Already he talked about returning to his "original obscurity".[39] He had hoped for little from Harrison, but he feared everything from Tyler.[40]

On the local scene the Loco Focos, radical Democrats, sniped at Wilson by spreading stories that he was an overeager office seeker. He denied the charge and claimed that he never would seek office as long as he could earn his bread. "I am not qualified to fill an office that would be an object of ambition and to fill one of the menial places under the government poor as I am I am too proud to take. The Locos feel mighty pleased when they can get a paragraph in a paper abusing me."[41]

Wilson won re-election to the 1842 session of the General Court and became a member of the Joint Standing Committee on Manufactures. A number of competent men of the State were members of the House that year. The Speaker was Thomas Kinnicutt from the politically powerful city of Worcester, a man widely respected for his fairness. John C. Gray, son of a leading Boston merchant, served as Chairman of the Finance Committee. George T. Bigelow, an able and even-tempered Whig, later became Chief Justice of the State. Many considered sensitive John P. Robinson of Lowell, an English and Classics scholar, as the best equipped member. John Palfrey, an antislavery Whig was on hand, as was Charles Francis Adams, at thirty-five already a leader in the debates on slavery, and perhaps the most illustrious of all.

Adams, once described by Marcus Morton as "the greatest iceberg of the Northern hemisphere", had the prestige of his family name, and all the advantages needed for political success except a warm personality. He was a nervous speaker and when he became excited his head would give a violent jerk as though he was about to be decapitated.[42] His aloofness kept more than one person at a distance, but not Henry Wilson. Eager to extend his friendships and political contacts, he talked to everyone high and low, and in future years he seemed to be personally acquainted with every citizen in the state. It was natural that he should cultivate Adams, and perhaps it was just as natural that Adams who was also politically ambitious, should cultivate Wilson. To Wilson, Adams was worth cultivating because he was a prominent member of the Whig party, with a common interest in the antislavery cause. To Adams, Wilson was a hard working practical politician who continually made the rounds collecting information about the party, people, and the antislavery fight, and who could be useful to him in fulfilling his own ambitions. In the next few years they kept in close touch with one another.

Wilson's major contribution during this session of the General Court was his participation in a report supporting discriminatory duties on imports, which claimed that "If protection is not afforded, the American laborer must compete with the half-starved laborer of Europe. He must work cheaper and live cheaper. Massachusetts cannot afford to sacrifice her working population. She is not ready to stop the music of the loom, the wheel, the spindle, and the hammer, or the more silent workings of the awl and needle."[43]

Although Wilson had done nothing remarkable in his first two sessions in the state legislature, it was an invaluable experience for him. His life took on new color; he liked the atmosphere of the state capital and he loved being with "the boys". More than that, he discovered people from strata of society that he had never before known; he heard ideas expressed and challenged; and he began to learn the intricacies of parliamentary procedure and political maneuver. If he introduced no significant legislation, he demonstrated to his associates a willingness to work and a strong personality.

By the summer of 1842 Wilson had decided not to run for re-election to the General Court, although he did flirt with the prospect of trying for the State Senate. He admitted to William Schouler, editor of the *Atlas*, "You mention about my being nominated for the Senate, and I should like it, of course most any young man would and I shall not go as representative this fall. No doubt I shall have liberty to stay at home and spend the long evenings with my wife so I shall not be disappointed at the result."[44]

Since he had just completed his new home on Central Street, and "snugly stored with it", he probably thought that he was sincere. But his anxiety for political advancement makes it hard to believe that it would not have been painful if he found that he had let a good opportunity pass by. As it turned out, he did accept the nomination for the Senate, but lost the election.

His association with Schouler was an early example of his lifelong practice of developing a close relationship with news-papermen, reporters, editors, and publishers. Among them, eventually, were William Robinson, Samuel Bowles, Horace Greeley, and Alexander McClure. He realized, perhaps before many of the politicians of his day, the importance of working for a good press. Often he would oblige by sending an article on some current issue that an editor might request. At first he did not like to write, but as the years passed he became quite prolific. He liked to give editors his views. In the summer of 1842 he told Schouler that he hoped the Massachusetts Whigs would not be foolish enough to commit themselves to the Ken-tuckian Henry Clay, General Winfield Scott, or anyone else for the 1844 Presidential nomination. He felt their friends should maintain their antislavery principles, and when the time came they would find the right man. He also thought that it would be a good idea to have old John Quincy Adams run for gov-ernor. "We could swamp the state with him."[45]

During the next two years Wilson tended to his shoemaking, but he was also active in party affairs and in the state militia. It was probably natural to expect that he would have an interest in military things. A student of the battles of the Revolution, and an outdoor man who was at home with the rougher elements of the town, he found that drilling on the village green was a congenial pastime. Popular with the men, they elected him a Major of the First Regiment of Artillery, Third Brigade of Massachusetts Volunteer Militia, of which his friend William Schouler was then a Colonel. He had a genuine interest in the regiment that went beyond a mere military pose, and he thor-oughly enjoyed his new-found status in the community as an officer and gentleman.

He was active in the affairs of the Natick Lyceum, too, particularly in trying to induce lecturers to appear before it. In a letter to the historian George Bancroft he once wrote, "We have a Lyceum composed of a few mechanics and we have obtained the services of some very able speakers and we are very anxious to have you come if you can do it—we are poor but if you can come we will give you ten dollars and pay your expenses."[46]

Wilson built an active life for himself. But behind his public interests was the continual struggle to make his way. In his strong desire to close the gap between the poor boy that he once was, and the member of the governing class that he hoped to be, he intertwined the joys of the strenuous life with intellectual pursuits, military affairs, and politics, but it was a harsh climb upward.

Henry Wilson's early days consequently set the pattern for his later political life. Poverty, limited schooling, and severe tasks were countered by boundless energy, enthusiasm, and ambition. Other self-made contemporaries, like Nathaniel Banks, "The Bobbin Boy", who rose to become Speaker of the House of Representatives of the Congress of the United States, would acquire the veneer of a Back Bay aristocrat, but "The Natick Cobbler", not given to affectation, would always remain the restless, unrefined man of the people.

NOTES

[1] *NYDT*, Nov. 24, 1875.

[2] Elias Nason and Thomas Russell, *The Life and Public Service of Henry Wilson* (Boston: B. B. Russell, 1876), p. 17.

[3] Jonathan B. Mann, "Henry Wilson's Boyhood," *The Historical Collections of the Historical, Natural History and Library Society* (South Natick, Mass., Publ. by the Society, 1910), p. 28.

[4] *The Natick Bulletin*, Dec. 31, 1875.

[5] *Henry Wilson* (Farmington, N.H.: The Farmington-New Durham Historical Society, Inc., August 21-22, 1954), p. 8.

[6] Mann was a personal friend of Wilson's from Natick. *The Historical Collections of the Historical, Natural History and Library Society*, p. 29.

[7] *The Natick Bulletin*, Jan. 28, 1876; *Boston Daily Commonwealth*, Sept. 24, 1853.

[8] Alexander K. McClure, *Recollections of Half A Century* (Salem, Mass.: The Salem Press Co., 1902), p. 237.

[9] *NYDT*, Nov. 24, 1875.

[10] Nason and Russell, *Wilson*, p. 21.

[11] *New Hampshire House Journal*, 1833, p. 28.

[12] Henry Wilson, Speech on "Prohibition", Tremont Temple, April 15, 1867, publ. by Mass. State Temperance Alliance.

[13] *NYDT,* Nov. 24, 1875; *Henry Wilson* (The Farmington-New Durham Historical Society), pp. 9-10.

[14] Blanche Evans Hazard, *Organization of The Boot and Shoe Industry in Massachusetts Before 1875* (Cambridge: Harvard University Press, 1921), pp. 3, 4, 48, 70.

[15] Nason and Russell, *Wilson,* p. 25.

[16] *NYDT,* Nov. 24, 1875, p. 1.

[17] Nason and Russell, *Wilson,* pp. 25, 36.

[18] *Ibid.,* p. 26.

[19] Wilson dated his opposition to slavery from the time of his first trip to Washington. He related this experience in a speech delivered in Philadelphia on the thirtieth anniversary of the American Anti-Slavery Society, Dec. 4, 1863, and reported in *The Liberator,* Dec. 25, 1863.

[20] *Ibid.*

[21] Nason and Russell, *Wilson,* p. 34.

[22] *NYDT,* Nov. 24, 1875.

[23] Jonathan B. Mann, *The Life of Henry Wilson* (Boston: James R. Osgood & Co., 1872), p. 15.

[24] Hazard, *Boot and Shoe Industry,* pp. 69-70.

[25] Wilson to William B. Claflin, February 1, 1858, Claflin MSS, Rutherford B. Hayes Library.

[26] Boston *Atlas,* March 25, April 8, 1840; Boston *Morning Post,* March 30, April 13, 1840.

[27] Boston *Morning Post,* May 22, 1840.

[28] Mrs. William S. Robinson, ed., *"Warrington" Pen Portraits* (Boston: Publ. by Mrs. W. S. Robinson, 1877), p. 20.

[29] Robert G. Gunderson, *The Log Cabin Campaign* (Louisville: University of Kentucky Press, 1957), pp. 7-16, 207, 216.

[30] George S. Boutwell, *Reminiscences of Sixty Years in Public Affairs* (2 Vols.; New York: McClure, Phillips & Co., 1902), I, 1, 79.

[31] Nason and Russell, *Wilson,* pp. 45, 46.

[32] Boutwell, *Reminiscences,* I, 71, 72.

[33] *Ibid.*

[34] Nason and Russell, *Wilson,* p. 46.

[35] Boston *Atlas,* Jan. 26, 1841; Feb. 1, 1841.

[36] Nason and Russell, *Wilson,* p. 48.

[37] Henry Wilson, "Lecture on American Slavery", n.d. (1855?), Boston Public Library.

[38] Mrs. W. S. Robinson, ed., *Pen Portraits,* p. 19.

[39] Henry Wilson to William Schouler, July 5, 1841, Schouler MSS, MHS.

[40] Henry Wilson, *History of the Rise and Fall of the Slave Power in America* (3 Vols., Boston: James R. Osgood & Co., 1875) I, 424.

[41] Wilson to Schouler, July 5, 1841; Schouler MSS, MHS.

[42] Boutwell, *Reminiscences,* I, 72, 73.

[43] *Massachusetts General Court Legislative Documents*—1842, House I-47, Report No. 22, Feb. 9, 1842, p. 8.

[44] Wilson to Schouler, June 2, 1842, Schouler MSS, MHS.

[45] *Ibid.*

[46] Henry Wilson to George Bancroft, Feb. 16, 1843, Bancroft MSS, MHS.

2
Free Soil

Wilson, like all politicians, loved to think and talk about possible presidential candidates. But the national scene in 1844 disappointed him. He believed that the Slave Power had forced the issue of immediate annexation of Texas upon the country, and he saw no prospect that the White House was ready to challenge this position. This struck him as wrong, sad, and humiliating. His own view was simple. He completely opposed annexation as part of a gigantic intrigue to perpetuate slavery. He saw the Slave Power as a commanding influence with the strength to make other interests bend to its wishes. Sometime later he wrote:

> It was as if somewhere some imperious autocrat or secret conclave held court or council, in which slavery's every interest, necessity, and demand were considered and cared for, and from which were issued its stern and inexorable needs.[1]

Wilson defined the Slave Power as the political influence which legally held four million men as property, with the desire to extend and perpetuate it. And this influence, he believed, made itself felt in party conventions, legislatures, churches, and schools. There was much talk of a Slave Power conspiracy, but Wilson knew that it was not a formal organization. Instead, it was a spirit, a growing terror, an influence, and certainly he had a basis for this view. There was common agreement among many Southern leaders that slavery was a good system, and when the occasion demanded, they did sacrifice basic civil and personal rights to protect its existence.[2]

Talk of the threat of the Slave Power affected the thought of the New Englanders as their section of the country became less effective in federal politics. Hatred of the South came from the fear of increasing control of the government by the slaveholders. Abolitionists claimed that the ambitions of the Slave Power were to extend slavery throughout the nation, and to remove constitutional guarantees of liberties. This picture of southern mastery made an impact upon the lower and middle classes in the North who were afraid of competition from slave labor and the infringement of their rights by aristocratic slaveholders.

In the early spring of 1844 Wilson visited Washington to sound out sentiments, search for news, and listen to gossip. Optimistic as usual, he found other optimists in the capital who believed that the Whigs could triumph in the coming campaign if they were not hurt by the Texas question. He came away convinced that the party should support its most popular aspirant, Henry Clay, on the condition that he oppose annexation. With a practical eye on party organization, Wilson also felt that Massachusetts Whigs should start immediately to organize the state, "everything depends upon getting the field first-one day in the field (early) is better than ten after the lines are formed."[3]

Clay's career gave no evidence that he opposed annexation as an extension of slavery. In 1844, he preferred to talk about economy in government, sound currency, reasonable protective tariffs, and distribution of land sales to the estates. But he had little choice if he wished to satisfy his long ambition for the Presidency. In April he therefore wrote that annexation had not been called for by any general expression of public opinion and that it was dangerous to the integrity of the Union, financially inexpedient, and involved certain war with Mexico. For these reasons he opposed annexation at that time.[4] To most northern Whigs and antislavery men like Henry Wilson this statement was satisfactory. Two weeks later the Whig Convention at Baltimore named Clay for President. While the antislavery Whigs may have held some reservations about the past history of their candidate, they were at least elated by his recent pronouncement. But their elation did not last long. The Democrats, with their nominee

James K. Polk, took a sufficiently strong stand in favor of the admission of Texas to force Clay to clarify his vague comments.

As Southern Whigs slipped away, Clay altered his position on Texas in an effort to regain their support. In July, he wrote to the editor of an Alabama newspaper that he did not personally object to annexation, but he did not want to dissolve the Union to acquire Texas. This appealed to nationalist opinion, but it did not solve the situation. Near the end of the same month Clay wrote another letter moving still closer to southern sentiment. He now wrote that he would be glad to see Texas annexed if it could be done without dishonor or war, with common consent of the Union, and upon just and fair terms. Slavery, he thought, should not affect the question in any way.[5] In the middle of the campaign the tables thus turned; the South became the assuaged, the North, the aggrieved section. Wilson and his friends were left with a candidate to whom they could not give their full support. Clay tried to defend himself against the charge of inconsistency by restating his opposition to immediate annexation, but his equivocation made his cause hopeless. The Whigs of Massachusetts found themselves the victims of a presidential nominee who desperately wanted to pacify both sides in a heated controversy so that he might gain his long sought goal, the White House. Antislavery men knew that a vote of Polk was a vote for immediate annexation, that for them the choice was between the lesser of two evils. The contest lost its heart and some threw their ballots away on James G. Birney, the abolitionist leader and candidate of the Liberty Party.

The Whigs lost the national election, but again Henry Wilson's career moved forward. Middlesex County was normally Democratic, but Wilson won election to the state senate when the voters failed to make a decisive choice among several candidates. Since the Whigs had gained a majority, they named Wilson to the seat.[6] Now he had the opportunity to speak out in the upper house where his views paralleled those of Charles Sumner, Charles Allen, Stephen C. Phillips, John Palfrey and Charles Francis Adams, all prominent "young Whigs". For a rebellious group they were, in terms of education and social class, well above Wilson, and it is a tribute to his political skill that they accepted him into their inner circle. Wilson and the young politicians became good political friends, but socially they moved in different worlds. Palfrey, fifty years old, was the eldest of the group. A Unitarian minister, who often mistook stubbornness for righteousness, he once edited the *North American Review*. Stephen C. Phillips was a wealthy Salem merchant, and Charles Allen had served in the legislature and as a Judge of the Court of Common Pleas. E. Rockwood Hoar, twenty-nine, the youngest, was a promising lawyer who eventually became Attorney General for President Ulysses S. Grant; and by 1845, Charles Sumner had attracted some attention as a social reformer and pacifist.

Wilson, as much as any man in Massachusetts, believed in fighting slavery by political action. While William Lloyd Garrison and his fellow abolitionists refused to take part in politics, firm in the belief that it was a matter of moral principles, Wilson, less sensitive about moral principles and perhaps more interested in people, grappled with the question in the political arena. A thorough-going politician, he saw no sense in waiting for a day of deliverance by some magical, moral stroke. He believed that slavery had to be fought step by step. He saw life as a battle, and he continually searched for weaknesses in the enemy camp where he could attack. But as a good politician, he carefully avoided extreme positions. He did his best to work with both the established leaders of the Whig Party and the abolitionists as long as they could serve his purpose. When abolitionists decried the Constitution, he was certain that he could accomplish more by working within the Constitution.

After the election of Polk, President Tyler moved quickly to win the distinction of bringing Texas into the Union. In December he recommended to Congress that Texas should be annexed by a joint resolution which would eliminate the need for more than a majority vote in each House. On February 28, 1845 Congress passed the resolution and provided that the Texas Constitution should be submitted for approval. In the fight against the admission of Texas in 1845 there seemed to be no soft spot in the wall of slavery. But if the opposition awed Wilson he did not show his feelings. He favored an all out offensive. He spoke at public meetings throughout Massachusetts and was one of those New England legislators who considered it a solemn duty to direct Congressional policy by resolutions from the state legislature for their guidance.

Wilson and other Young Whigs argued that the joint resolution of Congress had only allowed Texas to form a government and apply for statehood, and that she had not been
admitted. On the slight chance that Congress might still refuse
statehood, they continued to fight. When the Legislature convened in 184g, a resolution passed the lower house denying the
constitutional power of Congress to annex a foreign nation.
When this resolution reached the Senate, Wilson proposed an
amendment that any legislative act admitting Texas into the
Union could be repealed at the earliest date. The amendment
failed, but the original resolution passed. Next, Wilson introduced an order requesting the Judiciary Committee to report
a bill which would make it a penal offense to surrender an
escaped slave from Texas taking refuge in Massachusetts. That
too failed.[7]

During the presidential campaign of the previous year all
Whig leaders in the state had campaigned on a platform opposed to annexation. Abbott Lawrence, Nathan Appleton, and
other conservative cotton manufacturers had completely accepted
this stand. Now, the support of many party members for this
position began to dwindle. Lawrence and Appleton, along with
other influential leaders such as Webster, Choate, Everett, and
Winthrop, had little to say. They knew that the Texas issue was
a closed case, and they saw no reason for further assistance.
But this did not deter Wilson. He wanted to make a last ditch
stand. "Act, hold meetings in every district, town and county
of the state," he proclaimed.[8]

Following his own advice, Wilson worked hard for the organization of the Anti-Texas Convention to be held in the Fall.
The previous January Webster had instigated a non-partisan
state convention for the same reason, but Wilson believed that
Webster had withdrawn his active support when he learned that
Abbott Lawrence, Nathan Appleton, and Robert Winthrop did
not approve.[9] Wilson worked with Sumner and other young
Whigs who now operated as a well disciplined group. Heavily
committed to the Anti-Texas drive they dared to risk the wrath
of the party leaders. Still, they continued to avoid complete
association with their abolitionist allies. The cool, balanced
mind of Charles Francis Adams carefully planned their strategy.[10]

In September Wilson prepared a call for a meeting of men

of all parties at Concord to recommend action to resist the encroachments of the Slave Power. At the meeting Wilson offered a series of resolutions calling for constitutional resistance to slavery. The meeting adopted the resolutions and appointed E. Rockwood Hoar to confer with the general committee of the January Anti-Texas convention in order to hold meetings and organize efficient resistance.[11]

The next month the meeting reassembled with Wilson in the chair calling for bold and unified action. "Let us act, and as far as we have the constitutional right, go in favor of emancipation."[12] Garrison presented a resolution asserting that it would be the constitutional duty of the Massachusetts legislature to declare the act of annexation, if consummated, null and void. But Charles Francis Adams declared that this could not be a basis for union and action. The gathering passed resolutions to correspond with individuals in other parts of the state with a view to calling county and state conventions, and they appointed a large state committee, with Adams as Chairman. Further meetings took place throughout the state and antislavery petitions signed by tens of thousands were sent to this committee.[13]

All this activity culminated in a large rally of anti-Texas Whigs, abolitionists, and Liberty party men at Faneuil Hall on November 4 with Charles Francis Adams as chairman. Each faction, distrustful of the other, had its say. William Lloyd Garrison, Wendell Phillips, and William Henry Channing spoke for the abolitionists, Henry B. Stanton for the Liberty party, and George Hillard and Charles Sumner for the Young Whigs. Sumner called upon the audience to put aside party distinctions and to subordinate political and economic questions to the requirements of religion, morals, and humanity, and he again proposed the preacher William Ellery Channing's idea of a moral blockade against evil. This meeting seems to have only antagonized the leading members of the Whig party. Abbott Lawrence now openly denounced the work of the young Whigs and refused to give further support to their movement. "A majority of the people have decided in favor of annexation," he noted, "and . . . Texas now virtually composes a part of our Union."[14]

In December, the Anti-Texas Committee sent Henry Wilson and John Greenleaf Whittier, the Quaker poet, to Washington to present to Congress a petition of protest containing thirty thousand signatures. Charles Francis Adams gave Wilson a letter of introduction to his father, who presented the petition to the House of Representatives. A motion by the elder Adams to refer the matter to a special committee of one from each state, and another to refer it to a committee of the whole were simply rejected. The petitions were laid on the table, and Texas entered the Union. The trip was futile, the cause lost, but Wilson gained personal prominence, and he had an opportunity to meet with the members of the Massachusetts congressional delegation.[15]

By the end of the year it was clear that the split in the Whig party had deepened. Politics in Massachusetts, especially Whig politics, was in a turmoil. Henry Adams, literary son of Charles Francis Adams, said that in the forties lawyers, physicians, professors and merchants were the ruling classes and they acted as though they were clergymen and each profession a church. These were the kind of men who still held the real control of the Whig party in Massachusetts. They were good men, but under their leadership the Whig party had something of the atmosphere of an exclusive gentlemen's club. They subscribed to the Ciceronian idea of government by the best, but they also believed in defining who and what was best. This was not compatible with Wilson's nature, ambition, or antislavery views. As a young Whig he contributed to the deepening division despite his expressed appeals for greater cooperative effort. He worked for greater cooperation, but always from the antislavery viewpoint. The Democrats appeared more united than the Whigs, but in reality they too suffered factional troubles. One group, led by a conservative wholesale druggist, David Henshaw, favored Southern slavery, another led by George Bancroft and Marcus Morton favored Northern antislavery principles. Furthermore, the people in the state were not settled in their allegiance to any party. Loyalties once secure were now shaken and shifting, and it would be many years before the commotion would subside. In this atmosphere Wilson dreamed of some day building a permanent antislavery political organization.

During the year Wilson also found time to indulge his interest in military matters. In June the men of his regiment elected him Colonel, and six weeks later he became Brigadier General of the Third Brigade of Massachusetts Volunteer Militia. He held the post for the next five years, and became widely known as "General Wilson," a useful title for a politician. This interest extended into the legislature where he served as Chairman of the Joint Committee on the Militia which studied a former law compelling enrollment of all persons between the ages of 18 and 45. The Committee considered the proposal useless and placed its reliance upon the existing voluntary system because it was more efficient, economical, and "better calculated to cultivate the military spirit." Members of the committee believed, however, that an increase in compensation was warranted so they presented a bill to give officers an income of $5.00 a year.[16]

Wilson declined to run for the State Senate in 1846, preferring to return to the lower house. During this term he served as Chairman of a Joint Special Committee with instructions from that body to report whether or not the legislature should take any action in relation to the annexation of Texas. In April, six of the seven members agreed that the legislature was not required to take any further action. But the seventh member, Henry Wilson, issued a minority report which stated that:

It matters but little to us, whether other free States are ready to act with this Commonwealth. It is her duty, not to obey a vitiated public opinion, but to act up to her convictions of duty, and by the force of her example, elevate and combine the public sentiment of the country.

Wilson then recommended striking the majority report and substituting another resolution:

That Massachusetts distinctly and solemnly announce to the country her uncompromising opposition to the further extension and longer existence of American slavery; that she hereby deliberately declares her earnest and unalterable purpose, to use every lawful and constitutional measure for its overthrow and entire extinction; and she hereby pledges her cordial co-operation to the friends of civil liberty, throughout the Union in every just and practical measure, that shall tend to free our country from the dominion, curse and shame of slavery, and make her great and glorious among the nations.[17]

This was an advanced antislavery statement for any politician. Many Whig members criticized Wilson for whipping a dead horse, and denounced him for seeking to please a little knot of political abolitionists. Wilson defended himself against this charge by stating that he was not a political abolitionist, and by that he meant that he was not a member of the Liberty party. He believed that the Whigs had lost the sympathy and confidence of the South without gaining the confidence of the free impulses of the North. But, he announced that he was ready "to act with any set of men—Whigs, Democrats, Liberty men, or old organizationists—in all lawful and constitutional measures that shall tend to arrest the extension, and overthrow the entire system of slavery in America. . . ."[18]

In the ensuing legislative maneuvers to stall Wilson's resolution, Thomas G. Carey, a Boston merchant, said that this resolution would make an unfavorable impression in the South and injure business interests. E. Rockwood Hoar replied that he thought it quite as desirable that the legislature should represent the conscience as the cotton of the Commonwealth.[19] This remark gave rise to the popular distinction of the two factions of the Whig party as "Cotton" and "Conscience" Whigs, and identified the deepening division within the party. In reality it was the beginning of the Free Soil party.

The resolution did not pass, but a few days later the United States declared war against Mexico and for a brief period, the Conscience Whigs found many supporters because of the unpopularity of the Mexican War in New England, especially in the antislavery, rural areas of Massachusetts.

The military instincts of Henry Wilson did not take him to war. Instead he intensified his activities with other Conscience Whigs to take advantage of the change in public sentiment. One aspect of this activity was the purchase of a newspaper by some of his friends. In Wilson's mind both of the Whig newspapers, the *Atlas* and the *Advertiser,* served the manufacturing interests rather than courageously crusading for human freedom.[20] The party, Wilson felt, needed a vigorous organ to act as a mouthpiece, supply direction, and spell out issues. Wilson was not alone in his views. Charles Francis Adams, for one, was anxious to buy a newspaper that would speak for the Conscience Whigs. *The Daily Whig,* a far from flourishing newspaper, currently in debt, with only 212 paying subscribers, was a tempting possibility for purchase.

Adams got the printers' estimates, consulted further with John

Palfrey, and decided that a meeting should be held with S .C. Phillips, Wilson, and Sumner. They met in Lobby Number Thirteen at the State House, to consider the project. The scheme to buy the paper appealed to Adams, yet he worried about the financial risk, and Phillips had doubts about the expediency. The others wanted to go ahead, but both Sumner and Wilson's support was verbal rather than monetary since neither had funds to put into the venture. After some hesitation Adams and Phillips each bought two-fifths share in the paper, and Palfrey one-fifth. Adams would carry the burden as editor, and the others would contribute time and effort.[21]

On June 1, 1846 the initial editorial stated that the paper supported the policies established by the Whig Party since 1840. Despite their association with Garrison and other abolitionists the sponsors tried to make it clear that they were the true Whigs and that they did not wish to divide the party. This was a fine gesture, but Adams and his friends scarcely built party unity by their immediate criticism of regulars like Abbott Lawrence and Nathan Appleton.

During the summer of 1846 John Palfrey wrote a series of articles on the development of the Slave Power for *The Whig*. He charged that Appleton and his financial coterie were responsible for encouraging Polk to start war with Mexico when they gave up their fight against annexation in the Fall of 1845. It was now obvious that Appleton, Lawrence, and their conservative friends had received a challenge for the leadership of the party.

But perhaps the sharpest intra-party dispute involved Robert Winthrop, the scion of a great family and a likely successor to Daniel Webster and Edward Everett. Winthrop, a congressman from Massachusetts, held conservative antislavery views, but he was also conciliatory towards the South. Originally he opposed the annexation of Texas, but the declaration of war placed him in a delicate position. He was one of two members of the Massachusetts delegation in the House who voted for a bill providing necessary supplies for General Taylor's army even though it contained a preamble stating that the war had been caused by Mexican aggression. This gave the Conscience Whigs a special target, and Adams and Sumner, until then a personal friend, severely denounced Winthrop in the pages of *The Whig*.

Wilson was a constant visitor at Adams' office. He would stop by with subscriptions for *The Whig,* fill Adams in on "interesting details of party movement", deliver an article, gossip about state and national politics, or simply hold a friendly conversation with Adams or any of his other friends who might happen to be there at the time. Frequently, he ran into Palfrey, Sumner, or S. C. Phillips. Uppermost in their minds was the forthcoming Whig State Convention. The attack upon Winthrop had been part of their carefully planned strategy to take over party control, and they made certain that their faction appeared at primary meetings.[22] Slavery was now the great single issue as other public matters dwindled into insignificance. All shades of Whigs opposed war. As the slavery issue grew, the split within the Whigs, as well as the Democrats grew also. Citizens with life-long political associations cast away their old ties. This was an opportunity that the Conscience Whigs must grasp. It was this same summer that David Wilmot, a Democratic Congressman from Pennsylvania moved in the House that a pending appropriation bill be amended to bar slavery from all lands acquired in the war.

The State Convention met at Faneuil Hall on September 23, 1846. Speaking for the Conscience Whigs, Charles Sumner made a stirring speech on the antislavery duties of the Whig party and urged Daniel Webster to join the Conscience group. But the Cotton Whigs shrewdly managed the delegates. They inserted a strong antislavery plan into their proposed platform which made it indistinguishable from the rival platform. Then, at the right moment, Daniel Webster spoke for party solidarity, and the delegates, somewhat confused by the intricacies of the proceedings, followed the regular leaders and rejected the Conscience Whig resolutions. Wilson wrote to William Schouler that if they had been successful they would have nominated S. C. Phillips for Governor in place of George M. Briggs. He was personally fond of Briggs, who served seven consecutive terms as Governor from 1844 to 1851, but regarded him politically as an old line Whig.[23]

So a year of hard work produced nothing. Discouraged at times, Wilson said that he did not expect to be a candidate for public office again. The problem of making a living was still very much with him too. He was far from financial independence even though his business improved during these years. In 1845, his annual output was 38,000 pairs of shoes and he employed fifty-two workers. A glance at his accounts for January 1, 1846 show that he had property, including his house, shop and stock of raw and manufactured materials valued at $5,686, against notes of $3,765, and 1847 proved to be a big year for all Natick shoe manufacturers. Wilson was no exception. He made 123,000 pairs of shoes that year, a peak never again duplicated, and he had 109 hands working for him. It is surprising that his business flourished to this extent since he had devoted so much time and energy to politics.[24] He maintained a comfortable home on Central Street, and on November 11, 1846 his wife, after six years of married life, gave birth to a boy, a "first rate little fellow", according to Wilson, "fat and hearty." His wife had been very ill, but after a couple of weeks she appeared to be doing well, and Wilson's enthusiasm rose to new heights.[25]

Still only thirty-four, Henry Wilson led a varied life and thrived on the pressures, challenges, and combat. As new political alarms appeared he quickly forgot that he had ever thought about giving all his time to shoemaking.

The subject of principles irked Henry Wilson, practical operator that he was. Like most of his friends, he used the word frequently and loosely and referred often to the necessity for standing on principle. But what did Henry Wilson mean by "principle?" He asked himself this question and he found that opposition to slavery was the only principle which had any meaning for him. Everything else was insignificant. He was clear on this single point. As a political organizer, it bothered him to hear others talk about principles that he thought of little consequence.

Was the tariff a principle to stand on? Was the National Bank an issue to stand on? Wilson favored a protective tariff, and he knew that Daniel Webster had originally opposed protection. Now that Northern manufacturers prospered from protection, he supported it as a sound Whig practice. The debate over the years on the Bank of the United States had reached the proportions of a mania, but Wilson thought that the issue had died with the influx of gold after the discoveries in California.

When Wilson looked at the Mexican War he could not understand how anyone could claim to be against slavery and still vote for a man or party that supported a war for its extension. To profess opposition to slavery without wanting its abolition was simply hypocrisy in his mind.

Annexation of Texas had been a great issue, but Wilson knew that many Democrats had also opposed it. And he knew that many Democrats attacked slavery itself. So where were the principles that they stood upon? Why, Wilson wondered, could not the Northern Whigs and Democrats forget non-essential principles and combine to fight slavery.[26]

As General Zachary Taylor loomed as a possible Presidential candidate on the Whig ticket, Wilson made up his mind to oppose the nomination even if it broke "the party to pieces." A war hero had great appeal, yet Wilson could not support a man who owned slaves. Early in the spring of 1847 Wilson told Charles Francis Adams that he was disturbed at the possibility of Taylor's candidacy, but the more cautious Adams advised him to wait and watch events.[27]

By the middle of August Adams agreed that Wilson should write a letter to *The Whig* opposing Taylor and favoring Senator Thomas Corwin of Ohio who had made an eloquent denunciation of the war at the beginning of the year. Wilson wrote that a number of Whigs had hastily rushed to support Taylor without knowing his views. While Taylor would probably be a Presidential candidate, it was impossible for him to be a candidate of a united Whig party.

> The Whig party must go into the next election with a clear, distinct enunciation of its principles and measures . . . He (the candidate) should be in favor of rescuing the government from the grasp of the Slave Power . . . of arresting the present slave driving and land stealing war with Mexico. He should be opposed to the acquisition of territory, over which to extend the curse of human slavery . . . Thomas Corwin of Ohio, is the man for the occasion. . . .[28]

Wilson and other Conscience Whigs thought they had found a new leader in Corwin. Their enthusiasm faded, however, when the Ohio Senator refused to join the more radical antislavery groups.

The immediate concern for the Conscience Whigs in Massachusetts was the management of the forthcoming State convention. As a result of a bitter battle between two conservative factions, the Conscience Whigs received much attention from Abbott Lawrence on one hand, and Daniel Webster, on the other. Both were aware that the Conscience Whigs could play a pivotal part at the convention, and each intended to use them for his own ends. Webster, still pursuing the presidency, sought the endorsement of the convention. Tired of supporting Webster's ambitions, Lawrence decided that it was time to foster his own desires. He had his eye on a Vice Presidential nomination the next year, with Taylor heading the ticket. Lawrence believed that if the Northern Whigs dropped Webster they might reach an understanding with the Southern and Western wings of the party on the more important issues of the tariff, internal improvements, and banking.

This was a great opportunity for the Conscience Whigs. Sumner, Adams, S. C. Phillips, Palfrey, and Allen attended the convention, but their lack of political skill defeated their purposes. Webster made a strong antislavery statement which served only to injure him in the South, and to demonstrate that Massachusetts was not solidly behind him. This delighted Lawrence and his followers, but they held no lasting affection for the Conscience Whigs. When Palfrey moved that the Whigs of Massachusetts should not support any candidate for President or Vice President who did not oppose slavery, the Lawrence men quickly voted it down since the resolution might hurt Taylor. In the end, by their incompetence, the Conscience group hindered the antislavery Webster, aided proslavery Taylor, and ruined their own position as a significant faction in the party. At the end of the year Henry Wilson told a friend, perhaps overdramatically, that his association with the Conscience Whigs would prevent him from going to another Whig county or district convention.[29]

Wilson's relations with upper class politicians were always uneasy. They enjoyed his support, but feared his competition. For all their close cooperation, Charles Francis Adams seemed to regard Wilson favorably only when he played a subordinate role. When he shared similar ambitions, Adams became hostile. With the death of John Quincy Adams early in 1848, his son would have eagerly filled the vacant Congressional seat, and he seemed sensitive about Wilson's interest in the same place. In such a situation, Wilson could not count on Adams' close friends, Palfrey and Sumner. Writing to Sumner, Palfrey said:

Wilson has high claims. He is a man of great courage, as much, for aught I know, as Adams, as much as any man. He has also a superior mind and uncommon powers of speech and action. But it is no disparagement to any man in New England . . . to say that in the proper studies of a statesman, Adams is a head taller than any other living man (except Webster), who had been in public life among us. . . .[30]

But as it turned out neither Adams nor Wilson got the nomination for Congress. At a Whig convention held at Dedham, Wilson withdrew in favor of Horace Mann, and then received a unanimous appointment as a delegate to the Whig National Convention.[31] This may have been a consolation prize for Wilson, but it was an important one because it officially gave him a national role at a time when the Conscience Whigs of Massachusetts intended to take a strong stand concerning the next Presidential candidate. For years Wilson had looked beyond the local scene and had corresponded with antislavery leaders in other states, such as Joshua Giddings of Ohio. Now he would have a chance to speak out at a national gathering. Sumner had made an effort to have Adams chosen as delegate, but the convention must have sensed that this was a job for a thick-skinned politician, not for a sensitive would-be statesman. Adams must have realized this too. When he later learned of Sumner's try he told him "he was dreaming."[32]

While Taylor was the leading contender for the presidential nomination under the Whig banner, there were other possibilities still to be considered. Henry Clay and Daniel Webster were ever hopeful. General Winfield Scott, another Mexican war hero and John J. McLean, an Associate Justice of the United States Supreme Court, were also avowed aspirants. Senators John J. Crittenden of Kentucky and John M. Clayton of Delaware were among the potential "dark horse" candidates. Aside from Taylor these were simply a collection of regional anti-Democrats who had no broad appeal. Wilson wanted a candidate from the Free States who could command the strongest support among the people, and preserve the integrity of the party in accordance with his antislavery views. He would have supported Webster, Clay, or Scott, but he believed that John McLean would make the best nominee and for a time he had hopes for his selection. J. B. Mowrer, a New York backer of McLean, opened a correspondence with Wilson with the approval of Horace Greeley, and looked to him for advice and guidance in New England. Later Wilson said that if he could have determined the candidate at the convention, McLean would have been his choice; but if he could have made the President, Webster would have been his nominee. Wilson's esteem for Webster was not shared by all Conscience Whigs. Charles Francis Adams had to reconvince Sumner that Webster lacked moral principles.[33]

It was typical of Wilson that he would propose a member of an opposing faction of the Whig party for the presidency. He quickly forgot past differences when there was an opportunity to build a stronger antislavery party. The antislavery movement was a mass of splinter groups and some of Wilson's contemporaries behaved as though there was an advantage in alienating people, but he would have gladly bowed to a major political figure like Webster to unify their position.

In the pre-convention days Wilson made no secret of his opinion that he would bolt the party if Taylor received the nomination, and some of his Whig friends advised him not to be foolhardy in the matter. When Wilson talked of a new and independent candidate, Joseph Brewer wrote to William Schouler of *The Atlas* that he had no objection because, "the Whig party could run off a good deal of cumbersome material, and thereby purify itself." But he hated to see Wilson leave the party even though there were others that he could see depart with "gratification and delight."[34]

When news reached Massachusetts that Lewis Cass had received the Democratic nomination for President, Charles Francis Adams called a meeting at his office with his "Conscience" cohorts, Wilson, E. L. Keyes, E. Rockwood Hoar, Sumner and Francis Bird. They unanimously agreed to oppose Taylor in an organized manner and prepared to call a state convention if he received the nomination.[35]

A few days later Wilson wrote to Daniel Webster concerning the plans at the national convention in the event that Taylor headed the ticket. He outlined the arrangements for calling a state convention and predicted that they would carry at least twenty thousand Whigs with them. In addition they would try to hold a convention of the free states. A movement was underway in Ohio, and New Hampshire and Maine would follow shortly:

We want just such a man as you are to lead us and I have wished for years that you would feel it to be your duty to take the lead in a movement of this kind. The people would rally around you as no man of our time ever saw men rally . . . You may think it strange that I should presume to say what I have to you, but I trust you will excuse me for it. I say what I feel and think. You are and ever have been my first choice for the Presidency and I would work harder for you than any man although I have sometimes thought you ought to take stronger ground against slavery. . . .

Wilson told Webster that he would give him his vote at the Whig convention, but he wanted assurance that neither Webster nor his friends would aid Taylor's nomination directly or indirectly. He continued:

Some of your friends assure me that all is right with them but I want to feel very sure for we are to have trouble if Taylor is nominated and I do not want to make any mistake in my vote. If you see fit you can write me at Phil—care of your friend Ashmun . . . I shall leave the Convention as soon as Taylor swallows the Whig party if I go alone. . . .[36]

It was a frank, perhaps presumptuous letter that apparently never received an equally frank reply. But on the day Wilson left for the convention he ran into Tolman Willey on Court Street in Boston. Willey, a close friend of Webster's, pressed Wilson into visiting Webster's office. A number of members of the Young Men's Webster Club who were gathered there were anxious to see him before he left.

Wilson found Daniel Webster's son, Fletcher, Anson Burlingame, and several others present. Concerned about Lawrence's plan to support Taylor and seek the Vice Presidency, they asked Wilson what he intended to do. He replied:

If the Convention adopted a resolution in favor of Wilmot Proviso, or if General Taylor pledged himself for it, although a slaveholder, I would support him, but if the Convention refused thus to pledge him to the doctrines of the Whigs of Massachusetts, I should, if he were nominated, leave the convention and come home, and unite with any body of men in supporting the position of the Whigs of this State against the extension of slavery. . . .

When the Websterites heard this, they exclaimed, "Go ahead, Wilson, and we will back you!"[37]

With these thoughts in mind Wilson and Charles Allen went to Philadelphia in June as delegates to the National Whig Convention. The Massachusetts contingent, one of the stronger delegations, also included the prominent lawyer Rufus Choate and George Ashmun, a Webster lieutenant.

The Whigs were popular with the more prosperous and conservative citizens, but lacked appeal among the masses. They needed color, they needed enthusiasm, they needed a vote-getter. A military hero, William Henry Harrison, had solved the problem in 1840; perhaps another military hero, Zachary Taylor, might do so in 1848. Wilson, always attracted by the military, would have been the first to agree with these tactics if his chief aim had been preservation of the party.

The usual air of excitement surrounded the convention. Stalwart Clay men were claiming victory for their hero. Astute politicians like Thurlow Weed of New York and Truman Smith of Connecticut skillfully worked for Taylor. There were some, too, who still preferred Webster, while other delegates supported Scott. To many of the delegates, Taylor seemed to be the most reasonable choice because he had no political enemies and could best keep the party together.

The antislavery northerners talked much of Taylor's "noncommitalism", but it had little effect when delegates cast their votes. As the hours passed, Taylor became such a certainty that John McLean's name never appeared before the convention. The South solidly supported Taylor, Pennsylvania was split, and Ohio divided the opposing strength by backing Scott. On the first ballot, Taylor received 111 votes, Clay 97, Scott 43, Webster 22, and a few scattered. The next two ballots showed gains for Taylor, and on the fourth he received the nomination without having endorsed the Wilmot Proviso.

When a delegate moved to make the nomination unanimous, Charles Allen quietly stated that Taylor was "a man who will continue the rule of slavery for another four years. . . . We spurn the nominee." Then, referring to Abbott Lawrence's Vice Presidential hopes, Allen said, "Massachusetts will spurn the bribe. . . . I say that the Whig party of the United States is dissolved."[38]

Lewis Campbell of Ohio tried to introduce an antislavery resolution, but the chairman ruled him out of order. Wilson indignantly arose and announced, "I will not be bound by the proceedings here." The chairman shouted for order amidst hisses and cries of, "Then you don't belong here." George Ashmun, a conservative Massachusetts Whig, demanded: "My colleague has a right to be heard." A Southern delegate endorsed his plea: "As a Southern man, I too beg that he may be heard. He'll express nothing but his own sentiments. They'll do no harm here, nor elsewhere, and I hope they won't hurt him."

Wilson continued, "As a Whig I came here fully committed to its proceedings and organization and I am willing to be bound by its acts provided we act as Whigs. But we have come here and nominated a man. . . ." Hisses and cries of "Stop" and "Go on" interrupted him. Wilson asked, "Is it out of order to comment on the proceedings of this convention?" The Chairman said, "The gentleman will proceed." A voice shouted, "Is he a Whig? Hasn't he been identified with another party? (Abolition)."

Wilson adamantly bellowed, "We have nominated a man who said that he would not withdraw his name for Clay, or for anybody, and gentlemen ask us to support him. I have always voted the Whig ticket. I ask nothing more than to have a good government. If any Whig, from any section, had been nominated, I should have felt bound by the nomination . . . I go home and so help me God, I will do all I can to defeat that nomination." Out he stomped to the clamor of hisses and a few hurrahs and with him went the chance of Abbott Lawrence to win the Vice Presidency. In an attempt to appease free soilers and to make New York safe in the coming election, the convention quickly turned to Millard Fillmore.[39]

That evening Wilson and Samuel Galloway of Ohio called a meeting. It was attended by fourteen delegates from Maine, New York, New Jersey, Ohio, and Massachusetts. Wilson called the meeting to order and stated that the purpose was to take measures to combine the friends of freedom in a movement to prevent the extension of slavery. They proceeded to elect a chairman, John C. Hamilton of New York, a son of Alexander Hamilton. A number of speeches expressed the belief that the Whig party was lost to freedom. Wilson then moved that a National Convention be held at Buffalo early in August and that a committee be appointed to prepare a plan for the call. The motion was passed and Charles Allen, Joshua Giddings, and John C. Vaughn were selected to make up the committee. The body instructed them to persuade the Ohio Convention, which was to meet about the twentieth of June, to call for the Buffalo Convention.[40]

Wilson returned to Boston and on the following Monday, a cold, windy June day, walked over to Sumner's office where a large number of his friends had gathered. Adams, S. C. Phillips, E. L. Keyes, and Anson Burlingame were there. Wilson reveled in reporting his part in the proceedings, and roused them all to a high pitch of excitement. He moved Adams to write, "A more high handed piece of abominable villainy never was attempted in this Union, and the mortifying part of it is that Massachusetts through Robert C. Winthrop, and Abbott Lawrence has been a party to the bargain from the first."[41]

Speaking to the Whigs of the Eighth Congressional District who had sent him to the convention, Wilson publicly asked: "What was I, your delegate, known to be opposed to slavery in all its forms, to do? Should I, by approving this course, give lie to my own professions, and to your unanimously recorded votes . . .?" These were rhetorical questions which he believed needed no reply. "I ventured the assertion, in your behalf," he went on, "that the Whigs of the district that had sustained John Quincy Adams in his long and glamorous career would spurn a nomination forced upon them by the arrogance of the South, aided by the servility of the North. . . . Bitter denunciations have already been heaped upon me, yet I see nothing to retract. . . ."[42] The remarks were probably sincere, but it was a part that he loved to play.

There were denunciations, public and private. Not all quarters appreciated Henry Wilson's heroics, and some suspected his motives. The Boston *Daily Atlas* noted, "The Whig party . . . is not to be dissolved so easily, nor is it the power of Mr. Wilson or any other man to defeat the nomination. He will find plenty of Whigs in the old Bay State, young men, like himself, who stand ready to meet him on the stump and discuss the question before the people. . . ." The *Salem Gazette* made the more basic criticism that Wilson and Allen should not have assumed the duties of delegates unless they intended to abide by the fairly expressed decisions of the body. "They knew the responsibilities they would incur upon entering it. . . . Those implied pledges they forfeited, in a manner which we should think dishonorable, if we were not perfectly sure, from the characters of the individuals, that was honorably meant."[43]

But not everyone was so certain of Wilson's honorable character. Chester Adams wrote to Horace Mann from Natick that Wilson made a loud noise there, and that in his heat and zeal he may have taken a judicious course, but he added:

> It is however the opinion of men that his ambitious notions of conspicuous preferment have placed him in an uncomfortable position. The knowing ones seem to think he is looking to a seat in the next Congress by a vote from the eighth district . . . Soon after the last election, he said, 'If Horace Mann had not been nominated he should himself be sure of election.' Should he fail of this object and could be persuaded to wait until Daniel Webster's term expired, he would no doubt think himself well qualified and entitled to fill the vacancy . . . It is said by some that if he had as much modesty as he has of assurance and brass, it would much better comport with his standing and talents. . . .[44]

But this was simply criticism, and criticism, known, unknown or suspected, meant little to Henry Wilson. Perhaps he was insensitive, but with a careless shrug of the shoulders he ignored most attacks, personal and political, and rushed forward on the road that he set for himself.

The call for a state convention at Worcester on June 28, invited all Massachusetts voters opposed both to Taylor and Cass. It attracted a collection of unhappy Conscience Whigs, some Webster adherents and some Democrats and Liberty party men. Fletcher Webster was there to look after his father's interests, and he gave Wilson the impression that his father would go along with the new party. But if he did so, it was without the sanction of Daniel Webster. Ten days before the Worcester convention the elder Webster had written to his son, "These northern proceedings can come to nothing useful to you or to me. The men are all low in their objects—if the conscience men at Worcester were to ask to put me on their ticket what would it come to . . . ?[45]

Wilson harbored different thoughts of the Senator's intentions as a result of the friendly attitude of Fletcher Webster and his friends. One of these friends, E. Rockwood Hoar, in a speech at Worcester, stated that he had been authorized to say that Webster had not committed himself to Taylor, and that he sympathized with the purpose of the convention.

The large crowd enthusiastically listened to other speeches by Giddings, Adams, and Charles Allen. Sumner expressed views that paralleled Wilson's when he said that all the old party issues, the tariff, the bank, internal improvements were dead, and that the one genuine issue remaining was the extension of slavery into territory acquired from Mexico.[46]

The delegates denounced the national Whig convention, selected six delegates for the Buffalo convention and passed appropriate resolutions. They declared that they would only support men for President and Vice President who had shown by their acts that they opposed the extension of slavery. Van Buren received a commendation for his wisdom, but received no commitment in his behalf. Daniel Webster received applause for withholding his endorsement of Taylor, and a resolution looked to him to uphold the policy of the Free States before the country. They also gratefully remembered the work of Wilson and Allen at Philadelphia, and officially thanked them for their boldness territory acquired from Mexico.[46]

A day or two after the convention Charles Allen and Wilson received a pressing invitation from Fletcher Webster to confer with the elder Webster. They rushed to Boston, but when they arrived the Senator was out of town. When Webster returned Wilson called again at his office. According to Wilson, Webster expressed confidence in the men of the Worcester convention, many of whom, he pointed out, were personal as well as political friends, and he commended the resolutions that had been passed. Wilson told him that they would support those who favored the Wilmot Proviso, and that their primary aim was to overthrow the dominating influences of the Slave Power and make a "North". Webster replied that there had never been a North; when he and others tried to resist the South they had been beaten by representatives of the New England States, New York, and Pennsylvania. It seemed to him that if the forthcoming Buffalo convention could concentrate public sentiment on Northern rights, they would achieve a much desired result. But he doubted their ability to do it because of Southern strength. Wilson, always the optimist, led himself to believe that they could count on Webster's support, and that perhaps he would lead the ticket.[48]

On the ninth of August, thousands of men from all parts of the country gathered in and around a circus tent set up in the Buffalo city park. From this sweltering crowd, four hundred and sixty-five were chosen as delegates. They were a motley group made up of antislavery Democrats and Whigs, Liberty men, and various other shades of free soil advocates. There were some big names, too, among them. None of the leading candidates for the presidency attended the convention, but each party sent men of prominence. In attendance were Preston King and Benjamin F. Butler of New York for the Democrats, Salmon P. Chase and Joshua Leavitt for the Liberty men, and Charles Francis Adams and Joshua Giddings for the Whigs.

Adams regarded the meeting as unequalled for high purpose, but he must have been aware that there were many followers of Martin Van Buren, who as President had blocked the abolition of slavery in the District of Columbia, and catered to many Southern rights. Many delegates obviously wanted to use the convention to settle Democratic quarrels by striking back at Polk and Cass. But spirits were high, free soil songs filled the air, and the party had a slogan, "Free soil, free speech, free labor, free men!" It was probably worth more than the platform which offered something to everyone. The endorsement of cheap postage, election of all civil officers, and economy in government conformed to Democratic views; revision of the tariff, a homestead act, and federal funds for internal improvements, pleased the Whigs, and the promise that the federal government would never establish slavery anywhere, and abolish it where it could, appealed to the Liberty men. But such practical considerations did not prevent the belief among many that the new Free Soil party was "The Party of Freedom", long sought by John Quincy Adams and William Ellery Channing.

There were few real possibilities for President. Wilson found that his high hopes for Webster for President had no substance, and Salmon P. Chase withdrew the name of his choice, John McLean. Others favored John Hale of New Hampshire, but he had previously failed as the Liberty party candidate and could not summon wide support. Martin Van Buren, the strongest of the lot, easily won the nomination, with Charles Francis Adams as his running mate. Wilson later implied that Webster would have accepted the Free Soil nomination and that it was not until after

Van Buren had been nominated that Webster publicly endorsed Taylor. But Richard Henry Dana who served as a delegate from Boston appraised the situation more clearly when he said that Van Buren owed his candidacy to the simple fact that there was no prominent, acceptable Whig who would permit himself to run.[49]

Wilson, always ready to join forces for the cause, spearheaded a Massachusetts state Free Soil convention which met in September. A Democrat, John Mills, served as President, and Charles Sumner was chairman of the state central committee. The delegates endorsed Van Buren and Adams as the standard bearers, and nominated Stephen C. Phillips for Governor. Most of the Free Soil leaders were Conscience Whigs, but one Democrat, Amasa Walker, Wilson's young opponent of some years back, assumed a place of first rank.

No one held much hope for the Free Soilers at the polls, but the leaders of the new party, and Wilson in particular, fought hard. There was much talk from men of standing like Richard Henry Dana and Anson Burlingame, a rising young orator, but the day to day work, much of it behind the scenes, required Wilson's shrewd, opportunistic approach. And Wilson did his share of speechmaking and parading in torchlight processions too. A typical schedule found him within a few days addressing the friends of Free Soil at Greenfield, North Bridgewater, New Bedford, Nantucket, Springfield and Northampton.

Neither Wilson nor other Free Soilers received any help from the Garrisonians. Wendell Phillips, one of the group, carried on a running battle with politicians and parties, and denounced their trimming. It seemed to him that politicians talked one way at antislavery meetings, and another way during election campaigns when they scurried for votes. What he wanted was aggressive trampling on all slave laws, defiance of their legality, and repudiation of the government. The moral battle could not give way to the political battle.[50]

By these exalted standards Wilson was not so noble. He needed people. He was out to get votes, and he was happy to have anyone from any party join his side. He used his forceful personality to attract people from all walks of life, and his method was to be every place at once. He might spend a day visiting forty shops and factories in Boston, then take a night train to Springfield arriving at two or three o'clock in the morning, rouse some local chief from bed and ask for a night's lodging. More likely than not, however, he would talk over local conditions with his friend and see very little of bed. Sleep was a time consuming nuisance. Then he would be off again, perhaps to Northampton or Greenfield to see some other local factotum who could give him a sense of things in his town.[51]

As the campaign progressed Wilson's reputation for political scheming blossomed. He saw no wrong in trades, bargains, agreements, or temporary alliances. When Charles Sumner broke with his old friend Samuel Lawrence, the harshest insult Lawrence could make was "you have joined a Faction whose leaders are [Henry] Wilson and Mr. Martin Van Buren!!!"[52] Facts often justified the criticism, but jealousy, snobbery and sensitivity served to multiply unfounded suspicions. Entering active politics for the first time in 1848, the patrician lawyer Richard Henry Dana viewed Wilson with skepticism that lingered through his lifetime. Years later when Wilson was Vice President of the United States, the less successful Dana sneered at his "slovenly dress" and "imperfect English". "He can never get over that *hang-dog* look, as if he had stolen sheep in his boyhood, and was afraid you knew it."[53] Yet when Dana and his friends needed help, the ill-bred Wilson was often the man they found most helpful. A contemporary journalist, C. T. Congdon, thought Wilson honest in the main, "but he had an incurable propensity to manage and maneuver, and though direct enough in his purposes he did not hesitate to promise them by indirect methods."[54]

Yet with all the strife that he caused or suffered, with all the attacks that he faced, with all the social snubs that he encountered, Wilson neither bore malice nor remained angry overnight. Wilson once received a letter from Benjamin Butler of Massachusetts, a master of diatribe, which poured invective on his head. When he showed it to his friend Samuel Hoar, his only comment was "That is a cussed mean letter," and apparently he never spoke or thought of it again.[55]

Despite all the effort expended, the election results simply confirmed that the Free Soil campaign had been hopeless. Probably no candidate could have carried the day, and the light vote showed the indifference of the electorate. Both Taylor and Cass carried fifteen states each, Van Buren none. The results in Massachusetts, however, indicated that the cause was far from lost for the future. The Free Soilers could see progress. In the Presidential election of 1844, the Liberty party received nine percent of the entire vote in the state, while in 1848 the Free Soil party received twenty-nine percent. Equally significant was the shift in major party support. In 1844, the Whigs received fifty-one percent of the entire vote compared to forty-five percent in 1848. The Democrats had forty percent of the vote in 1844, and only twenty-six percent in 1848. For a new party dominated by former Whigs, a surprising number of Democrats had transferred their allegiance, another clue to future political combinations.

No one was less likely to give up the battle than Wilson, particularly now that he pictured himself as a newspaper editor. Adams had dejectedly terminated his brief tenure as editor of the *Republican* and Wilson found himself tempted to try his hand where his friend had failed. For all his courageous lashing out against conservative Whigs, Adams had been a nervous editor from the start. He continually worried about the expense of operation, poor circulation, and lack of support from his friends. But during the campaign subscriptions had increased and the time seemed more propitious for such an undertaking. Even Adams thought that Wilson might be the man to give the project the effort that it required to make a success. Besides, Wilson's shoe business had suffered from his political position and he was not averse to finding a more lucrative line of work.[56]

The name of Henry Wilson appeared on the masthead of the *Republican* as early as September 1848, but it was not until November 11, 1848 that he formally signed a partnership agreement with William S. Damrell, Francis and Martin Moore, and Curtis C. Nichols. They became known as the Wilson, Damrell Company for the purpose of publishing the *Daily Republican, Semi-weekly Republican* and *Weekly Emancipator* and *Republican*. They began with high hopes and a plea for wider circulation. The basic idea of the paper was to advance antislavery and the Free Soil organization, but they also planned to create broader appeal by printing all current news.

Shortly after Wilson started with the paper, Adams submitted a series of pieces "On The State of the Parties" and caused something of a stir in Boston. He asked, "Shall State Street rule Massachusetts? Shall a money influence dictate to her the terms of her own degradation, making her the mere football of the South. . . ."[57]

Wilson, through the pages of the *Republican,* concentrated on keeping the Free Soil party alive on all levels of government. "We trust that the Free Soil men in Boston and in other cities and towns, will keep up their organization, make it complete where it is defective, and never yield an inch before the opposing parties . . ." In answer to questions as to the need for a separate political organization, the *Republican* replied that only an independent party would have the power to oppose the inroads of slavery.[58]

But all was not smooth with the management of the paper. William Robinson, an antislavery journalist, later known as "Warrington," served as editor for a time and he claimed that Wilson's partner Damrell was afraid of Milk and State Streets, Adams to the contrary; that on more than one occasion he had altered his editorials after they had been sent to the printer. When Robinson found out that changes had been made he finally threatened "to have the type distributed" if it occurred again. So the journalistic ambitions of Henry Wilson dissolved into a sorrowful experience as wrangling among the staff and complaints among the faithful followers replaced thoughts of high purpose. Too many friends had ideas about how the paper should be written, and too few friends had ideas about offering financial support.

Wilson made many mistakes and the biggest of all was to rush into the venture in the first place. Even though many of his associates thought he could turn his hand to anything, it was simply not his business. His inexperience, coupled with lack of sufficient capital crippled him from the outset. As time passed his difficulties multiplied. Complaints about Robinson's editorship forced Wilson to bring in another man, Eugene Smith, formerly editor of the *Hartford Courant.* Smith received twelve dollars a week, while Robinson got a five dollar reduction in pay to fifteen dollars a week. He was also informed that if something more promising turned up he could feel free to leave. Smith and Robinson served on an equal basis, but they did not appear in the paper as editors. In this unhappy arrangement their task was to follow Wilson's instructions to make the paper become what he wanted. Wilson intended to spend more time in the office, and eventually he hoped to organize a group of writers who would furnish the quality that he desired. Control rested with him, but at that time he did not wish anyone's name, including his own, to appear as editor. He considered bringing in someone else in the near future who would serve in that position, possibly John G. Palfrey.

A guiding influence in Wilson's decisions was the necessity to cut expenses. He told Robinson that this was the best arrangement that he could make, but it was a poor one that satisfied nobody. Dissatisfied, Robinson left the paper. Wilson took his troubles to Charles Francis Adams, but Adams could still vividly recall his own unhappy experiences, and wanted no part of the headache.

In June 1849, a few interested Free Soilers, including Adams, met at Sumner's office to try to improve the deteriorating situation. The group listened to a letter from Wilson which clearly indicated that he had failed, and that publication would stop if he could not sell his interest. There was much talk, but no tangible assistance.

By August the masthead stated that a new firm Wilson & Bent, had taken over publication. Wilson delayed the termination of the paper by bringing in new blood. But he made matters worse by supporting coalition views contrary to the advice of his close friends, Adams, Palfrey, and Phillips. The *Republican* made increasing references to the possibility of a union ticket for the next election. "We shall not stop to inquire where a man has been, but only inquire where he is right now. Most of us are too young in our conversion to the cause of the slave to be overdistrustful of new converts. . . ." Such hints of coalition only embarrassed and alienated his friends.[59]

Anson Burlingame, a henchman of Charles Francis Adams, thought the *Republican* a sickly paper. "It is in the hands of General Wilson, a good man in his proper place, but who is altogether beyond his depth in editing a newspaper. He is, or has been, anxious to get another truck and dicker. We Whig Free Soilers knocked that Democratic move in the head after considerable trouble and have not the least idea of being traded off to Democracy to gratify anybody's desire to go to the United States Senate. . . ."[60]

On November 15, 1849 the *Republican* announced that publication would stop, but again some last minute aid arrived which delayed the demise. Finally, in January 1851, Wilson gave up with a loss of about seven thousand dollars.[61] Wilson was a failure as a newspaperman, but staggering under the crushing blow, he still had the strength, ability, inclination, and resilience to try to organize a coalition that might elect at least one antislavery United States Senator from Massachusetts. It was a difficult, treacherous, unpopular path before him. Still, it was a job for his talents. Unwilling to despair too much over his publishing troubles, he plunged into his new self-appointed task with all his vigor.

NOTES

[1] Wilson, *Rise & Fall,* II, 188.

[2] Wilson, *Rise & Fall,* II, 188-189; Russel B. Nye, *Fettered Freedom* (East Lansing, Michigan State College Press, 1949), pp. 218-249.

[3] Wilson to Schouler, April 16, 1844, William Schouler MSS, MHS.

[4] Glyndon G. Van Deusen, *The Life of Henry Clay* (Boston: Little, Brown & Co., 1937), p. 365.

[5] Van Deusen, *Clay,* pp. 373-375.

[6] *New York Times,* Nov. 23, 1875.

[7] Wilson, *Rise and Fall,* I, 623, 636.

[8] Wilson, *Rise and Fall,* I, 640.

[9] William Gleason Bean, "The Transformation of Parties in Massachusetts . . . from 1848 to 1860" (unpublished Ph.D. dissertation, Harvard University, 1922), p. 55.

[10] David Donald, *Charles Sumner and the Coming of the Civil War* (New York: Alfred Knopf, 1960), p. 138.

[11] Wilson, *Rise and Fall,* I, 641.

[12] *Ibid.,* p. 643.

[13] *Ibid.,* p. 645.

[14] Donald, *Sumner,* p. 141; Martin B. Duberman, *Charles Francis Adams* (Boston: Houghton Mifflin Co., 1961), p. 108.

[15] Charles Francis Adams, *Diary,* Dec. 16, 1845, MHS.

[16] Massachusetts General Court, *Legislative Documents,* Senate No. 28, 1846.

[17] Massachusetts General Court, *Legislative Documents,* House No. 89, 1846.

[18] Nason and Russell, *Wilson,* p. 67.

[19] Wilson, *Rise and Fall,* II, 117-118; George F. Hoar, *Autobiography of Seventy Years* (New York: Charles Scribner's Sons, 1903, 2 vols.), I, 134.

[20] Wilson to Schouler, Nov. 26, 1846, William Schouler MSS, MHS.

[21] CFA, *Diary,* May 23, 1846.

[22] Donald, *Sumner,* pp. 146-148; CFA *Diary,* June, July, 1846, Sept. 21, 1846.

[23] Wilson to Schouler, Nov. 26, 1846, William Schouler MSS, MHS.

[24] Hazard, *Boot and Shoe Industry,* p. 213.

[25] Wilson to Schouler, Nov. 26, 1846, William Schouler MSS, MHS.

[26] Boston *Daily Whig,* March 11, April 3, June 17, 1847.

[27] CFA, *Diary,* April 7, 1847.

[28] Boston *Daily Whig,* August 18, 1847.

[29] John Palfrey to CFA, Dec. 15, 1847, Adams, MSS, MHS; Donald, *Sumner,* pp. 156-159.

30 John Palfrey to Charles Sumner, Feb. 28, 1848, John G. Palfrey MSS, HL.
31 Charles Francis Adams to John G. Palfrey, March 15, 1848, CFA Letterbook, MHS.
32 *Ibid.*
33 Donald, *Sumner,* p. 163; *Boston Republican,* Oct. 5, 1848.
34 J. N. Brewer to W. Schouler, May 21, 1848, William Schouler MSS, MHS.
35 CFA, *Diary,* May 27, 1848.
36 Wilson to Webster, May 31, 1848, Daniel Webster MSS, Baker Library, Dartmouth College.
37 *Daily Commonwealth,* July 14, 1852.
38 Holman Hamilton, *Zachary Taylor—Soldier in The White House* (New York: The Bobbs-Merrill Company, Inc., 1951), p. 95.
39 *Daily Republican,* Springfield, Mass., June 12, 1848.
40 *Daily Commonwealth,* July 14, 1852.
41 CFA, *Diary,* June 12, 1848.
42 Wilson, *Rise and Fall,* II, 144, 145.
43 Boston *Daily Atlas,* June 13, 1848; Salem *Gazette,* June 23, 1848.
44 Chester Adams to Horace Mann, June 14, 1848, Horace Mann MSS, MHS.
45 Bean, "Party Transformation," p. 25.
46 Donald, *Sumner,* p. 166.
47 Wilson, *Rise and Fall,* II, 146.
48 Wilson, *Rise and Fall,* II, 146, 148.
49 Bean, "Party Transformation," pp. 24-26.
50 Oscar Sherwin, *Prophet of Liberty* (New York: Bookman Associates, 1958), pp. 145, 146.
51 George F. Hoar, *Autobiography,* I, 217, 218.
52 Donald, *Sumner,* p. 170.
53 See Samuel Shapiro, *Richard Henry Dana* (East Lansing: Michigan State College Press, 1961).
54 Charles T. Congdon, *Reminiscences of a Journalist* (Boston: James R. Osgood & Co., 1880), p. 132.
55 Hoar, *Autobiography,* I, 217.
56 CFA, *Diary,* August 24, 1848.
57 *Boston Republican,* Dec. 13, 1848.
58 Boston *Republican,* Nov. 30, 1848, Dec. 14, 1848.
59 Boston *Republican,* June 25, 1349.
60 Bean, "Party Transformation," p. 55.
61 Nason & Russell, *Wilson,* p. 91.

3

Coalition

By 1849, Massachusetts politicians had started thinking in terms of coalition. The election the year before clearly showed that the Whigs were now a minority party in the state, and delegates to county conventions, haggling for political plums, awakened to the possibilities of a new combination. Then too, the suggestion of a temporary alliance to gain antislavery representation was not unique. In 1847, the fused strength of New Hampshire Whigs and antislavery Democrats sent John Hale to the United States Senate, and similar conditions elected Hannibal Hamlin of Maine and Salmon P. Chase of Ohio. Other Northern states, New York and Wisconsin among them, also fashioned loose mergers which met with varying degrees of success at the polls.

The hope of winning the majority vote in the state legislature alleviated the difficult task of hammering out specific arrangements between the widely differing Democrats and Free Soilers in Massachusetts. Democrats hungry for office, and a strong faction of the Free Soil party led by Henry Wilson, tired of "petrified Whiggery", were anxious to join forces for practical aims. To Wilson gaining power meant everything; noble sentiments were fine, but he wanted the authority of office more than the emptiness of exalted talk. In the spring of 1849 an editorial in the *Republican* quoting Charles Sumner claimed: "Should the

59

opposition combine its energies it will crush forever the power of 'the lords of the lash and the lords of the loom.' "[1]

Wilson and Sumner were ready to form an alliance with the Democrats at the 1849 Free Soil State convention. Wilson managed the floor of the convention, and Sumner, as chairman of the committee on resolutions, asked the delegates who opposed slavery not to forget the tyrannical money power of the Commonwealth. His resolutions called for cheaper postage, the election of postmasters, the free grant of land to settlers, and the retrenchment of federal expenses and reduction of patronage. There was also an expression of alarm about the tendency of legislation to consolidate wealth in corporations. All of this had the sound of radical Democracy. Some former Whigs, Charles Francis Adams among them, had misgivings about these resolutions, but under Wilson's skillful guidance the convention accepted them.[2]

In September, 1849, the Democratic State Convention at Springfield flirted with the idea of coalition too, when it passed resolutions opposing slavery and its extension to the territories. The Democratic state leader, Benjamin F. Hallett, drew up these resolutions and showed them to Wilson prior to the convention. The Democratic *Post* supported the move and expressed the view that the two minority parties would act together in the state.[3]

Such thoughts were far from pleasing to Adams, Dana, and Palfrey with whom Wilson associated as a "Conscience" Whig and Free Soiler. They considered all attempts to organize a coalition a complete surrender of principle and the work of the devil. To their statesmanlike eyes the scheme was the same as the throwing of a race by jockeys.[4] In the fall of 1849 Adams and Wilson held a heated discussion over party policies which only strained their previously friendly relationship.[5] Adams had rationalized running with Van Buren on the national Free Soil ticket, yet now he took a moralistic stand against Wilson for advocating expediency. Ironically, William Robinson, the journalist, said that he heard Adams suggest expedients by the hour.[6]

New factors which Adams did not care to admit to himself were creeping into the situation. Wilson was no longer simply a lieutenant useful for running errands and collecting information. Rapidly stepping forward as an appealing political figure in his own right he aroused considerable personal jealousy. More than one New England gentleman considered Wilson a good man in his place, but felt that he had neither the background nor the proper education to challenge men who were confident of their natural right to govern.[7]

Opposition to the coalition on the basis of righteousness was oversimplification. The coalitionists wanted their cooperation to pay off with immediate rewards, but it was also true that they shared some ideas to develop the affinity. Free Soilers like Wilson, Keyes, and Bird had far more in common in matters of manner and principle with Democrats like Boutwell and Banks than they did with the Dana-Adams-Palfrey trio.

A confusion of principles ran through the three state parties. Differences and similarities concerning state and national affairs within each group set men of the same party against each other and fused others from opposite parties into a common front. In the midst of ties which thus criss-crossed party lines, some of the ideas of the Locofocos attracted men of Wilson's ilk.

Adams, a conservative in local matters, abhorred the radical Democrats. Wilson fought Locofocos too, but he was a reformer at heart and sympathetic to the workingman. Pledging support to reforms for the sake of coalition and the possibility of forming a permanent antislavery party was easier for him. The Locofoco cry against the money power and monopoly was, after all, not too far removed from the old Free Soil complaints about State Street and Cotton Whigs. Wilson knew, moreover, that the protective tariff, the National Bank, and opposition to the annexation of Texas and the war, had been espoused at one time or another by members of both parties.[8] Now the Whigs in control of the state were deaf to change and disgusted Wilson. He described the State Senate as "a great body; stupidity and gross ignorance are its chief characteristics."[9] So without any difficulty Wilson could support the Democrats in measures to give greater representation to small towns, to elect state senators by districts, to adopt the secret ballot, a mechanics lien law and a homestead law.[10]

Despite little preparation and a haphazard organization, the election of 1849 produced some mutual agreements between the two parties in local contests and laid the groundwork for the future. But the great impetus for the continuance came from the

imminence of the Compromise of 1850 with its Fugitive Slave
Law which served as an excellent target for all foes of slavery.

On the seventh of March, 1850, Daniel Webster made his
famous speech supporting the Compromise measures. Feeling in
the state against Webster immediately intensified. The speech
seemed like treason to antislavery workers. The next day, Wilson,
highly overwrought, walked around the Boston Common with
two Democrats, Nathaniel Banks and George Boutwell, and in
an animated conversation he declared war on Webster and put
forth his plan for a coalition. Banks asked him if he was fool
enough to believe that he could succeed by breaking with Webster. Boutwell showed interest, but suffered from doubts and
said little.[11]

Banks and Boutwell were personal as well as political friends
who had risen from poverty, but their warm friendship did not
extend to Wilson. Their working class backgrounds were similar,
and as nimble opportunists they might now have shared common
political interests with Wilson. But they had for years moved in
different circles and regarded him with a certain amount of
suspicion. The conditions of the times, rather than personal
friendship, formed the basis of their eventual alliance.[12]

While the notion of coalition had wide appeal there was no
spontaneous surge among politicians to follow Wilson's lead.
Their sentiments were with him, but they knew that there were
many practical perils in accomplishing such a task. The subject
was good for conversation, a delicate one for action. A report of
the Massachusetts Antislavery Society contained the observation
that a coalition could control Northern politics if it existed in
good faith. But the report noted also:

> There are disturbing influences which are at work on both
> sides to prevent a cordial understanding—an entente cordiale
> —between the treating powers. The mutual fear of being
> overreached in the bargain, the hungering after the fleshpots
> of office which the Democratic Israel will remember to have
> been enjoyed in the Egypt of a Southern Alliance, and the
> apprehensions of the Free Soilers that the little they ask for
> will be conjured away from them in the hugger-mugger of
> political intrigue, must make the union of the parties difficult
> where it is in opposition, and dubious where it has been
> imperfectly effected.[13]

The abolitionists clearly appraised the forces at work. Wilson was aware of these hazards and knew that a false step would finish him politically. Yet with all the dangers, he could not resist the temptation. The job called for a professional, and he was confident that Henry Wilson was that professional.

Some of the Democrats who had toyed with thoughts of coalition in 1849 were now distant. Hallett had cooled to the plan, and Marcus Morton and Caleb Cushing, conservative leaders in the party, were far from enthusiastic about the emphasis upon labor. But Banks and Boutwell agreed to work with Wilson, and they enlisted the aid of two promising Democrats, Robert Rantoul, Jr., and Benjamin Butler, who began to organize the towns throughout the state.

Ignoring criticism, Wilson feverishly worked to construct a Free Soil machine which derived support from pro-labor politicians. John Quincy Adams Griffen and Francis Bird were two of his allies. As usual, he looked to newspapermen for assistance. He found pugnacious William Robinson, who he had dismissed from the *Republican,* and James Stone, "the worker's editor,"[14] both ready to help. Robinson, married to a former Lowell factory girl, was partial to the issue of shorter hours for workingmen.

Anson Burlingame and Samuel Hoar, political friends of Wilson in his home county, Middlesex, withheld their support. Hoar favored a coalition, but a coalition of Whigs and Free Soilers, to win Congressional seats for John Palfrey and the educator Horace Mann.[15] A Democratic-Free Soil partnership seemed unthinkable to him. It was one more example of confused principles and party politics.

In August Free Soilers met at Charles Sumner's office to discuss the appointment of a conference committee to work with the Democratic party "to mature a system of union". A number of members of the State Committee were present. Wilson may have been present, but if not, Keyes and Bird reflected his views by favoring the organization of the committee. Charles Francis Adams vehemently opposed the plan. Although outnumbered, he stalled the plan by persuading John G. Whittier to move to table the question. Adams was certain that the Democrats were moving towards the slave state policies and that the Free Soilers were carrying things too far for the sake of a deal that might give them a United States senatorship. He believed that such action would lose all moral character and ruin the Free Soil party. Accidental combinations born of the necessity of the moment were one thing; a treaty of alliance for a purpose running counter to established principles was quite another.[16]

The equally righteous Sumner was not so strong in his opposition. At this date he may have suspected that he might benefit from a bargain, and he seemed to find ready reasons for turning the state over to the Democrats if one seat in the United States Senate could be gained.[17]

The tension between the Adams wing and the Wilson wing of the party increased. It was, in fact, a struggle for the Free Soil state leadership. At a meeting early in September Wilson, unable to restrain himself, practically read Adams, Palfrey, and their coterie out of the party. This was the first clear break in their relations. Adams angered Wilson by blocking his idea of practical progress for the antislavery cause. Wilson angered Adams by his disregard of principle and lack of respect for Adams' established leadership. To make matters worse, Adams also learned that Wilson wanted to prevent his friend, Stephen C. Phillips, from getting the Free Soil nomination for Governor.[18]

A few days later two large parlors of the Adams House in Boston filled with prominent Democrats and Free Soilers to confer once again on the possibility of union. The evasive words of the speakers indicated that no one wished to assume direct responsibility for making a deal. Marcus Morton, the last Democratic Governor of Massachusetts, reported to be against a coalition, spoke against any agreement to divide offices, and then proceeded to present a picture of how it could be done. The oratorical fog did not lift until Adams announced his complete disapproval of any plan of union. In this timid and confused atmosphere he found support among subsequent speakers until Wilson had his turn. Even Wilson, while defending the proposal, lowered his sights and settled for a concession which simply gave individuals leeway to act for union in minor elections. The meeting prohibited any action by the central organization.[19] Adams felt that he had won something of a victory, but Wilson refused to admit defeat.

The 1850 Free Soil State Convention met at Washington Hall on Bromfield Street, Boston. Most of the real action took place behind the public denunciation of Webster and the Compromise. Wilson apparently saw little hope in openly pledging the party to a coalition, but behind the scenes he was busy. Prompted by Wilson's intimations, Stephen C. Phillips wanted to drop out as a candidate for Governor. He had no wish to be a scapegoat in any trade for office, but Adams and Sumner ignored Phillips' wishes since they felt that it would be playing into the hands of coalitionist conspirators if he did not try for the nomination. After an adjournment, the delegates reconvened at the Beech Street Theater, and Wilson, for the Committee of Nominations, reported the names of Phillips for Governor and Amasa Walker for Lt. Governor. But even then Wilson and his friends aimed to trade Boutwell for Sumner; the Democrat Boutwell to be Governor, the Free Soiler Sumner to be Senator. This objective was widely known.[20]

Disgusted with Wilson's covert maneuvering, Adams regarded him bitterly. "If I could be astonished at anything," he wrote, "it would be the proclivity of Wilson of whom I once thought well. But politics are in their essence corrupting, and they seem to have done their work upon him. . . ."[21] Adams had misgivings about Sumner too, whom he thought to be playing a game of duplicity. He believed that Sumner's perceptions of men were poor and that his stand had encouraged profligate maneuvers of others who had worse motives. Mingled with Adams' bitterness over "circuitous tricks to gain power", was the realization that his own ambitions were collapsing. There was no question that he would have jumped at an opportunity to be Senator, possibly as an antislavery Whig candidate.[22] Now hope faded because of a man he considered far beneath him in intellect and ability; a man capable only of political intrigue.

Wilson's leadership in building a political organization, based upon minute division of labor, brought the voters to the polls and helped win the election for the coalition.[23] In both Houses of the legislature they controlled the majority vote. The election of the Governor was left to the legislature and it was certain that Boutwell would be named without difficulty. Wilson would keep his part of the bargain. The next move would be to place Sumner in the Senate. The procedure was simple, the understanding was clear, and there was no reason to anticipate any stumbling; yet the trouble had just begun. Would the Democrats act in good faith to carry out the bargain? After the election, with the governorship assured for them, their attitude seemed to change. The thought frightened Wilson. He fought hard for the arrangement. Now he must have asked himself a thousand questions. Had he gone too far? Would he be sold out by the Democrats? Could he hold the coalition together long enough to elect Sumner?

Walking along the street in Boston one cold day in November, Wilson ran into Adams. He frankly admitted concern about the outcome of his plans and he told Adams that he did not trust the Democratic leaders who now seemed to be against conceding the Senatorship. In his predicament Wilson received little comfort from Adams who informed him once again that he did not believe in any position except one of principle. Wilson assured him that he would settle for nothing less and that he might blow up the coalition and make terms with the Whigs. But this was an impractical remark born of worry and Adams pointed out that only a great probability of union with the Democrats would secure any advances from the Whigs. Adams realized that Wilson and his friends scarcely knew where to turn and that to achieve success from this ticklish situation would require the nicest management. As Adams walked away he congratulated himself that he had stood upon principle and avoided the affair.[24]

The following month brought no lessening of tension. Wilson saw signs of treachery on every side. Distressed with events, he called on Adams to discuss his troubles. But their divergent views kept them apart. Wilson's interest in placing antislavery people in places of power seemed to Adams nothing more than an unworthy sacrifice for the sole interest of gaining office. "He is lax in principle," Adams wrote, "without absolutely wanting it, and wavering in purpose."[25] But the conversation made Adams sorely conscious that he was no longer in the confidence of the Free Soil leaders.

Wilson, on the other hand, may have appreciated Adams' principles, but the state political machinery was his chief concern at this time. All the parts of the jerry-built organization troubled him, but he did his best to make it work. Ironically, as he grappled with an organization on the verge of collapse, he was becoming, despite all the headaches, the acknowledged leader of the antislavery politicians in the state. Still this fact did not diminish his trouble.

On New Year's Eve members of the two parties met at the State House to make arrangements for the organization of the government. The Democrats met in the Green Room; the Free Soilers, Wilson among them, met in Attic #1 directly over the Democrats. Before long, the Democratic caucus sent word to the Free Soilers that they had named a committee of five to discuss arrangements with them. The Free Soilers promptly agreed to meet, and appointed a similar committee. That evening the two groups met. The Democratic leader announced that the two Houses should be organized by giving the Democrats the Speaker and Clerk of the House, and the Free Soilers, the President and Clerk of the Senate. The proposal seemed reasonable to the Free Soilers and they concurred.[26]

There was still much to be arranged, but this was an amicable start. The next day, January 1, 1851, saw something of a social and political revolution in Massachusetts. The proud, aristocratic Whigs were no longer the proprietors of power in the state. The common man, prominently represented in the coalition, invaded the domain of the elite in the persons of Henry Wilson, "The Natick Cobbler", who became President of the Senate, and Nathaniel Banks, "The Bobbin Boy", who became Speaker of the House.

That evening members of the two parties met again to continue the negotiations of the previous night. The Free Soilers, eager for a quick settlement, expressed their desire to meet the whole subject with fairness, frankness, and good faith. They proposed to concede the governorship to the Democrats on the condition that they would receive the long term United States Senatorship. Wilson later reported they were willing to elect Boutwell as Governor without any pledges for principles, measures, or offices, and would take no responsibility for his administration. In return, the Free Soil Senator would go to Washington unpledged and uncommitted to any party or group of men. The conference weighed the comparative value of Governor versus Senator, and finally approved the agreement.

Wilson made another suggestion. He proposed that the Free Soilers also take the Senator for the short term and let the Democrats have the Lieutenant Governorship, and a majority of the Council. But this was not accepted. The negotiations continued with further proposals and counter proposals. The Democrats were insistent on getting the Lieutenant Governor, five Councilors, the Treasurer, and the short term Senator. They would concede the Secretary to State, four Councilors, the Auditor, and Sergeant-at-Arms to the Free Soilers. This required a concession by Wilson and his friends, but in their anxiety to secure the long term Senator they were ready to go to great lengths. At last the Democratic terms were adopted by the Free Soilers with only one dissenting vote; the Democratic caucus concurred without any dissenters.[27] "Truck and dicker" divided the highest offices in the state and nation. The results delighted Wilson. He had achieved his primary objective against strong opposition.

The agreement worked according to plan at first. Both parties agreed to Robert Rantoul, Jr., for the Senate short term, and the Free Soiler, Charles Sumner for the long term. Only one Free Soiler opposed the Democrat Rantoul, and only six Democrats opposed Sumner. Democrats assured Wilson that Sumner's election was certain by a majority of at least twenty votes. After the first week of the New Year all difficulties appeared to be settled.[28]

The legislature elected Boutwell Governor. A motion then passed to follow with the remaining selections on Friday, January 10, but the Whigs and a few Democrats brought a delay until Saturday; and on Saturday someone blundered with a poorly formed motion that put the vote off until Tuesday, the fourteenth.[29] Wilson may have felt some uneasiness over this time lag, but he continued to receive assurances that all was well. Not wishing to show any distrust of their allies, the Free Soilers lived up to their bargain and participated in the election of the Councilors. The Democrats, third party in the legislature, with less than one third of the Senate seats, and scarcely more than one quarter of the House were now the party in power.

Securely in office, the discontented rumblings of the Democrats intensified. On Monday a number of Democrats who had taken part in the New Year negotiations held a private meeting to defeat Sumner. Caleb Cushing, the leader of this faction who was destined to be nominated by President Grant, but not approved by the Senate, for Chief Justice of the United States, considered Sumner an abolitionist agitator and he now claimed that he had not been bound by a caucus that had been held to bind the Democrats together. At a meeting on January 6, James M. Usher, a Senator from Middlesex County had offered a resolution pledging the Democratic legislators to abide by the final caucus decision. Concerning their selection of candidates, Cushing had voted for this resolution which passed 74 to 6.[30]

The *Post* quickly forgot that Boutwell could not have been elected without Free Soil support. It maintained that the coalition had been formed for state, not national, affairs. This was not so. It had been generally known that the Free Soil goal was the United States senatorship. During the campaign the newspaper, *Free Soiler,* edited by F. W. Bird, openly stated, "Our paramount object is to advance the cause of freedom by breaking down a proslavery organization and electing a U.S. Senator."[31]

The change of heart among the Democrats did not result from any misunderstanding. The revulsion that revolved around the personal and political beliefs of Charles Sumner, "the classical ornament of the antislavery party", caused the trouble. And there may have been side issues too. Senator Usher said that a factional quarrel within the party stirred up opposition.[32]

January 14, the date set for the election of Senator, brought throngs to the door of the State House. Spectators, anxious to follow the proceedings, filled the galleries. The members cast their vote. Sumner received 186; 110 cast by Free Soilers, 76 by Democrats. Robert Winthrop, the Whig candidate, received 167, and there were 28 scattered votes. Sumner needed five more votes to win the election. The Free Soilers had been betrayed. Another vote taken the same day left the results unaltered.

The next day the vote showed worse results, and the day after that, there was simply a gain of one ballot for Sumner. Wilson was infuriated, and to make matters more difficult a host of new strategies and viewpoints appeared from all sides. John Greenleaf Whittier, who may have been the first person to suggest Sumner for the Senate, now thought he made a mistake in supporting the coalition. Distressed by the rough battle, Whittier advised Sumner to abandon the contest.[33] Sumner maintained a lofty pose, but he had an agonizing time in his efforts to present an indifferent appearance with his proper friends and at the same time show his eagerness for the post among his rowdy allies in the coalition. Upset by the rush of events, he told Adams that he wished the whole thing had been sunk; that he had been swept

along in the beginning without carefully looking into the
situation.[34]

When still others, such as John Bigelow, an active politician in
the state, counseled Sumner to give up, Wilson refused to countenance the idea and expressed every confidence of final victory.
His great hope was that Banks would adhere to the bargain and
have sufficient weight to carry the Democratic side. But Banks
had his troubles too. He came into conflict with Cushing, and
behind Cushing was the slick state boss, Benjamin Hallett.[35]

On January 17, the Massachusetts correspondent for the *New
York Daily Tribune reported:*

> No Senator yet. Further balloting has been postponed a
> week. The probability is there will be no election. It looks
> very much as though the Free Soilers had been sold.[36]

On January 22, the Senate elected Sumner over Winthrop,
but it was a hollow victory since there was still no progress in
the House. As time dragged on, Wilson became the chief target
of criticism for the handling of the situation. Stephen Higginson,
brother of the prominent abolitionist Thomas Wentworth Higginson, thought Wilson's temperament was too sanguine and that
he had been misled by vague promises into a condition of help-
lessness.[37] The newspapers were busy too. The *Atlas* and the
Advertiser feuded with the *Commonwealth* and freely referred to
"bargain and sale" and "the impossible Senator". Edward Everett,
ready to believe anything evil about Wilson, wrote an article for
the *Advertiser* on "Bribery and Corruption" in which he charged
that an agreement between candidates for high office to vote for
each other was essentially as corrupt as getting votes by giving
money.[38]

The situation became so desperate that Wilson, in an effort to
win public support, wrote a letter to *The Commonwealth* airing
all the negotiations between the Democrats and Free Soilers. He
made no secret of the State House conferences, and reviewed
their action step by step.[39] Wilson continued to fight, but more
and more it looked like a battle against windmills. Yet he refused
to give up. He had counted on so many who now offered nothing.
Boutwell, comfortably ensconced in the Governor's chair, could
have broken the logjam, but now he preferred to take a hands
off attitude and announce that the matter was in the control of

the legislature.[40] Marcus Morton withdrew his support, too. He gave as his reason that coalitions brought out the worst elements of both parties, but he was probably unhappy that his own role was not larger. Wilson blasted Morton's "croaking, paltering . . . duplicity."[41] Still, Wilson searched for any hopeful trend. Through February the ballots continued. From one tally to another there were differences of no consequence, and it was generally conceded that Sumner could not be elected.

From day to day party complications and personal jealousies multiplied. As the legislature lingered, attention focused increasingly upon Cushing and Wilson. Cushing, a charming, learned man, in contrast to the crude Wilson, contended that the election of Sumner would bring disunion. For added measure he had a distinct dislike for shoemakers in politics. As he looked around the State House, he saw not only "The Natick Cobbler," President of the Senate, but also Amasa Walker, Secretary of the Commonwealth, and John E. Alley, a Senator and member of the Council. All were shoemakers, or held an interest in the shoe trade. There were others too, and the shoe towns generally supported the Free Soil party. Cushing asked Boutwell, "What I wish to know, Governor, is whether this state is to be shoemakerized or not?"[42]

At more than one conference Cushing said that any Free Soiler other than Sumner would be acceptable to his group. Despite his dislike for shoemakers he urged Wilson to come forward as the compromise candidate.[43] Perhaps it might have been arranged. Certainly no one would disagree that it had become impossible to elect Sumner. Yet Wilson, regarded by so many as a self-seeker, turned a deaf ear to the offer and left no doubt in anyone's mind that his man was Sumner.

Wilson proved to be an able leader under pressure. With his close associates, Bird, Keyes, and Alley, he weaved his way through a maze of contradictory forces. He was everywhere. He gave encouragement where needed, conciliated where needed, and talked roughly where needed. He hustled for extra votes in the lobby of the State House, buttonholed others at the Marlboro Hotel, and tracked some to their rooms. Then there were the incessant meetings. To some he seemed a coarse operator, but he remained loyal to Sumner. A contemporary said that other men could carry organization to a finer point, but for the job before them Wilson had no peer.[44]

Through March the battle raged. "It is now certainly known," the correspondent for the *New York Daily Tribune* wrote, "that Sumner cannot be elected; and as the Free Soilers resolutely refuse to put up another candidate, the election goes over."[45]

On April 23, the first ballot of the day required 194 votes for a Sumner victory. Sumner received 193 certain and one doubtful which had his name written with a pencil mark drawn across it. After a half hour debate the election committee reported that two more votes were cast than there were members present. The electrified House refused to adjourn and another ballot was ordered. An erroneous report of Sumner's election spread around the town and *The Commonwealth* prematurely hung out a dozen flags. Crowds formed around the State House and excitement grew as the decision seemed near. But after three indecisive ballots the House adjourned.

The next day the returns of the first ballot indicated two more votes then there were members present. Rumors ran riot about pressures and counter pressures, promises and threats. Edward Everett heard that there were strong suspicions that there were attempts to gain votes by holding out hopes that some Free Soilers might support the Hoosac Tunnel, a much debated local project.[46] Sidney Bartlett, a Boston Whig, moved that they use envelopes for the next vote. He hoped to prevent mistakes and perhaps give the Democrats an opportunity to vote against Sumner. So there were sealed envelopes for the twenty-sixth ballot. One hundred and ninety-three votes were necessary to win this time. The clerks counted exactly 193 for Sumner, and he became the new United States Senator. No one seems to know who changed his crucial vote, but Wilson intimated that it was one Israel Haynes of Sudbury.[47]

Sumner received the news calmly at the Adams home on Mount Vernon Street where he was, by plan, having dinner with his friend and great foe of the coalition. At this moment of victory Sumner illustrated his preference for Charles Francis Adams and respectability over the riff-raff of the coalition. Henry Adams later wrote that his father and his friends held the correct and noble position concerning the coalition. While they were too good to take part in it, they were not too good to take profit, and Charles Sumner was "the partner to receive these stolen goods."[48]

Wilson was far from calm when victory came. His joy knew no bounds. By evening thousands of people were crowding about the Commonwealth office and Wilson joined the celebration. When he spoke in praise of the election some hecklers interrupted him with shouts for Daniel Webster, and he proudly answered, "Victory this day consummated dates from the 7th of March, 1850, when that great man stood up in the Senate and repudiated the long cherished sentiments of Massachusetts."[49]

The next day Sumner wrote to Wilson:

> To your ability, determination, and fidelity our cause owes its present success. For weal or woe, you must take the responsibility of having placed me in the Senate of the United States.[50]

In many ways the Sumner victory was a greater victory for Wilson. Generally recognized as the prime mover of the coalition, he skillfully directed it through agonizing months, with odds against him, to a succesful conclusion. From the battle he emerged as a symbol of the workingman's triumph over the inheritors in state politics. The glory had gone to Sumner, but Wilson's stature as a practical operator of the state machinery in the struggle against slavery reached new heights as he became the chief working politician of the Free Soil group. He had taken a long hazardous step and won.

NOTES

[1] Boston *Republican,* June 27, 1849.
[2] Boston *Republican,* October 11, 1849; Donald, Sumner, p. 182.
[3] Wilson, *Rise and Fall,* II, 339.
[4] Henry Adams, *The Education of Henry Adams* (New York: The Modern Library, 1931), p. 49.
[5] CFA, *Diary,* October 15, 17, 1849.
[6] Mrs. Robinson, ed., *Pen Portraits,* p. 418.
[7] Bean, "Party Transformation," p. 55.
[8] Boston *Daily Whig,* April 3, 1847.
[9] Bean, "Party Transformation," p. 41.
[10] *Ibid.,* pp. 34-38.
[11] Mrs. Robinson, ed., *Pen Portraits,* p. 405.
[12] Fred H. Harrington, *Fighting Politician* (Philadelphia: University of Pennsylvania Press, 1948), p. 9.
[13] Massachusetts Anti-Slavery Society, 18th Annual Report, January 23, 1850, p. 38.
[14] *Harrington, Fighting Politician,* pp. 9, 10.
[15] Bean, "Party Transformation," p. 51.
[16] CFA, *Diary,* August 10, 1850.
[17] *Ibid.,* August 12, 1850.

[18] *Ibid.,* September 5, 1850.

[19] CFA, *Diary,* September 10, 1850; Donald, *Sumner,* p. 186.

[20] CFA, *Diary,* October 3, 1850; Bean, "Party Transformation," p. 56.

[21] CFA, *Diary,* October 8, 1850.

[22] *Ibid.,* November 15, 1850.

[23] Bean, "Party Transformation," p. 62.

[24] CFA, *Diary,* November 22, 1850.

[25] *Ibid.,* December 27, 1850.

[26] Boston *Commonwealth,* January 30, 1851.

[27] *Ibid.*

[28] *Ibid.*

[29] *Ibid.*

[30] *Ibid.,* February 18, 1851.

[31] Bean, "Party Transformation," p. 66.

[32] *Ibid.,* p. 69n.

[33] John Whittier to Charles Sumner, January 16, 1851, Sumner MSS, HL. Albert Mordell, *Quaker Militant* (Boston: Houghton Mifflin Co., 1933), p. 164.

[34] CFA, *Diary,* January 12, 1851.

[35] Harrington, *Fighting Politician,* p. 11.

[36] *NYDT,* January 17, 1851.

[37] S. Higginson to C. Sumner, January 17, 1851, Sumner MSS, HL.

[38] Edward Everett, *Diary,* January 31, 1851, MHS.

[39] Boston *Commonwealth,* January 30, 1851.

[40] Boutwell, *Reminiscences,* I, 120.

[41] Donald, *Sumner,* p. 198.

[42] Boutwell, *Reminiscences,* I, 119.

[43] Claude M. Fuess, *The Life of Caleb Cushing* (2 vols.; New York: Harcourt, Brace & Co., 1923), II, 103.

[44] Edward L. Pierce, *Memoir and Letters of Charles Sumner* (4 vols., Boston: Roberts Brothers; 1878-93), III, 248.

[45] *NYDT,* April 3, 1851.

[46] Edward Everett, *Diary,* April 25, 1851, MHS.

[47] *NYDT,* April 24-28, 1851; Fuess, *Cushing* II, 104.

[48] Henry Adams, *Education,* p. 49.

[49] Boston *Commonwealth,* April 25, 1851.

[50] Nason & Russell, *Wilson,* pp. 93-94.

4
Success

The governorship was soon on Wilson's mind. The personal success that he gained as a leader of the coalition increased his stature and he felt certain that if he exerted his usual energy he could reach his goal in 1852. The people were with him, he believed, even while he recognized that he would have to battle the same opposing factions. John Palfrey and Horace Mann were now his chief Free Soil competitors, and some Whigs talked of throwing their support to Palfrey in order to break the Democratic-Free Soil coalition.[1]

Wilson, still the strong advocate of coalition, worked hard to retain the friendship of the Democrats. He believed that it was important to get along well with them, but it was not a simple job and he had many difficult moments organizing the state government at the start of the year. Sumner comfortably ensconced in his Senate seat, could not understand why he should be having any such troubles. Wilson replied that the Whigs were doing all in their power to destroy the coalition.[2] But finally the Democratic-Free Soil coalition established its control of the legislature, and once again Wilson served as President of the Senate, a good springboard for his ambitions.

A variety of activities engaged Wilson during the year. Another presidential campaign loomed ahead, but this time it concerned him primarily in relation to state affairs. The Free Soilers had not decided on a candidate for the presidency, which complicated the local elections; party loyalties in a national election were usually too strong for new groups to form. In Wilson's opinion the Convention might have elected another United States Senator, and a majority of the Massachusetts delegation to the House if the national question had not interfered. For some time Wilson had expected that General Winfield Scott would be the Whig candidate and he respected the soldier's drawing power. He calculated that Scott's military reputation was worth 200,000 votes. If Scott avoided a positive expression of support for the Compromise of 1850, and endorsed the cause of the Hungarian patriot, Louis Kossuth, who was now a popular hero in America, Wilson believed that he would sweep the country.[3] By now Wilson had developed a reputation as a political prognosticator that remained with him for the rest of his life. But, like all such seers, he could be very wrong. Despite many poor forecasts his reputation for this particular talent remained untarnished.

Never one to turn his back on a popular cause, Wilson had quickly identified himself with the enthusiastic supporters of Kossuth, who had been hailed by the American public as a champion of liberty for having established the short lived Republic of Hungary. Wilson could not understand why any one should refuse to give Kossuth whole-hearted support. He wrote to Sumner:

> I hope soon our country as one of the Nations will have it distinctly understood that she is in favor of allowing all nations to settle their own affairs and adopt the form of government they wish and that she opposes the intervention of any other nation in the affairs of other nations—that she will regard such intervention as a violation of the rights of nations and that she will call down upon any nation violating this doctrine the condemnation of the world and if the case demands it I hope she will indicate this doctrine with the thunder of her guns. Let this country and England adopt this policy and who thinks Russia or Austria would violate it.[4]

Wilson was undoubtedly happy to go along with the masses on this soul stirring issue, yet he expressed sentiments that were a genuine part of his nature. If he was guilty of saber rattling in speaking up for Kossuth, and if he seemed overly sympathetic towards the stricken Hungarians, no one could claim that his heart was ever callous to the needs of the underdog. So vigorous was he in his support of Kossuth that many of his friends believed he was ready to endorse the Democratic candidate, Lewis Cass who had spoken for intervention. They warned Wilson to move slowly even though the Hungarian cause was especially popular with coalitionists. Sumner was far from pleased by Wilson's remarks and he made it clear that he did not favor an extreme position.

Before the Kossuth fad dissolved Wilson found that it had served him well by giving him an opportunity to speak out on a subject of some significance other than slavery. When Kossuth visited Massachusetts, Wilson, as chairman of the legislative welcome committee, told him:

> Your victories were our victories. And when by the treachery of Gorgey, Hungary fell before the armed intervention of Russia, they felt and still feel that the Czar had not only violated the rights of Hungary, but had outraged the Law of Nations, and the sentiments of the civilized world.[5]

His speech was well received and widely read. William Seward told Sumner, "What a magnificent speech Wilson made to Kossuth! I have read nothing for a month which took such hold of me."[6]

But the Kossuth fashion faded and once again interest centered upon presidential candidates. Free Soilers faced contradictory frustrations over the presidency. Wilson wanted to support a winner, and believed Winfield Scott the man. But he told Sumner, "We cannot support Scott yet I hope he will be elected and I feel confident he will be. I have for nearly two years believed that he would be nominated and elected and for months I have had no doubt about the adoption of a platform adopting the Compromises."[7] The Whigs discouraged him, but the Democrats offered less comfort with their likely candidate Franklin Pierce. Wilson had occasional hopes about an assortment of men who might accept the thankless job of running as the Free Soil candidate, David Wilmot, Salmon Chase, John Hale, and Charles Francis Adams among them, and he periodically changed his mind about each. He realized too that they might end up without making a nomination, but he did not relish the idea.[8]

In state affairs Wilson's aim was simple, to cultivate the coalition and crush the Whigs. But the coalition was a matter of continual anxiety, and Sumner's delay in speaking out against slavery during his first months in the Senate did not help the situation. Wilson was aware that many suspected him of political machinations for personal advantage, and now that Sumner failed to speak up for antislavery cause he appeared in a worse light. He did not bitterly criticize Sumner, as many did, but he told him frankly of the feeling at home. "You know that some of us have been complained of much and distrusted but we went ahead and now some few of our men do not yet see that our coalition was for our interests. . . ."[9]

In less than a month Wilson wrote to Sumner again in reply to inquiries about sentiments at home and he minced no words:

> Do not for Heaven's sake fail to speak, cost what it may of effort or trouble. I tell you frankly that our people are in a state of disappointment and almost of despair . . . One of our leading men said that if your time was out you could not get a vote for reelection and several gentlemen to whom this was said agreed with him . . . at the Worcester Convention some of our leading men wanted to put in a resolution you would consider as a hint that we were not satisfied with your silence. I state these things to let you know the feeling of our friends for you must not fail to do away with their feelings by making such a speech as all know you can make.[10]

When Sumner finally gave his "Freedom National" speech attacking the Fugitive Slave Act in the Senate, Wilson congratulated him for his "glorious speech", and reminded him none too subtly that he owed his place to his support. "How proud I am that God gave me the power to aid in placing you in the Senate of the United States where you can utter such glorious sentiments."[11]

As the national Free Soil convention approached Salmon P. Chase of Ohio and John Hale of New Hampshire were the leading contenders to head the ticket. Wilson preferred Chase because he thought that his nomination would prove pivotal in the key states of New York, Pennsylvania, Ohio, Indiana, Wisconsin, and Michigan. But he retained an open mind on the candidate and even asked William Seward for his views. "I cannot feel that you and I belong to two parties. I feel and for years have felt that I would fully agree in your principles and now we differ not much in our opinions as to the best result for the cause of freedom. . . ." Again Wilson moved outside party boundaries in search of new alignments.[12]

The Free Soil National Convention met in Pittsburgh. Wilson went as a delegate, and served both as Chairman of the convention, and as Chairman of the National Free Soil Committee, his first national assignment. When Hale received the nomination, Wilson rationalized that it was for the best. With his usual optimism he saw indications that Hale was at once popular among the Democrats and feared by the Whigs.

But the main business of the year, the governorship, now approached a decision, and took precedence over Wilson's other exertions. The threat of Wilson becoming Governor intensified the bitterness of the Adams coterie, and they cautioned each other about preventing a destructive contest among themselves that would end in a Wilson victory by default. Adams continued to have difficulty containing himself when he thought of Wilson. He was certain that he had been undermined by the crafty maneuvering of an inferior. In true Adams fashion he wrote: "Palfrey is to be sacrificed to this insane thirst for official distinction of a third rate man, with the arts of a first rate demagogue!"[13]

As the time for the nominating convention drew near, Adams' suspicions of Wilson seemed to have substance. Playing a double game, Wilson publicly claimed that he was entirely averse to the nomination, while privately he took soundings among the delegates for support at the convention.[14] Clearly, he was guilty of dissimulation. By the middle of September Judge Charles Allen and Wilson wrote to the *Commonwealth* declining the nomination for Governor, but Wilson's letter had a ring which invited further effort in his behalf.

At the state convention at Lowell large crowds noisily supported Wilson, but when the delegates cast their ballots Horace Mann received a larger plurality. The loss of the nomination was a great blow to Wilson. However, he remained at the head of the state committee with every intention of trying for the nomination another year.

Some state politicians thought that Wilson was so shaken by his defeat at the convention that he would have trouble controlling his own district. But they underestimated his resiliency.

Wilson received the Free Soil nomination for Congress, gained thirteen hundred votes over the previous candidate when there was a majority of thousands against his party and lost the election by only ninety-three votes. His strength seemed to suggest that he would either represent the district some day or win the governorship in 1854.[15]

Still, these were dark days for Free Soilers, coalitionists, and for Henry Wilson. The Whigs lost the national election, but they regained control of the state, and the Democrats, now looking for federal patronage, developed a strong anti-coalition faction. They knew that Franklin Pierce did not approve of cooperation with Free Soil. The only remaining hope for the coalitionists was their proposal for a constitutional convention in 1853. Wilson strongly supported the convention and he believed that it could also serve as a stage for his personal ambitions.

Following agitation by the coalitionists, the people voted for the constitutional convention and chose delegates from every town regardless of size in March 1853. It was not necessary for a delegate to be a resident of the area that he represented, and this leeway permitted many prominent men to obtain seats when their local constituencies failed them. Sumner represented Marshfield, Richard Henry Dana, Jr., sat for Manchester instead of Cambridge, and Anson Burlingame, also of Cambridge, represented Northborough. Wilson took the precaution to run for election as a delegate in two towns, Natick and Berlin, and won in both. He had never visited Berlin in his life and he good-naturedly said, "perhaps if they had known me better they would not have elected me. . . ."[16] With the consent of the town, he resigned as their delegate and made way for his friend, George Boutwell, who had failed of election in his home town of Groton.

Wilson arranged for other absentee elections too. Where he succeeded he made friends with his "betters," temporarily at least, where he failed he increased enmity towards himself. Anxious to be a delegate, Richard Henry Dana sought the assistance of Charles Francis Adams who spoke to the crusader, Samuel Gridley Howe. Howe, in turn referred the matter to Wilson who arranged it. Pleased with the result, Dana softened his view of Wilson. "He has shown himself a good-natured, well disposed man, with no personal enmities. I think he is considered by his personal opponents a more honest man than they were disposed to regard him. . . ."[17] But there were times when he was not successful. Wilson worked equally hard to gain seats for Palfrey and Adams, and when he failed they were certain that they were victims of his treachery. Wilson explained that he had tried without success to induce the Irish voters to support Adams.[18]

Despite its waning power, the coalition carried most of the leaders into the convention and dominated the proceedings. Crowding themselves into Representatives Hall at the State House, the delegates elected Nathaniel Banks president of the convention over the Whig ex-Governor George N. Briggs by a vote of 250 to 137. A number of prominent citizens served as delegates. Among the Whigs were Rufus Choate, and Harvard Law School professors, Simon Greenleaf and Joel Parker. Among the coalitionists were the humanitarian Robert Rantoul, Sr., and aggressive politician Benjamin F. Butler of Lowell. But of the total number of delegates, little more than half actively participated in the proceedings. Many elected to the convention were farmers from the western part of the state who were frequently absent. Wilson served as a majority leader with support from George Boutwell, Francis Bird, and Edward L. Keyes. Ben Butler, a ready debater, also helped with his wit, sarcasm, and combativeness. On the Whig side Richard Henry Dana made several speeches, but he was too independent to obtain a following. His voting and influence went against his former Whig associates even though he did not identify himself with the coalition.

The convention gave Wilson an opportunity to exhibit his skill in a deliberative body. He spoke frequently, but rarely for more than ten or fifteen minutes at a time, and he understood the swift currents of the convention. Since he wanted to gain concrete results he tried to pacify various reform elements. He knew that the loose coalition majority was not a dedicated band of reformers and that its strength could easily drift away, so he tried to bind together only when opportunities arose to make plausible changes.

When the eloquent Rufus Choate pleaded to "spare the rust of the constitution", Wilson replied that he thought that their free institutions were to be "ever new, bright, perennial . . . ever to be renewed by the popular intelligence."[19] Wilson wanted to draft a modern constitution which would meet with the approval of the people, and he never hesitated to tell the delegates when he thought a provision might jeopardize their success. Wilson had a larger following than any other single delegate because of his personal acquaintance with all Free Soil and Democratic members, his experience with the coalition from its inception, and his activity. When he rallied forces at any given moment there were probably a hundred delegates ready to follow his signal.

Wilson stood in sharp contrast to his friend Charles Sumner who was much in evidence at the convention but unable to give any practical direction. His lengthy, overly prepared speeches only bored the delegates. On one issue he devoted an entire forenoon to a learned oration filled with ancient and modern historical allusions. As a result the convention voted to limit all future speeches to one hour. George Boutwell, for one, had little regard for Sumner's faculty for handling legislative business. "He was not only not practical, he was unpractical and impracticable."[20]

For all Wilson's ability, he found himself supporting weak measures. The gathering discussed a wide variety of issues, but attention centered upon three, the representation system, the plurality rule in elections, and judicial tenure.

Town representation against district representation was an old feud between town and country. Heavy immigration in the forties had increased the population in the cities, but the declining rural areas retained their representation; still, the small towns were unhappy too since they resented city domination in the legislature. By the use of a general ticket system Boston Whigs continually sent a bloc of forty-four members to the legislature even though Democrats and Free Soilers polled as much as forty percent of the vote. Disgruntled farmers formed a temporary alliance with disgruntled city workers who were unable to win a ten hour law from the Whig legislature.

Richard Dana denounced a logical Whig proposal of representation based upon population by claiming that it disregarded the "little rural towns, where every man has his property, every man his fireside, every man has his family [and a] strong . . . interest in the soil. . . ." He also sneered at "the floating alien population" of Boston. Such statements surprised and delighted

Wilson and Ben Butler who sponsored the coalition plan to under-represent the cities. They knew that their scheme was partisan, but Dana, a man above party ties, defended it as "practical and humane conservatism."[21] In a move to gain permanent control of the House of Representatives, Wilson had introduced the plan to restore annual representation to the smallest towns and reduce Boston's delegation by one-third. Even Wilson could only defend it as a temporary measure that a subsequent legislature could alter. The Natick Cobbler had taken an undemocratic stand on a significant public issue. If he apologized, it must have been on the basis that citizens of rural areas favored the antislavery cause.

The representation resolutions finally adopted gave the small-est towns a representative in the lower House for six years out of ten, and districts based upon population were established for the State Senate. As the Whigs pointed out, one-third of the peo-ple in the state could elect a majority in the House of Repre-sentatives.

Coalitionists had campaigned for a plurality system, but now they defended a majority system as the only hope of restoring a coalition. Very clearly political events rather than principle de-termined their position on this issue. Finally a plurality rule passed, but it did not apply to the election of the governor and congressmen.

On the question of changing judicial tenure the convention held three views. One group, including Ben Butler, wanted an elected judiciary, a second wanted limited, appointive tenure, and a third wanted to retain the *status quo*. Wilson held the sec-ond viewpoint. "I am not ready," he said, "to peril the Constitu-tion in an effort to gain an elective judicial system."[22] But he would have been far wiser to have avoided the entire subject. The question of judicial tenure eventually became a major factor in carrying the people against the new constitution and showed that Wilson had made a grave error in judgment. A large number of delegates, irritated by the life tenure of judges, favored an elec-tive judiciary but many recognized the danger of meddling with such a delicate matter. Marcus Morton, Sr., Chairman of the committee on amendments, wanted to restrict changes in the judicial system, but Wilson led a more radical majority in over-riding the suggestions of Morton's committee. Wilson's resolution, adopted by the convention, proposed to reduce the term of Justices of the Supreme Judicial from life, or "good behavior", to ten years. In lower courts the term would be seven years. Continuance in office would also depend upon a Governor elected for a single year.

There was much good work accomplished in committees which produced a number of suggested revisions in the constitution. Among them were the secret ballot, abolition of property qualifications for Governor and Lieutenant Governor, abolition of imprisonment for debt, election rather than appointment of Attorney-General, Secretary of State, Auditor and Treasurer, and a constitutional convention once every twenty years. After a session of three months and two thousand pages of reported talk the convention submitted eight propositions encompassing their recommendations to the people.

They were:

1—To adopt this preamble, declaration of rights, and frame of government as the Constitution of the Commonwealth of Massachusetts.

2—To enlarge present remedies of habeas corpus.

3—To give juries the right to determine the law and facts in criminal cases.

4—To make judicial investigation of claims against the Commonwealth.

5—To increase the restraints upon imprisonment for debt.

6—To prevent use of the school fund for the benefit of any religious sect.

7—To provide for business incorporation under general rather than special laws.

8—To allow bank incorporation under general law.

Considering the many problems involved, Wilson believed that the convention had done a good job. He also believed that he had accomplished his personal purpose when he received the Free Soil nomination for Governor at the State convention at Fitchburg in September.

Harmony prevailed throughout the optimistic, animated meeting that nominated Wilson. Sumner was absent, but he sent a letter endorsing the new constitution. Amidst unanimity and enthusiasm Wilson received 610 of the 615 votes cast for governor, and his old acquaintance, Amasa Walker, became the nominee for lieutenant governor.[23] While it was a jubilant gathering for those present, there were some former Free Soilers prominent by their absence. Charles Francis Adams, of course, was one such. When he learned the news of Wilson's nomination he declared that "it has given the character by which the party must hereafter bear. A party of dirty, negotiating, trading politics. . . ."[24]

One observer outside the state held a different view. The New York Whig, William Seward, wrote, "If Henry Wilson must be elected over my friends the Whigs of Massachusetts, I shall have two solaces. First in the fact that cause of political justice will have a worthy and noble supporter. Second that those same friends will have a lesson which cannot be read without profit to themselves and the country. . . ."[25]

At later conventions the Whigs nominated Emery Washburn, and the Democrats, Henry W. Bishop. The coalitionists behind Wilson appeared confident of success. Charles Sumner planned to make about twelve speeches during the campaign, the young orator Anson Burlingame intended to speak about thirty times, and George Boutwell and Nathaniel Banks also had heavy speaking schedules. Stumping the state in this fashion disturbed Edward Everett who regarded it as "one of the downward tendencies," and an activity that devolved upon adventurers.[26]

As the campaign progressed Wilson and his friends found opposition in all quarters. Among the bitter opponents of the new constitution were Adams and Palfrey. Unhappy over their exclusion from the convention they energetically fought acceptance of the proposals. There was opposition from many other corners of the state too. To defeat the Constitution aristocratic Whigs combined with Boston Irish, administration Democrats with Independent Free Soilers, pro-slavery proponents with antislavery proponents, large city inhabitants with small town inhabitants. The cry, "Wilson for Governor," seemed to spur many of them to fiercer opposition.

Late in October Caleb Cushing, Attorney General in Franklin Pierce's cabinet, wrote a letter to Robert Frothingham explaining the President's views about the coalitionists in Massachusetts. The letter received wide publicity. Cushing reported the President as believing that "To support or vote for the Free Soilers of Massachusetts is to give countenance and power to persons avowedly in the persistent agitation of the slavery question and therefore hostile in the highest degree to the determined policy of the administration. . . ."[27] Some Free Soilers attacked the letter with great ferocity, while others claimed that it would help their cause. But the letter hurt. Later Whittier told Sumner "up to the time of Cushing's letter I had little doubt of his [Wilson] being Governor."[28]

Wilson lost the election. It was a bitter disappointment and a stunning blow to his hopes and aspirations. Although he gained about two thousand more votes than John Hale received in the Presidential election the previous year, he was a badly beaten man. The year 1853 thus ended in a personal defeat for Henry Wilson, a stillbirth for the new constitution, and the death knell of the coalition. The Whig party remained in complete control of Boston and the state. The bitter opposition of Irish Catholics to the new constitution and the coalition also planted the seed for the growth of the Know Nothing party in Massachusetts. The voters rejected all eight propositions for the new constitution, but the one against appropriation of school funds for parochial schools lost by only a few hundred votes and indicated rising nativist sentiment.

The Whigs poured their taunts upon Henry Wilson, the defeated candidate. It was almost more than his thick skin could stand and for weeks after the election he took unfrequented streets on his way from the railroad station to his warehouse. Once again, without enthusiasm, he returned to manufacturing shoes and delivering lectures to supplement his income. Politics was his life. Now he had little but despair, and his chagrin increased when he realized that men like Palfrey and Adams had misunderstood his methods, purpose, and friendly assistance.[29]

Samuel Gridley Howe told Sumner that their people were scattered and discouraged, and that Wilson had little heart for a fight.[30] But Wilson's mood could not long remain despondent. The Nebraska Bill sponsored by Illinois Senator Stephen Douglas shook him from his lethargy and gave him an opportunity to speak up again. In February 1854 he attacked the bill at a meeting at Faneuil Hall. He also held meetings to raise a "Million Fund" to promote the antislavery cause. On one occasion he raised $70,000 on the spot. He wanted to encourage antislavery sentiment and thought of organizing antislavery leagues throughout the state. He also hoped that the free state Whigs would break away from Southern Whigs. Always on the lookout for possibilities for forming an antislavery party, he tried to arrange for the free-soil Democrats to call a convention to denounce the Nebraska Bill.[31]

By the spring of 1854, he thought of a united Whig party of the sort that Seward seemed to favor had become anathema to Wilson. He told Seward that his own views paralleled Seward's more than that of any other public man from his own party, that he considered Seward the wisest statesman in the union, and hoped that some day he would occupy the White House. But he bluntly told Seward that he would not vote for him against Stephen Douglas if he ran on a united Whig ticket and that he would take that position at the forthcoming Free Soil state convention. He continued:

> I think the time has come to dissolve the infamous union of the Whigs of the north and south. If the northern Whigs will now act they can unite with them 160,000 Free Soilers and tens of thousands of Democrats and carry with a rush every Free State . . . [W]e can make a power that will crush forever the slave propagandists of the free States . . . Under your lead we can go to battle and to victory. For one I shall do all in my power to defeat any efforts to reconstruct and build up the national Whig party.[32]

While Wilson wrote these words he was already a secret member of one of the many Know Nothing Councils that had sprung up in Massachusetts. But he saw no conflict between this action and his statements to Seward. He convinced himself that he could not exclude himself from any organization that might fight slavery. His ambition gave room for rationalization. At the Free Soil state convention held a few days later at the Music Hall in Boston he enthusiastically spoke about the "one great Republican party" which should consolidate all enemies of slavery.[33]

The "American party" or Know Nothings came abruptly to the forefront in Massachusetts in 1854. But the causes for a nativist party had seethed for years. In the early nineteenth century thousands of Irish had immigrated to Boston to escape famine and poverty. As they settled in the city they formed a distinct, closely knit, segment of society. Unskilled, and often resourceless, many found work at starvation wages while others remained perennially unemployed. In the crowded slum areas near the waterfront where they lived, vice, illiteracy, disease, and crime flourished. Between 1845 and 1854 Irish transient paupers at Massachusetts almshouses outnumbered the total of all others, and their frequent intoxication led to a reputation for criminality.

The New England Puritan dislike for Catholics had declined during the eighteenth century, and almost disappeared in the early nineteenth century as a result of good feelings produced by collaboration with the French and general growth in tolerance. But now the Irish migration shocked the tastes and sensibilities of native Americans who failed to analyze social causes and still regarded England as the mother country. As time progressed the Irish also became a political power in Boston, and a conservative power at that. Their leaders encouraged group solidarity and virtually maintained an Irish party which sought public funds for parochial schools and blocked humanitarian reforms which might weaken religious forces. Since they feared freed Negroes in the labor market they also stood in the way of the antislavery cause.[34]

By 1853, as the old political parties crumbled, the Irish had sufficient strength in combination with the Cotton Whigs to defeat the Constitution that had meant so much to Wilson. He would have been less than human if he had not resented their political influence. And other disturbing factors appeared in 1854. The Irish received blame for failure to enforce prohibition laws; they defended the Burns fugitive slave rendition, and the Kansas Nebraska Act. Their position on the Kansas Nebraska Act drew criticism from such highly respected sources as the *Commonwealth, Worcester Spy,* and Theodore Parker. In this atmosphere tolerance dwindled and thousands of Whigs, Free Soilers, and Democrats flocked to the nativist movement.

Henry Wilson sensed that this popular upsurge could aid both his personal and political ambitions. One Know Nothing lodge refused to admit him, but he joined another.[35] From the beginning, however, Native Americans regarded him as suspect. It was not his nature to oppose anyone for reasons of birth, and at the State Constitutional Convention he had objected to placing anything in the Constitution which would make any distinction under any circumstances whatsoever between any man or race of men. He made it clear that he placed men of every race, religion, and country upon terms of perfect equality. Moreover at a reception for an Irish patriot in 1853, he had welcomed the oppressed from all countries regardless of race, land, language, or creed.[36] When Wilson talked of American principles he preferred to talk about antislavery, anti-fugitive slave laws, and anti-Nebraska rather than nativist sentiments.

As late as September 1854 *The Boston Daily Bee,* an official Know Nothing newspaper, found it difficult to believe that Wilson had joined their ranks because his principles did not seem to jibe with their own. Another newspaper, *The Boston Know Nothing,* classified Wilson and his lieutenants as:

> that class of needy adventurers, which has for some years past attempted to scramble into office and to impose upon the people by the false pretend [*sic*] of Free Soil, and the fiction of anti-slavery, has, by cunning maneuvering and adroit management succeeded in hood-winking and bamboozling the good honest Native Americans of this state, in such a manner as to ride themselves into power or position, without any regard to the ultimate result of their selfish trickery and management, upon the welfare of the cause, they pretend to advocate.[37]

When Robert Winthrop heard that Wilson might be a Know Nothing he noted, "If it be true that they have enlisted Wilson, they are not unlikely to become a power. He is far too shrewd to allow himself to be made a catspaw."[38] This was the thought that disturbed the hard core nativists. They feared that Wilson would capture their party. A true nativist like Samuel F. B. Morse of New York regarded the Massachusetts Know Nothings as "a Jesuitical ruse,"[39] while others thought that the new party was simply the coalition or Free Soil in disguise.

So, ironically, while Wilson cynically planned to use the Know Nothing organization for his own desires he became tarred for an offense of religious intolerance of which he was largely innocent. If the Irish Catholic bloc had held antislavery views there can be little doubt that Wilson would have feverishly courted them to form a political alliance. But it is true that Wilson was guilty of complete opportunism, perhaps a greater sin, and he should be severely condemned for his behavior.

In September, the Republicans gathered at a state convention at Worcester under the chairmanship of Robert Rantoul, Sr. It was evident, however, that this was still the same old Free Soil group. Without too much enthusiasm, Wilson received the nomination for Governor by a vote of 316 as compared to 68 for Stephen C. Phillips, his closest opponent. A motion to make the decision unanimous failed, but after some hesitation the nominee received three cheers. The convention endorsed repeal of the fugitive slave law, no more slave states, no more slave territories, no acquisition of Cuba without prohibition of slavery, abolition of slavery in the District of Columbia, and encouragement of Western emigration.[40]

The anti-State Constitution Free Soilers of 1853 remained aloof from this meeting, but *The Springfield Republican* thought that it was a case of a rose by another name and that "essentially, practically, and resultingly, it was a thoroughly Massachusetts free soil gathering."[41]

Charles Francis Adams sent his son, John, to the convention to observe the proceedings, and when he learned the name of the gubernatorial candidate he acidly exclaimed, "This dissipates the whole of my expectations founded on this movement. It now takes the twang of intrigue which marks the character of that man, and renders any amalgamation of parties impracticable . . . it demolishes all my hopes of being useful this year."[42]

Henry Wilson must have realized that the nomination for Governor from this small band of Free Soilers meant little. No sooner had he been named than politicians immediately suspected, with good reason, that he would work something out with Know Nothings. Francis Bird wondered whether or not the Know Nothings would support Wilson. John Palfrey viewed the nomination as the beginning of a coalition with Nathaniel Banks and the Know Nothing party; and Adams believed that Wilson sought control of the Know Nothings.[43]

It seems probable that Wilson hoped and worked for an endorsement of his candidacy from the Know Nothing party. But if he did, his plans did not develop as he expected. In the latter part of October, a Know Nothing Council secretly met in Boston to select a ticket. While Wilson appeared to have influence in this group he was unable to obtain their backing for the governorship. At any rate he made a conciliatory speech, and Henry Gardner, a Boston businessman of conservative Whig views, received the nomination to the displeasure of the old native Americans.

The Boston Know Nothing commented:

> Good men and true have been kept out of the American ranks to make room and place for a set of political jackals, who have betrayed their trust and betrayed those that trusted to their good faith. We have cried out against demagogues and old party hacks till we have fallen into the hands of hacks of the worst kind. . . . The amount of wire pulling and log rolling that has been carried on within a few weeks past in all parts of the State is absolutely alarming. . . . The peculiar organization of the American party has afforded extraordinary facilities for the exercise of undue influence.[44]

Oddly enough, the Catholic *Pilot* and Brownson's *Review* were not immediately hostile to the American party. Brownson advised his readers to vote as American citizens, not as Catholics. He made a distinction between native American and anti-Catholic feeling and warned Irish Catholics not to become too partisan. Since 1852 Catholic immigration had been supplanted by non-Catholic immigration that the Irish Americans regarded as revolutionary and atheistic. So they had no desire to see the naturalization laws made less restrictive.[45]

There can be little doubt that Wilson made some deal with Gardner at the Know Nothing Council or shortly thereafter. *The Springfield Republican* claimed that Wilson and Anson Burlingame managed the nomination of Gardner as a part of an arrangement by which Wilson would go to the Senate and Burlingame to the House of Representatives. At the end of October, only a few days before the election, Wilson sent a letter to the chairman of the Republican State Committee declining to run on their ticket. Upon receipt of the letter the committee excitedly met to determine what they should do. Judge Allen attacked Wilson and the Know Nothing conspiracy and there were intimations that they would name a new candidate. But the meeting adjourned with a vote not to accept Wilson's resignation. It was too late to put another candidate into the field even though they were certain they had been sold out.[46]

On election day, to the surprise of many, the Know Nothing party swept into office. Gardner received more than 80,000 votes, the Whig, Governor Washburn, received 26,000, the Democrat received about 13,000, and Wilson fewer than 7,000. The Know Nothing success was without precedent. They carried every city and town in the state, elected 362 out of a total of 365 members of the legislature, and every Congressional contest.

Wilson, again a defeated candidate, was nevertheless jubilant over Gardner's victory. But many of his friends, former friends, and enemies registered shock and dismay. Stunned by the results, Samuel Gridley Howe said, "The prestige of family standing-respectability-character even has gone. . . ."[47] Edward Everett regarded the election as a revolution that paralyzed the minds of men. He was certain that there had been a Wilson-Gardner deal, but he thought that it might not be ratified. "Rockwell, they say, is a Know Nothing and will be chosen. But if, as is alleged, the Freesoilers have a majority in the legislature they will choose Wilson. . . ."[48]

Although prospects for a seat in the Senate looked good, the next few weeks must have been a strain on Wilson. He knew from past experience with coalitions that promises could be quickly withdrawn or forgotten. Too, with his ear ever close to the ground, he probably heard rumbles of discontent and rumors of other men winning the Senatorship that he desperately desired. On January 10, the *New York Daily Tribune* reported that Wilson's chances for the Senatorship were lessening. His major opponent was Alfred B. Ely, an original and determined Native American. His supporters said, "It won't do to elect Wilson to the Senate, for he is more a Free Soiler than a Know Nothing; he will not be cordially received by our Carolina and Louisiana brethren; his appearance at Washington as a Know Nothing Senator will cause a jar in the machinery and perhaps prevent an agreement on Houston, or Rayner, or Garrett Davis, or Fillmore, as our candidate for President. . . ."[49]

As the senatorial election in the legislature drew closer the doubts of the Native Americans persisted concerning Wilson's principles. With the date for the election in the House of Representatives set for January 23, 1855, one Robert Hall wrote to Wilson on January 18 asking for a clarification of his political position. Realizing his delicate position, Wilson replied on January 20 with admitted reluctance:

> Summoned into action by the evils and abuses which have grown out of the annual immigration into America of hundreds of thousands of men reared under the influences of social, religious and political institutions differing from, or antagonistic

to our own, the American movement proposes to correct these evils and abuses by wise and humane legislation; to protect ourselves from the organized system in the old world, which subjects us to the support of foreign paupers and the depredations of alien criminals; to thoroughly revise the naturalization laws; to destroy the political element of foreign influence heretofore so potent in public affairs; to counteract the insidious and malign tendencies of that sectarian power that instinctively sympathizes with oppression in the Old World and in the New, and to place the government of America in the hands of Americans who are imbued with the spirit of her Democratic Institutions. Guided in its action by love to all men and hatred to none.[50]

This represents Wilson's most extreme nativist position under great pressure. It apparently staved off further serious attacks, but it was still a relatively mild statement for the time which could be shared by many who were not Know Nothings. Charles Francis Adams, for one, refused to join the Know Nothings, but he had expressed the wish that the new party would check the tendency of politicians to court the Catholics as a sect.[51]

When the legislature cast their ballots for United States Senator, Henry Wilson, the Know Nothing candidate, was victor. Defeat had been turned to success, frustration to happiness. The scrambling done, the battle over, Henry Wilson was now ready to take his seat in the United States Senate. It pleased some, and disturbed others to see this unpolished, undignified man succeed to the chair of the polished, dignified Edward Everett. The news upset none more than Everett who noted in his diary, "He was himself [Wilson] till quite lately a shoemaker. He is not to be disparaged for his origin or his trade; but he has all the furtive arts, the vindictive passions, and the mean ways that might be expected from such an origin. . . ."[52]

Shortly after Wilson's election, Theodore Parker, the crusading Unitarian minister, could not resist writing frankly to him about the results:

If I had the power to put whom I would in the Senate, my first choice would have been C. F. Adams or S. C. Phillips— though for either I have not half the personal friendship I feel for you. After them you would have been my man before all others in the State. Besides, there is one reason why I wanted you before even either of them, viz. I wanted to see a shoe-maker get right off his bench and go to the Senate, and that from Massachusetts. . . .

You have done more than any political man in Massachusetts or New England—in the last ten years perhaps, certainly in the last seven—to liberalize and harmonize the actions of the political parties. . . . There is only one thing which made me prefer C. F. A. or S. C. P. to you—here it is. You have been seeking for office with all your might. What makes it appear worse is, you have no mean thing or secretiveness, and so your efforts for office are obvious to all men. Now I don't like this hunting for office in foes; and yet less in my friends. . . .

Now for the noble things I expect of you. By nature you are a very generous man, sympathizing with mankind in all lofty aspirations—a man of the people—with the popular instincts warm and powerful in you. I look to you as a champion of justice to all men; especially to the feeblest and most oppressed. I know you cannot fail to be faithful to this great question of Slavery. But your connection with the Know-Nothings makes me fear for other forms of justice. The Catholics are also men, the foreigners are men, and the world of America is wide and waste enough for them all. I hope you will never give up to Know-Nothings what was meant for mankind. . . .[53]

Theodore Parker knew his man. Other men might have been offended by such a presumptuous letter, but not Henry Wilson who showed his strength when he replied:

I shall keep it and often read it as the plain and frank views of a true friend . . . I will say, however, that I shall give up no votes here which will infringe upon the rights of any man, black or white, native or foreign.[54]

Henry Wilson, the bound out boy and Natick cobbler, had come a long way. Charles Francis Adams had thought that, lacking financial means, this upstart would eventually settle for a place in the Customs House. But Adams, like many others, under-estimated Wilson's ability, activity, and ambition. Success had been built upon hardship and defeat combined with optimism, opportunism, and resiliency. His service in the legislature, practical outlook, and eagerness to form a strong antislavery political organization guided his career. Some thought that he would forget the slavery issue now that he had achieved office. But it would only be a matter of weeks before the new Know Nothing

Senator would threaten to break up the party if it did not sponsor the antislavery cause.

Samuel Bowles, publisher of *The Springfield Republican,* thought that there was too much emphasis upon artifice in the last election and too litlte appeal to the moral sense of the people. But he believed that Wilson would be a truer representative of the practical opinions of the state and a more effective operator than Sumner. Among the most "moral", the non-voting abolitionists who sacrificed all immediate results in politics to an abstract idea, there appeared to be more pleasure than dismay. Wendell Phillips could somehow support Garrison's burning of the Constitution and, at the same time, be glad to see Wilson elected. Many moralists looked askance at political manipulations, but others may have realized that they lacked the skill, the stomach, and the capacity for the job. There were many twists and turns in public opinion and the slow, puzzling work required intricate talents that went beyond the set speech on the lecture platform. "The destructive energies of the Know Nothings," read the salty Annual Report of the American Anti-Slavery Society, "which seem to be directed for the demolition of both parties, may produce a political Chaos, out of which a new and better Creation may yet spring."[55]

Wilson took his seat in the Senate on February 10, 1855, and this, in itself, caused a slight tussle. The Whigs made a place for him on their side, but Chase and Sumner wanted him in the Free Soil locality. Finally, as a compromise, he sat alongside an Anti-Nebraska Know Nothing.[56] His first business in the Senate was the presentation of two petitions, on praying for the repeal of the fugitive slave law, the other for the repeal of the naturalization laws.[57] These were simple formalities for a freshman Senator, but in a day or two he aroused suspicion among his antislavery followers by voting to lay the bill for the admission of the free state of Oregon on the table. Secure in the Senate, it now seemed true that he would forget to fight against slavery. In contrast Sumner voted against shelving the Oregon bill. "It is not too much to say," claimed the *New York Daily Tribune,* "that the very weakest doughface, or the most unprincipled renegade who ever yet represented that State in Congress, would not have been guilty of such an act."[58] But this was an exaggeration. The bill had little chance of passing and Wilson thought that this gave him an opportunity to assuage Southern members of his party by voting with the majority on an already decided issue. It was a futile gesture, but in his mind was the possibility of unifying his party. Much of his opposition among the Know Nothings came from an element that hoped for a national American party, but feared that he was simply a regional abolitionist.[59]

Presidential candidates and party structures were never far from Wilson's thoughts. "What is the position of affairs in your state?" was a favorite question he asked of Salmon Chase and other prominent politicians. He wondered with misgivings about the frequently mentioned Garrett Davis of Kentucky and Texan Sam Houston. And he wondered about the West. In the spring both Sumner and Wilson lectured throughout the country, for a fee, on slavery, and Wilson continually sounded out political sentiment as he traveled from state to state. Sumner may have kept an ear to the ground too, but Adams claimed that, "His head is now so exalté that he lives in a pure atmosphere of his own."[60] The same criticism could never be applied to Wilson.

In his lectures Wilson hammered against the ignominy of the Know Nothings for their refusal to take a strong antislavery position, and at this early date he probably realized that the American party could not be transformed to meet his desires. Edward Everett, skeptical of motives, noticed that both Sumner and Wilson enjoyed drawing a contrast in their talks between the antislavery battle in 1835, when men blazed new trails among hostile citizens to 1855, when they were honored by sympathetic audiences. But, Everett acidly added, they never reminded their audiences that they were silent during the early martyr age. He was sure that it was only when the slavery question held the balance between parties and abetted corrupt coalitions that either of them had championed the cause.[61]

Everett may have been fair or unfair, but Wilson's position on slavery was never extreme. He clearly stated that slavery should be abolished in the District of Columbia and the territories of the Federal Government, and that the Fugitive Slave Act should be repealed. In the South he hoped that the people would voluntarily get rid of the institution in the not too distant future. This was the only way, he thought, that slavery could be peacefully abolished. At no time did he ever demand immediate emancipation everywhere. But it was realistic politics that enabled him to advance an antislavery position without being branded an extremist. It probably represented his true sentiments too. He had always respected states rights, and had never called for sweeping intervention in the South by the Federal Government.

In May the Massachusetts State Convention of Know Nothings adopted strong antislavery resolutions. Wilson preached that the only hope the American party had of avoiding the fate of the Whig party was to take an antislavery stand. Slavery agitation in Congress in the coming session would swallow up all other questions, and Catholicism, foreign influence, and naturalization would be scarcely heard. It was idle. he said, to think of establishing a party on a platform ignoring slavery. He also denounced the secrecy of the Order and advocated an open political organization with open nominations openly made. Remarks of this kind were enough to set off predictions that he would bolt the forthcoming national Know Nothing Convention.[62]

Wilson argued that the object of the American party was to infuse vitality into effete political organizations. This interpretation allowed him to tread lightly on nativism which he tried to minimize or make believe did not exist. Admittedly, this was political trimming. But the nativist element was very real and strong in numbers. In acknowledging their presence Wilson attempted to attribute loftier motives to them than they deserved. He claimed that it was neither the intention of the party to restrain immigration nor to cease serving as an asylum for the oppressed of Europe. He saw America as a land open to people of all nationalities and religions who sought to improve their lot by hard work. He liked, too, to consider Know Nothings as a labor uprising by saying that employers had used the foreign vote against the native masses. He deplored the Massachusetts legislature for passing an amendment excluding naturalized citizens from office in the Commonwealth. But the American party, he said, opposed European governments sending shiploads of felons and paupers to their shores. And he objected to the formation of distinctive bodies within the country according to their nationalities which would influence the politics of the nation. Last, he disliked the interference of the Roman Catholic church in the free school system which he regarded as deplorable politico-religious action.[63]

Moral courage is a difficult quality to measure, and whether or not Wilson's views on nativism exhibited a noble trait or not is a question. He could afford to be outspoken now without immediate loss of offices. But he also had to contend with two rivals who were powers in the state and in the Know Nothing party. They were the Governor, Henry Gardner, and Nathaniel Banks, a former Democrat with antislavery leanings who was now a member of the United States House of Representatives. Wilson and Banks had worked well together in the past, and they were both jealous of Gardner. But Banks, more cautious than Wilson, feared Gardner sufficiently to refrain from bolting the Know Nothings.

Early in June the Know Nothing Council met at the Assembly Rooms at the corner of Tenth and Chestnut Streets in Philadelphia. The Southern delegates were bitter about Wilson. The Virginians regarded the swarthy, ungrammatical Northerner as coarse and vulgar, the cause of their woes, a disorganizer, and an abolitionist. They waged a strong battle to block his admission to the Council, and managed to keep him out of the first day's business. Oddly enough, there were also admittance problems with the Louisiana delegation which had some Roman Catholic members.

In one of the preliminary meetings before the convention one delegate heatedly pointed at Wilson and charged him with defeating the Know Nothings in Virginia. Wilson cooly replied that he was the last man to shrink from the frank avowal of his opinions and that he would not submit to dictation and threats. His reply made a favorable impression at a time when the Boston papers were attacking him. The *New York Daily Tribune* correspondent thought that except for Andrew Jackson, no one in history was as much indebted to his enemies for helping him as Henry Wilson. His assailants overlooked his innumerable weak points and attacked him where he was invulnerable. Wilson's critics, he reported, did not know him personally and "revile him for qualities which he does not possess and accuse him of doing things which he could not do if he wished to, and then wonder that their attacks have only resulted in leaving Wilson stronger than before. . . . Instead of shaking his friends' confidence, the unjust criticism he received only created a certain enthusiasm for him while the real causes for dissatisfaction were forgotten or forgiven." Unfortunately, the correspondent, "Oliver," did not describe Wilson's particular characteristics.[64]

Slavery split the National Council and the party and Wilson played a major role in creating this division which, in turn, was a significant step in forming the Republican party. At Philadelphia he conferred with Samuel Bowles and Ezra Lincoln, former Whigs, and urged them to gain Whig support for a new antislavery party in Massachusetts. Wilson reputedly told Bowles and Lincoln to inform Robert Winthrop, a former Whig Governor, that he would go into the ranks and work for him in return for his endorsement of a new party. The honors of victory might have been Sumner's seat in the Senate. But Winthrop shied away. His conscience would not permit him to accept. "Had I been a soldier of fortune," he later wrote with perhaps a tinge of regret, "I should have closed with it."[65]

Wilson received no comfort from another respectable leader, Charles Francis Adams, who saw no hope for any antislavery combination in the state.[66] And Edward Everett, never a help to antislavery forces, could still criticize the Northern members of the Know Nothing Council for conceding too much to the South.[67] But Wilson, insensitive to opposition, was ready for a showdown. He decided to move ahead with his plans to build an antislavery party made up of Know Nothings, old Free Soilers, anti-Nebraska Democrats, and antislavery Whigs, with or without Henry Gardner. The Massachusetts State Convention of Know Nothings held the latter part of June under the influence of Wilson, adopted an antislavery platform and invited all persons in the Free States of whatever political creed to join them.[68]

But Wilson's simple vision of joint action, and his continual calls for banding together for a common purpose did not automatically bring forth the cooperation that he sought. Following the state convention, Wilson wrote to Wendell Phillips expressing hope for unity. He hoped "that we shall forget each others faults and shortcomings in the past, and all labour to secure that cooperation by which alone the slave is to be emancipated." Phillips responded to the letter cordially in a Fourth of July speech at Framingham, but still objected to the spirit of cooperation. "If there is anybody here," he said, "who does not like quarreling, I advise him to go and join the conservatives, for he will find reformers always in a tempest."[69] Conflicts of conscience were no help to the politician who wanted to mesh a variety of aims, ambitions, and motives for combined action.

Wilson talked harmony while the political condition turned to absolute chaos. Amidst speculations and schemes that came to nothing he traveled around his state and other states asking for union to defeat the national administration. "We must not quarrel about nice shades of words. We want to defeat the Black-power with a name and a man, and once defeated the battle will be ended forever. Establish the fact that the power is not invincible and the Republic passes out of the hands of an Oligarchy. . . ." In carrying the message Wilson seemed to be everywhere at once. "Confound the man," a Know Nothing Hunker exclaimed, "he has at least one attribute of Deity—he is omnipresent. If there is a Convention today in New Hampshire, there General Wilson, will be. If there is one tomorrow in Ohio, there also will General Wilson be."[70]

It was a busy summer for one Massachusetts Senator, not so busy for the other. Aware of the uncertain political situation, Sumner convinced himself that it was time for a vacation. He saw competition for his seat in the Senate on every side, and by disappearing he avoided embroilments.[71] But Wilson operated in the middle of confusion. In August he attended the Know Knothing State Council at Springfield which adopted a platform similar to the Know Somethings. They abolished secrecy and ceremony, but adopted a clause denouncing foreign elements which Wilson opposed. They adjourned in apparent harmony, but already the party was a dying institution. The previous year there were 1,000 delegates present compared to less than 200 in 1855 and experienced observers felt that they were attending the last rites for a passing political organization.[72]

Later in the month a Fusion group gathered at the United States Hotel. It included a Chapman Hall Committee, Free Soil Committee, Know Nothing Committee, and a Know Something Committee. The Chapman Hall Committee, led by Charles Francis Adams and Charles Allen, considered themselves a complete fusion group and met with the other factions with considerable reluctance. A newspaper report charged that Adams wanted to form an antislavery organization excluding Wilson. But Adams regarded the story as pure mischief. Meeting Wilson in the street, Adams told him bluntly that he had disapproved of him and his course for some years, but he would not take public action for personal reasons. Wilson agreed that the report was mischievous, but never petty about criticism, he assured Adams that he had not suspected him of any such motive. He added that he knew that many of his acts had caused some of his old friends to distrust him, but he hoped in time he could clear up this misunderstanding to their satisfaction. Wilson was usually generous in his remarks, but he must have taken a certain delight in knowing that the same newspaper report stated that Adams and Charles Allen "represent nobody-politically speaking," and that Henry Wilson "is unquestionably the most popular man in the State, with perhaps the single exception of Charles Sumner."[73]

Each committee had a different idea about Fusion, but somehow, they found enough in common to enable them to move towards a state convention. Adams wanted a real fusion and feared a simple coalition. His fears were not put to rest when the Know Nothings advised him that they intended to remain in their Orders. But in the interest of the national stake he clung to the fusion. Despite his firm conviction that Wilson was the source of attacks upon him as one of the "aristocratic freesoilers," he knew that the alternative was the triumph of Democrats, "aided by the opponents of the liquor law, the foreigners, and the junker Whigs, and Know Nothings."[74]

Out of the committees, conflicts, and chaos came the real formation of the Republican Party at Worcester. Nathaniel Banks accepted the presidency of the Convention held in September only after he received assurance that Gardner would cooperate. The convention turned out to be a wild affair. The Gardnerites demanded the gubernatorial nomination for their man, while Wilson and his followers refused to go along. Wilson won, and Gardner lost, for the time being. Julius Rockwell, an antislavery Whig, received the nomination.

Nothing distressed the Americans more than the actions of Wilson. They repented the support that they had given his election to the Senate and felt that they had been sold out by him. Following the convention *The American Bee* castigated him in almost every column. The *Charlestown Advertiser* noted approvingly the remarks of the Springfield *Republican* that "Henry Wilson was a political harlot;" and the *Atlas* fully endorsed the sentiment, and said that Henry Wilson was a "humbug, proslavery at Washington, and anti-slavery in Massachusetts." Wilson, "had denounced the pair a hundred times; but they all sleep in one bed now, and ere another week they will be found dressed in each other's breeches."

In a long and convincing letter in the *Bee,* E. C. Baker, Secretary of the State Council of the American party of Massachusetts, reminded Wilson that at meetings at the State House, United States Hotel, and other places, he had said that his only object was to incorporate the antislavery planks in the American Platform; and have the two ideas of Americanism and Anti-Slavery go "neck and neck" in the great Presidential campaign of '56. He claimed that Wilson had told him that this was the only course that could kill Charles Allen, Charles Francis Adams, and R. H. Dana. He claimed that Wilson said that these men had broken the back of every party with which they had ever been connected, and would by their presence and support curse the best party that could be formed in Massachusetts. There were also recollections that Wilson had said that he would use his personal and political influence for the renomination of Gardner. Baker concluded that a study of the fusion movement would show that "Pilate and Herod made friends," men who but five months before had been stigmatizing each other, and he was sure that opposition to slavery was not even the principal object of the fusion.[75]

Nor was Gardner any more pleased with Wilson's actions. He did not take the defeat in the convention gracefully. Instead, he reconsidered his support of fusion, accepted a nativist nomination for Governor for himself, and eventually won the election. Even Banks hedged during the campaign. He let Republicans use his name, but dropped some of his speaking dates. When he did appear he did not denounce Gardner, and some of his close associates worked for the Governor.[76]

The strength of the nativists was still real, and the Know Nothings did not follow Wilson in sufficient numbers. The political manipulator failed for lack of popular support, and the immediate outlook for a consolidated antislavery party seemed dismal. The Know Nothing Party may have been dying, but it was not dead. Crushed in their hopes for national success, they were sufficiently strong to embarrass the new Republican Party and helped the Democrats recover control in New Jersey, Pennsylvania, Indiana, and Illinois; and to carry for itself the states of New York, California, and Massachusetts.[77]

Wilson, in the tradition of seers, had been found wanting. "The fusion fraud is utterly discredited," wrote Everett. "Never in my time has there been so much boasting, so much bragging, so such lecturing, so much lying and the whole 'republican' vote is less than the free soil vote in 1853 and 1854."[78]

Many Whigs had quietly voted for Gardner to put down Wilson whom they had sought so long to kill politically. But Wilson refused to give up. One Whig reflected, "I have helped to kill that Wilson three [sic] several times, and thought we had him in his coffin six feet under the ground; but I verily believe that if we were to cut his head off and drive a stake through his body and bury it under cross-roads, he would be up again more formidable than ever at the next election."[79]

Wilson confided to Salmon Chase, who had just been elected Governor in Ohio, that it was a hard blow. He admitted that he had overestimated the power of antislavery and underestimated the power of old organizations. He thought, too, that their friends had delayed too long before entering the canvas. He had taken to the field several days before he could get others to move. "Our friend Sumner would not speak until eleven days before the election and then we were beaten beyond the hope of recovery. . . ." He estimated that fewer than twelve thousand old Free Soilers voted for Gardner, and at least ten thousand Whigs went over to him to destroy the Republican movement. "Your election," he told Chase, "is the only bright spot in the political sky of this autumn."[80] But he had hopes for next year, and he was no longer a Know Nothing. As one Know Nothing charged, "All our Philadelphia delegates but Wilson and Foster were true as steel."[81]

NOTES

[1] Wilson to Charles Sumner, December 15, 1851, Sumner MSS, HL.

[2] *Ibid.,* January 5, 1852.

[3] *Ibid.,* February 17, 1852.

[4] *Ibid.,* January 5, 1852.

[5] *Daily Commonwealth,* April 27, 1852.

[6] Nason & Russell, *Wilson,* p. 101n.

[7] Wilson to Charles Sumner, June 23, 1852, Sumner MSS, HL.

[8] CFA, *Diary,* June 2, 1852.

[9] Wilson to Charles Sumner, July 7, 1852, Sumner MSS, HL.

[10] *Ibid.,* August 3, 1852, Sumner MSS, HL.

[11] *Ibid.,* September 5, 1852, Sumner MSS, HL.

[12] Wilson to William Seward, July 8, 1852, Seward MSS, University of Rochester.

[13] CFA, *Diary,* September 11, 1852.

[14] *Ibid.,* September 13, 1852.

[15] James W. Stone to Charles Sumner, December 27, 1852, Sumner MSS, HL; Alexander McClure, *Recollections,* p. 288.

[16] *Official Report of the Debates and Proceedings in the State Convention* (Boston: White & Potter, 1853), p. 24.

[17] Samuel Shapiro, *Richard Henry Dana,* p. 151.

[18] Wilson to Sumner, March 10, 1853, Sumner MSS, HL.

[19] *Official Report State Convention,* p. 94.

[20] Boutwell, *Reminiscences,* I, 227.

[21] Samuel Shapiro, "The Conservative Dilemma: The Massachusetts Constitutional Convention of 1853", *The New England Quarterly,* XXXIII, No. 2, June, 1960.

[22] Bean, "Party Transformation," p. 158.

[23] James Schouler, "The Massachusetts Convention of 1853," Proceedings of the Massachusetts Historical Society, November 1903, pp. 2-17.

[24] CFA, *Diary,* September 16, 1853.

[25] William Seward to Charles Sumner, September 23, 1853, Sumner MSS, HL.

[26] Edward Everett, *Diary,* October 20, 1853, MHS.

[27] *NYDT,* November 1, 1853.

[28] John Greenleaf Whittier to Charles Sumner, November 15, 1853, Sumner, MSS, HL.

[29] E. L. Pierce, *Memoir and Letters,* III, 342.

[30] Laura E. Richards, ed., *Letters and Journals of Samuel Gridley Howe* (Boston: Dana Estes & Co., 1909), II, 398.

[31] Wilson to Charles Sumner, February 26, 1854, Sumner MSS, HL; *NYDT,* February 17, 1854.

[32] Wilson to William Seward, May 28, 1854, Seward MSS, University of Rochester.

[33] Bean, "Party Transformation," p. 245.

[34] Oscar Handlin, *Boston's Immigrants* 1790-1865 (Cambridge: Harvard University Press, 1941), pp. 48-205.

[35] Harry J. Carman and Reinhard H. Luthin, "Some Aspects of the Know Nothing Movement Reconsidered," *The South Atlantic Quarterly,* XXXIX, April, 1940, p. 221.

[36] Bean, "Party Transformation," p. 245.

[37] *Ibid.,* p. 248.

[38] Robert C. Winthrop, Jr., *A Memoir of Robert C. Winthrop* (Boston: Little, Brown & Co., 1897), p. 168.

[39] Handlin, *Boston's Immigrants,* p. 211n.

[40] Bean, "Party Transformation," p. 193.

[41] Francis Curtis, *The Republican Party* (2 vols., New York: G. P. Putnam's Sons, 1904), I, 198.

[42] CFA, *Diary,* September 7, 1854.

[43] *Ibid.,* September 9, 15, 1854.

[44] Bean, "Party Transformation", p. 249.

[45] *Ibid.,* pp. 254, 255.

[46] CFA, *Diary,* October 25, 1854; George Merriam, *Life and Times of Samuel Bowles* (New York: The Century Co., 1885), p. 125; Henry Greenleaf Pearson, *The Life of John A. Andrew* (Boston: Houghton Mifflin & Co., 1904), p. 65.

[47] Pearson, *Andrew,* p. 65; Boutwell, *Reminiscences,* I, 238; Harrington, *Fighting Politician,* p. 23; Richards, *Letters and Journals,* II, 403.

[48] Edward Everett to Mrs. Charles Eames, November 16, 1854, Everett MSS, MHS.

[49] *NYDT*, January 10, 1853.

[50] *The Campaign Bee*, October 1855. Reprinted Wilson's letter of January 20, 1855.

[51] CFA, *Diary*, August 30, 1854.

[52] Edward Everett, *Diary*, January 12, 1855, MHS.

[53] John Weiss, *Life and Correspondence of Theodore Parker* (2 vols., New York: D. Appleton Co., 1864), II, 209, 210.

[54] *Ibid.*, p. 210.

[55] Annual Report Presented to the American Anti-Slavery Society, New York, May 9, 1855; Merriam, *Samuel Bowles*, pp. 131-132; Irving H. Bartlett, *Wendell Phillips, Brahmin Radical* (Boston: Beacon Press, 1961), pp. 189-190.

[56] *NYDT*, February 12, 1855.

[57] *Cong. Globe*, 33 Cong., 2 Sess., pp. 1051, 1052.

[58] *Ibid.*, 1150; *NYDT*, March 6, 1855.

[59] Edward Everett, *Diary*, March 28, 1855; Bean, "Transformation of Parties," p. 270.

[60] Wilson to Salmon P. Chase, April 16, 1855, Salmon P. Chase MSS, HSP; CFA, Diary, May 24, 1855.

[61] Edward Everett, *Diary*, May 9, 1855; CFA, *Diary*, May 24, 1855.

[62] *NYDT*, May 21, 1855.

[63] *Ibid.*, June 2, July 18, 1853.

[64] CFA, *Diary*, June 10, 1855; Edward Everett, *Diary*, June 14, 1855; *NYDT*, June 7, 10, 11, 12, 1855; Bean, "Transformation of Parties," pp. 295-306; W. D. Overdyke, *The Know Nothing Party in the South* (Baton Rouge: Louisiana State University Press, 1950), pp. 128, 29; Francis Curtis, *The Republican Party* (2 vols., New York: G. P. Putnam's Sons, 1904), I, 219, 220.

[65] Edward L. Pierce to George Julian, undated letter, 1855, Julian-Giddings MSS, LC; Robert C. Winthrop, Jr., *Winthrop*, p. 171; Wilson, *Rise and Fall*, II, 433, 434.

[66] CFA, *Diary*, June 10, 1855.

[67] Edward Everett, *Diary*, June 14, 1855.

[68] *NYDT*, June 29, 1855.

[69] *National Anti-Slavery Standard*, July 21, 1855.

[70] *NYDT*, July 14, 18, 19, 26, 1855.

[71] Donald, *Sumner*, p. 272.

[72] *NYDT*, August 10, 1855.

[73] CFA, *Diary*, August 27, 1855; *NYDT*, August 24, 25, 1855.

[74] CFA to Bailey, September 2, 1855, Adams Letterbook, Adams Family MSS, MHS; Duberman, *Adams*, pp. 201-203.

[75] *The American Bee*, October 1855.

[76] Harrington, *Fighting Politician*, pp. 24-25.

[77] Wilson, *Rise and Fall*, II, 433, 434.

[78] Edward Everett, *Diary*, November 7, 1855.

[79] *NYDT*, November 9, 1855.

[80] Wilson to Salmon P. Chase, November 17, 1855, Salmon P. Chase MSS, HSP.

[81] Letter by an unknown member of American Party recently elected to office, to unknown person, November 17, 1855, Misc. MSS, RBH.

5

Kansas

The year 1855 had left its scars on Henry Wilson. To some he would always be a political adventurer. The reformer, Francis Bird, for one, never fully recovered his respect for Wilson even though he would be closely associated with him for many years to come. Bird later claimed that Wilson admitted that the Know Nothing episode was a blot on his record.[1] But events moved rapidly and there was little time for remorse. 1856 was a presidential year and there was much to do.

Affairs in Kansas gained an increasing amount of attention and alarmed Wilson even though he must have privately appreciated the appearance of a national problem that heavily contributed to the new realignment of political parties and revolved around slavery. The enactment of the Kansas-Nebraska Bill in 1854, based upon the principle that the people in the territories would decide whether or not slavery would be permitted in their areas, aroused Wilmot Proviso supporters and other antislavery groups into uniting under the banner of the Republican Party.

Kansas became the battleground for Missourians to express fears of abolition in an emerging neighbor state, and for New Englanders to send antislavery emigrants, for press propaganda, for fraudulent elections, for physical combat, and claims and counter claims. It was a continuing crisis with no quick settlement, and each incident gave Congress fuel for debates over rights and wrongs, real and imagined. When the first Governor of the territory, Andrew Reeder, held an election in March 1855 to elect a legislature several thousand armed Missourians invaded Kansas and fraudulently stuffed the ballot boxes. The elected legislature congregated at Shawnee Mission and adopted a severe slave code which limited office holding to proslavery men, and imprisonment for anyone who claimed that slavery did not legally exist in the territory.

The free state men repudiated the Shawnee legislature and took it upon themselves by equally illegal methods to hold a constitutional convention at Topeka which prohibited slavery, ratified the constitution by a vote which excluded proslavery men, and inaugurated a competing state government with Charles Robinson as Governor. As the new year began Kansas had two governments, both illegal, both creating a stalemate in the establishment of orderly constitutional procedures which could gain the respect of all the people of the territory. Ironically, this great commotion was over slavery, yet up to that time not a slave had been taken into the territory and the census of 1860 counted only two slaves in Kansas.

Wilson submitted a resolution in January requesting the President to communicate to the Senate all information in his hands concerning the disturbances in the Territory of Kansas affecting the freedom of elections. In February, three months before Sumner spoke on Kansas, he took the best part of two days to describe the violence of Missourians and the fraudulent voting, and to defend the New England settlers. He demanded the President show how the Emigrant Aid Society had violated the law, traced the belligerent activities of the Platte County Self-Defensive Association in opposition to the Northern societies in 1854, and recounted some of the election returns which exceeded the census. To the South he said, "vote down the Free State men of Kansas if you can; but do not send 'border ruffians' to rob or burn their humble dwellings, and murder brave men for the crime of fidelity to their cherished convictions."[2]

It was a forceful speech, melodramatic perhaps, and certainly not unbiased, but still thorough, and for the most part temperate. Yet one of his listeners, H. A. Wise, Governor of Virginia from 1855 to 1860, thought differently. He considered it a harangue and a severe "infliction" on the audience. "He repeats himself constantly; his language is disjointed and ungraceful, and altogether he seemed to me the least attractive speaker I had ever heard in the Senate."[3] Wilson's projecting underlip, he declared, gave him "a very coarse expression." But most Northerners disagreed. The speech and the reverberations improved Wilson's standing in Massachusetts. Even some of his ex-friends found some kind words to say about him. In early March, John Palfrey, who had done his part to spread distrust of Wilson, observed that he was received at the Revere House with unanimous cordiality and spoke well.[4] Palfrey glowingly acclaimed Wilson's Kansas speech as brave and able. But an unexpected event increased Wilson's stature in Massachusetts far beyond anything he could have done for himself. It was the attack on Sumner.

Like his colleague, Charles Sumner expressed concern for Kansas too. Both men followed the activities of New England Emigrant Aid Company and believed the same reports that came to them through these channels about Kansas. Under the influence of Eli Thayer and Amos Lawrence, 1240 free state settlers had migrated to Kansas in 1854 and 1855. Small in numbers, they were still effective provocateurs and had given Missourians an excuse for pro-slavery "border ruffians." The company had transported rifles as well as men to disturb the possibilities of a peaceful solution. Now that the regular government sought recognition from Congress tension and trouble grew. Settlement in an off year might have been accomplished, but in a presidential campaign, sectional interests intensified.

The Massachusetts Senators did not care to see the many ramifications that went beyond the slave question. They were blind to the problems of land speculation, railroads, local political rivalries and ambitions, and the reality that most Southern settlers in Kansas were non-slaveholders who wanted to ban free Negroes. They magnified the strife which was common to other frontiers. It was much easier for politicians to talk in terms of righteous indignation while they consolidated party lines.

The Democratic presidential hopeful, Stephen Douglas, watching his popular sovereignty theory struggling to become a reality, depicted Kansas in the Senate as a territory which naturally attracted settlers from the adjacent state of Missouri. But, he declared, this normal progress had been blocked by the New England Emigrant Aid Company which had imported armed antislavery men ready to do combat with peaceful Southerners. Despite these difficulties created by abolitionists, a territorial government had been established which drew upon the Missouri Code and protected slaveholders. Douglas upheld the "Law and Order" party and rejected the free state government of Kansas as revolutionary. Such a picture of events only infuriated men like Wilson and Sumner. The Republicans, seeking a firm foundation for their party, now found a cause in the fight against popular sovereignty and used Kansas as an example of its failure.

Douglas opened a debate in the Senate which lasted several weeks. When he spoke for the regular government of Kansas, Seward asked for the immediate admission of Kansas as a free state under the Topeka constitution.[5] Many Northerners joined in the fray, but Sumner, never one to speak impulsively, did not deliver his oration on the subject for two months. When he did speak the depths of his sentiments are seen in the one hundred and twelve page printed version of his address which cited British parliamentary debates, the Congressional Globe, the Statutes at Large, Florius, Cicero, Livy, Vergil, Dante, and Milton. Sumner turned to the classics where Wilson had turned to election statistics.[6]

The fierce speech, known as "The Crime Against Kansas," is now famous in history for its vituperative language and personal attacks upon Senators Stephen Douglas, James Mason, and Andrew Butler. Butler of South Carolina, the tall Massachusetts Senator announced, was the Don Quixote of slavery who "has chosen a mistress to whom he has made his vows, and who, though ugly to others, is always lovely to him; though polluted in the sight of the world, is chaste in his sight . . . the harlot, Slavery." Douglas was "the squire of Slavery its very Sancho Panza, ready to do all its humiliating offices."[7]

Sumner must have been carried away with preoccupation for literary style and forgot that he was talking about real people who felt the weight of his words. It was a bad speech in bad taste which taken alone, could only harm his cause. Sumner liked to think that he was "in morals" not "in politics." But the moralist would have done well, if he wanted to advance the fight against slavery, to retain some of the generosity and understanding that most politicians possess. Seward had advised him to tone down the speech, and Wilson, among other Republicans, regretted the vindictiveness. After the speech was given, Representative John A. Bingham, a Republican from Ohio, suggested that Wilson protect his colleague. Accepting the suggestion Wilson collected Anson Burlingame and Schuyler Colfax, Republican members of the House, and told Sumner: "I am going home with you to-day, several of us are going home with you." But this only irritated Sumner who sharply replied, "None of that, Wilson."[8]

The oration might have been remembered as nothing more than an embarrassing episode had it not provoked the inexcusable assault upon Sumner by Congressman Preston S. Brooks of South Carolina, a cousin of Senator Butler. On May 22, two days after Sumner had completed his speech, Brooks entered the Senate Chamber and waited for it to clear. As Wilson left the room he recognized Brooks and gave him a polite bow. After a time, when the room was almost empty, Brooks struck Sumner over the head with a gutta perch cane. Seated at his desk, the six foot four Sumner had difficulty getting up, but finally wrenched the desk from its fastenings and fell in the aisle, stunned and bleeding.

When Wilson heard of the attack he rushed into the Senate, but found that Sumner had been removed to the Vice President's room and that a doctor was in attendance. He helped Sumner into a carriage and went with him to his lodgings.[9] In the evening a small group of Republican Senators met at Seward's house and agreed that Wilson should raise the point that Brooks had violated the rules and decorum of the Senate. They did not want to create a party issue and decided that no Massachusetts congressman should take the lead in any investigation.

On May 23, Wilson made a simple statement in the Senate which explained the reason for Sumner's absence. Purposely underplaying his part, he did not submit a motion, but left it to senior Senators to develop "measures to redress the wrongs of a member of this body, and to vindicate the honor and dignity of the Senate." There was a pause when he finished, but no one offered a motion. As the presiding officer was on the verge of proceeding to other business, Seward moved for the appointment of an investigating committee. When formed, it did not have one Republican member, and produced a report on May 28 which stated that the assault was "a breach of the privilges of the Senate," but regarded any further action beyond their jurisdiction since Brooks was a member of the House.[10]

Such restraint was not natural to Wilson, but he handled himself well and the curbing of his own emotions did not curtail the general expressions of outrage. A wave of indignation swept the North, with feeling especially inflamed in Massachusetts. Editorials, protest meetings, and rallies all excited sympathy for Sumner. A gathering of 5,000 people in and around Faneuil Hall on May 24 consisted of men of a wide variety of political views. Governor Gardner pronounced that he would stand by Sumner in this hour of trouble, and he was joined by others who had never shown any fondness for the Senator.[11] "Bleeding Sumner" and "Bleeding Kansas" became slogans for the Presidential year.

The political aspect of the attack was not lost on Wilson and he did not restrain himself long. Within a few days he denounced in the Senate the "brutal, murderous, and cowardly assault." Butler cried out, "You are a liar!"[12] And two days later Brooks challenged Wilson to a duel. He formally replied:

I characterized, on the floor of the Senate, the assault upon my colleague as 'brutal, murderous, and cowardly.' I thought so then. I think so now. I have no qualification whatever to make in regard to those words. I have never entertained, in the Senate or elsewhere, the idea of personal responsibility in the sense of the duellist. I have always regarded duelling as the lingering relic of a barbarous civilization, which the law of the country has branded as a crime. While, therefore, I religiously believe in the right of self-defense in its broadest sense, the law of my country and the matured convictions of my whole life alike forbid me to meet you for the purpose indicated in your letter.[13]

Wilson sent the reply to Brooks by James Buffinton, a Massachusetts congressman, and then telegraphed his wife at Natick, "Have declined to fight a duel, shall do my duty and leave the result with God. If assailed, shall defend my life, if possible, at any cost. Be calm."[14] He also sent notes to his good friends William Claflin and John Alley to look after his ten year old son if anything should happen to him.

Wilson's reply was much more straightforward than the answer of Anson Burlingame to a similar challenge from Brooks. Burlingame, a Massachusetts congressman who faced a difficult election, half retreated from a challenge by Brooks, then accepted with the condition that they meet in Canada. But even that bumbling behavior made Burlingame something of a hero in the eyes of his constituents who returned him to Congress.

Wilson carried two Colts for several months and he later told a friend about constant threats that he received at the time. "My mind is made up—I shall walk the path of duty if it cost my life." He never left his lodgings, he said, without wondering whether or not his papers were in order if he did not return alive.[15] Many years later, in 1873, Wilson was told that a group of Southerners had met at the National Hotel to discuss the possibility of assaulting him.[16] There were dangers, but it is hard to believe that Wilson did not enjoy the excitement and dramatics.

Wilson returned to Boston for the Republican state convention and found that he was warmly greeted in the streets.[17] Even Charles Francis Adams found new virtue in his recent behavior and at Worcester presented a resolution complimentary to Wilson's handling of the Sumner attack. It was adopted amidst great applause, and beyond that, Adams pointed out his past differences with Wilson and recommended his case as an example for those who had prejudices to get over.[18]

The convention showed a new spirit in bringing members of all parties together. "Oliver" reported, "The change in popular feeling about Sumner and Wilson, about the South and the Union is really marvellous."[19] When Wilson spoke in this bright light of reflected glory he said, "I shall attack no man for words spoken in debate or elsewhere, but if attacked, by the blessing of God, whenever, however, and by whomsoever attacked, I shall defend my person and my life."[20]

The *Richmond Enquirer* listened to Wilson's words with different ears. "How very lustily the cock crows upon his own dunghill. At Washington, in presence of the persons with whom he is eager to grapple, he is as harmless as any other noncombatant. In Massachusetts he is all ablaze with indignation, and thirsts for blood with the appetite of a hungry tigress."[21]

As the South defended Brooks in the Senate, Wilson felt the continued responsibility to respond for his state. Since his initial arrival in Washington he had been exposed to "plantation manners." Now he asked Butler, "why did the 'chivalry' of South Carolina require that for words uttered on this floor under the solemn guarantees of constitutional law, a Senator should be met here by violence? Why appeal from the floor of the Senate—

from a judicial tribunal, to the bludgeon?" He wondered about "the gallant set," and it made good reading in Northern newspapers.[22] The Republican National Convention was also about to convene.

Wilson was not unaware that the Southern fire-eaters were excellent vote getters in the North. When William Yancey called for immediate secession, or Robert Rhett defended slavery and extolled the virtues of Mississippi and Georgia in violent language, Northerners reacted by joining the Republican ranks or, at least, thinking better of the new party. Extremists in both the North and South effectively obtained reactions that were the reverse of those that they desired in the opposing geographical areas. Psychologically, a frontal assault on a wrong never seems to correct the condition. Certainly Northerners were not ready to agree that Southern rights had been trampled upon, and that the time had come for revolution. Calls in the South to leave the union at once only horrified the North. Distrust grew on both sides; each felt threatened by the other.

Since the previous autumn, Wilson had shown an interest in the candidacy of John C. Fremont, the colorful explorer. Both Banks and Wilson thought he would make an ideal candidate. Fortunately he was an Episcopalian, not a Catholic, and he seemed right on the Kansas question.[23] But Wilson also had kind words to say about Seward and Chase and appeared more interested in stopping the perennial candidacy of Judge McLean of Ohio than in backing any particular man.

At the national convention Wilson appeared before the delegates following an evangelical address by Owen Lovejoy. As expected, he gave the more practical speech. Referring to his recent role, he declared that he was more accustomed to looking into the faces of foes than friends. He called on the members of the Republican Party to adopt a generous policy toward others and to lay a foundation for the union of all parties. Whigs, Democrats, and Americans had to unite to save the first principles of American liberty, Free Speech, Free Press, Free Soil, and Free Kansas. He depicted Franklin Pierce with the blood of freemen of Kansas dripping from his guilty hands. Douglas and Buchanan were victims of the Slave Power. When he referred to the stricken Sumner there was a sense of horror in the audience followed by three cheers for Sumner and three groans for Brooks.

He mentioned Fremont, McLean, Banks, Chase, and Seward as possible candidates and asked for full support for the one who might be named. "But whoever the nominees be let all unite for the common cause—Liberty and Freedom."[24]

Fremont became the Republican candidate, but Judge McLean claimed that money and corruption had been freely used to procure the nomination. He was certain, even though it may have been a streak of jealousy, that Blair, Greeley, Wilson, and Weed, "all of whom were corrupt," would control the nominee.[25]

In Massachusetts Wilson and Banks formed another coalition of Know Nothings and Republicans to gain Gardner's support for Fremont. In return the Republicans made no nominations for state office, thus assuring Gardner's election as Governor for a third term. Wilson said the Republicans could afford to be liberal in dealing with an expiring organization. The journalist, William Robinson, thought that passive support of the nativist Gardner was blasphemy for the sake of forming a sectional party and a high price to pay for unity in Massachusetts. But another journalist, Samuel Bowles, disagreed. He looked upon these coalitions as incidental to the destruction of old parties and the reorganization of the new. The Whigs, he said, were "selling out" to the Fillmore Americans and vice versa, and the Buchanan and Fillmore parties, consisting of fresh groups, were talking about a national bargain to stop Fremont.[26]

Actually, Wilson's ideas differed from the Know Nothings on how to defeat the Democrats. He wanted to attract foreign elements, especially in the West, into the Republican Party. The foreign vote gave the Democrats an advantage which he wanted to take away from them.[27] A united front was his objective. There was only one exception to Wilson's all encompassing party moves. When some of the extreme advocates of a free Kansas, such as Thomas Wentworth Higginson, urged resistance to the government he spoke decidedly against them. He associated disunionists with Democrats.[28]

Wilson's influence in the party grew and he received much credit for harmony among the Fremont men in Massachusetts. He worked hard in the campaign raising money in his own state and around the country. Frequently he appeared before workingmen's groups where he was always well received. Even a severe critic, *The Boston Traveler*, complimented him. "For the excellent and careful management with which the Republican organization has been conducted not only in the state, but in the nation, the party is much indebted to the sagacious counsels and indomitable perseverance and energy of Senator Wilson." They noted, too, his recent rise from a position of obloquy and contempt to new heights as a future White House possibility.[29]

Wilson's reputation also received a boost from Charles Sumner who publicly acknowledged upon his return to Boston in November that they both worked in mutual trust. "By my disability he was left sole representative of Massachusetts on the floor of the Senate . . . it is my especial happiness to recognize his unfailing sympathies for myself and his manly assumption of all the responsibilities of the hour."[30]

Massachusetts gave Fremont a two to one majority over his opponents, but the Republicans failed in their bid for the Presidency. Once again Wilson looked to the future and his ebullience in the face of defeat irritated some politicians. Since Cameron had told him that Blair, Weed, and he "didn't see much in future victories if they had to begin by waiting four years."[31]

In the campaign and immediately preceding years, Wilson had become, like Seward of New York, Chase of Ohio, and Lincoln of Illinois, a founder and builder of the Republican Party. Each of these men, and many others like them, had their own ambitions. Each trimmed, each conformed, and sometimes they followed instead of led. Each knew their limitations. Each knew the complex factors that went into making a political party. They did not claim to be idealists or moralists. But overriding their shortcomings they consciously combined a wide variety of social, political, and economic factions to build an organization to fight slavery. For the time being, defeat was the only reward for their efforts.

*   *   *   *   *

Writing to Sumner from his desk in the Senate Chamber at the start of 1857, Wilson could not resist making a snide remark about one of his Southern colleagues. "We have just put Mason in the chair, 'Plantation Manners' now settle over the Senate." Still the lone active Senator from Massachusetts, he suggested that Sumner not return until the following term so that all speculation would end about when he would take up his duties.[32]

Despite the loss of the Presidential campaign, Wilson was

hopeful about the antislavery cause, and thought that the atmosphere in Massachusetts had changed for the better since 1851. "All we have to do now is labor on in faith of ultimate success."[33] But not all antislavery people were hopeful about Wilson. The extremists held a Disunion Convention at Worcester in January which attracted kind words from many eminent men. The abolitionist objective of the gathering was to decry the Constitution and call for disunion rather than abide slavery. For years "No Union with Slaveholders" had been a prominent part of the creed of men like Garrison and Phillips. Disunion was their remedy. Thomas Wentworth Higginson told John Palfrey that one of the most remarkable features of the convention was that a dozen of the leading men in the country took the trouble to write sympathetically to the convention. But unlike Giddings and Wade, who were among the correspondents, Wilson refused to show any sympathy for their objectives.[34] "In my opinion," he told Sumner, "the Anti-Slavery cause would be advanced if some of them were ever more to keep silent."[35] He knew that Southern slaveholders enjoyed identifying all antislavery men as disunionists because they could characterize them as revolutionary and unpatriotic.

Wilson seemed to shrug off criticism from the abolitionist quarter, but being human, it must have nettled him too. "I see Garrison has read me out of the Senate," he wrote Sumner late in the month, "how little he knows about our position here. Is it not strange that a man who has acted for freedom often against his apparent interest for years—who now has to go daily with a revolver in his pocket should be accused of retreating by one who ought to have more charity. So goes the world."[36]

The Dred Scott decision came in 1857, but the big event for Wilson in that year was a trip to Kansas. He claimed that he simply wanted to see the country and had no political mission, but this was not quite true. Many of the Free State men in Kansas considered the territorial laws fraudulent and did not want to cast their ballot in the next election in October. This was too idealistic for Wilson. Part of the time he traveled through the territory with Samuel Gridley Howe who was undecided about the question. But Wilson had no doubt.

En route to the territory, Wilson boarded the steamer, New

Lucy, at Jefferson City, along with Governor Walker of Kansas. He visited Leavenworth, Lawrence, Lecompton, and Topeka and spoke to large crowds wherever he went, sometimes with Walker in the audience. He urged the people to make the territory an efficient free state. As he observed conditions and talked with the Kansans he became aware of the problem of land speculation. But he saw growth and settlement, too, and concluded that Kansas could become free with proper organization.

Wilson urged the Free State leaders to get out the vote. The officials had been neglecting the enrollment of voters and he was sure that the only hope for a free Kansas was to take possession of the territorial government; "secure the power under the forms of the Border-Ruffian Code, and then repeal that code." In the room at Lawrence of Free State "Governor" Charles Robinson, he urged the policy of voting at the October election. Some of the men present argued that they had refused to acknowledge the validity of the territorial laws and that to change their view would be inconsistent, divide the Free State men, and put their cause in peril. They believed, too, that they would be cheated at the polls even if they did cast ballots. To these objections Wilson realistically replied that they had lost the President, both Houses of Congress were against them, and the Topeka Constitution would not be accepted by Congress or recognized by the President. They must try to vote, and if cheated by officials or outvoted by Missouri invaders, they could then establish the facts. Wilson added that he would go home and raise three or four thousand dollars to help them organize for the election if they would decide to vote in October at their Free State Convention.[37]

Cancelling a proposed trip to Nebraska and Minnesota, Wilson rushed East to raise funds. Always proud of the speed of his travels, he arrived in New York in 117 hours, less than five days, with only one night's rest at St. Louis. He immediately solicited help from E. D. Morgan in New York, Amos Lawrence, Samuel Gridley Howe, and many others. In addition to money he wanted a good man to go out to the territory to see that the work of organization was done efficiently and the money judiciously expended.

In Boston, New Haven, and New York, Wilson received pledges for over three thousand dollars, and then set his sights on reaching five thousand. Reporting his progress to Robinson, he said, "you must be organized or all is lost. Will you see to it. What you want is the *Power*. That you must have or you are broken and lost. Pray do heal up all quarrels and act together in a practical way. Walker will, in thirty days, destroy you unless you are ready to act in some practical way to save Kansas to freedom."[38]

Pressure in the money market and a business depression prevented Wilson from raising all the money he wanted, but enough was raised, perhaps $3,000, to send Thomas Marsh, a previous Republican candidate for Treasurer in Massachusetts, to Kansas as agent. Wilson paid all his own expenses in this fund raising campaign, which included three trips to New York. And he did this at a time when his personal finances were at a low ebb. Not having an independent income, he was obliged to borrow money frequently from Sumner, William Claflin, or Amos Lawrence. But he meticulously paid his debts, and insisted upon paying interest.[39]

As the Fall elections approached Wilson was not too optimistic. He surveyed the scene late in August and was sure that the Democrats would give Chase a hard battle in Ohio; he feared the results with Wilmot in Pennsylvania, and in New York he saw a close race brought on by bad management. And at that moment he did not think things looked good in Kansas. In Massachusetts he did believe that Banks would be elected Governor even though affairs there were complicated. A few of his friends were not enthusiastic about the Banks candidacy, but they were too weak to do anything. He worked for Banks and his prediction proved right when the Republicans won the governorship.[40] At last Gardner had been defeated.

Wilson's anticipation about the elections in the other states proved to be quite accurate too. In Ohio the Democrats won the legislature and almost defeated Chase for Governor. In Pennsylvania Wilmot lost. And in New York the Republicans gave up control of the legislature.[41]

For all his work and expense, Wilson faced criticism in the Fall for presumably advising leaders in Kansas to let the legislative election go by default. These complaints were completely unjustified. Howe, no great friend of Wilson's, believed that the funds that he had raised were the reason for the Free State voters carrying Kansas in October.[42]

Wilson had considered Walker a tool of the Slave Power, but actually the Governor, a friend of Stephen Douglas, wanted a fair election in Kansas to exemplify popular sovereignty and develop the moderate wing of the Democratic Party. The Free State voters, Republicans and Democrats, accepted Walker's promise of impartiality and came out in droves to cast their ballots. The final tally, to the surprise of many, showed that the Republican candidate to Congress had won by a majority of more than four thousand, but the newly elected legislature, contrary to any logical pattern, was pro-slavery.

Closer examination of the suspect electoral results revealed that McGee County, with fewer than a hundred qualified voters, had recorded 1,266 proslavery votes. And the sparsely populated village of Oxford on the Missouri border reported 1,628 ballots cast. Governor Walker visited both areas, checked the returns, concluded they were fraudulent, and threw them out. One Oxford list which Walker discovered contained 1,601 names all written in the same handwriting on a roll fifty-four feet long with nearly 1,500 names copied in consecutive order from Williams' Cincinnati Directory. If the Governor's decision to exclude these fraudulent ballots remained unchallenged the Kansas legislature would have a Free State majority.

It would be several months before the Free State legislature became a legitimate instrument of government, but antislavery men had won an upset victory. Wilson's tactics had paid off. Others had shared his views, but no New Englander, no Republican, and no member of the Senate had worked harder to translate his conviction into action.

The October election took on special significance because it immediately preceded the final session of the Kansas constitutional convention at Lecompton. As the proceedings commenced, Stephen Douglas, as spokesman for the Democratic Northwest, announced that the election had proved that the voters wanted a free soil state. But the delegates to the convention turned a deaf ear. The majority, determined to produce a proslavery document, wanted to forward the results of their work directly to Congress for approval. A minority, guided by the principle of popular sovereignty, wanted to submit the proposed constitution to the people of the territory. After a severe battle, many conferences, and some late hour Presidential influence, a compromise permitted the Kansans to vote, not on the constitution itself, but on a choice between "the constitution with slavery" and "the constitution without slavery." But this meant a stacked deck since the proposal preserved existing slave ownership. This unfair choice only opened a new and prolonged fight between the North and the South and those for and against slavery and and popular sovereignty. It also pitted Stephen Douglas against President Buchanan.[43]

Affairs in Kansas threatened to split the Democratic Party. Buchanan removed Walker from the Governorship and supported the Lecompton Constitution. Douglas moved to the center stage as an enemy of the Slave Power in his revolt against the President, but Wilson, working with all his might in the preliminaries, had done his part in setting that stage.

In Congress there were some other matters claiming Wilson's attention. One was the Tariff Bill of 1857 which established duties lower than at any time since 1812. With his constituents in the Massachusetts textile industry who wanted lower tariffs very much in his mind, Wilson voted for its passage. Late in the year he also introduced a bill to appropriate one million acres of the public lands of the United States for the benefit of free public schools in the District of Columbia.[44] But in the main it was a hard year of campaigning for a free Kansas.

As the New Year began, Wilson admiring Douglas' struggle against Buchanan, saw possibilities for another coalition. Some politicians thought that he deluded himself in thinking that Douglas would espouse Republican principles. But this is unlikely. Wilson was far from naive in the ways of politics. More likely, he simply knew that the Republicans must win a large bloc of new votes if they wished to win a national election, and working with Democrats was not a novel experience for him. Besides, many free soil Democrats had already joined to build the Republican Party. Greeley, Banks, and he thought that they could win over about a hundred thousand Illinois Democrats for their cause.[45] "Depend upon this." Wilson advised William Schouler, "Douglas is as sure to act hereafter with the opponents of Slave Power as you or myself. We must deal kindly with these men and adopt a liberal policy."[46] And he disagreed with Theodore Parker about Douglas. "I leave motives to God, but he is to be with us, and he is today of more weight to our cause than any ten men in the country. I know men and I know their power, and

I know that Douglas will go for crushing the Slave Power to atoms."[47]

Douglas did nothing to discourage such sentiments. He was perfectly willing to be re-elected to the Senate without any opposition. With him it was now "we could do this, and we could do that." And Eastern Republicans responded to his ideas. In June 1858, *The Springfield Republican* rationalized, "The Republicans of 1856, in order to turn out the present slavery administration of 1860, must have help from somewhere— from men who voted for Buchanan or for Fillmore, or from both, and who, if they did not applaud the Nebraska bill and the assault on Sumner, at least acquiesced in them both and were silent."[48]

This seemed reasonable in the East, but in Illinois local politicians had their own jealousies, ambitions, and ideas. Senator Trumbull warned Abraham Lincoln that the seaboard outlook threatened the success of the Republicans in Illinois. "Some of our friends here act like fools in running after and flattering Douglas . . . He [Douglas] encourages such men as Wilson, Seward, Burlingame, Parrott, etc. to come and confer with him and they seem wonderfully pleased to go."[49] Westerners did not trust the Douglas overtures and suspected that he did not expect any more than a suspension of hostilities until after the election. They were probably right in their appraisal. At any rate, Wilson's courting of Douglas simply proved to be one more blind alley. Besides, Wilson had to mind his own business in Massachusetts where his own re-election would soon come up for consideration. He seemed well entrenched, but there were competitors. Charles Francis Adams was a ready replacement even though he had no desire to tangle with Wilson for the seat.[50] But Wilson always retained friendly relations with Douglas who later told him, as he faced the Senate race, that Lincoln was "an able and honest man, one of the ablest men in the nation. I have been in Congress sixteen years, and there is not a man in the Senate I would not rather encounter in debate."[51]

Wilson revealed some of his personal philosophy about this time in a letter to William Claflin seeking patronage for an old friend, Rev. E. D. Moore. "He was a Minister in Natick when I went there twenty-four years ago and in a position of influence and power. I made his acquaintance and he was to me a friend at a time when I had neither friends or power in the town or state. His kindness to me was of great value and I am not the man to forget an act of kindness. . . . You know that I gave six or eight weeks of hard work to the organization of the canvas and I think I ought to be able to obtain all that I have asked or shall ask of the new Administration the continuing in office of one personal friend."[52]

He was also frank about the question of social equality of the Negro in Massachusetts, and did not claim that the situation was perfect. "There is prejudice, and an unjust prejudice, in regard to men of intelligence and of personal character, men in every proper sense of the word highly respectable.. I do not think in social life they are fully recognized; that colored men, with the same intellectual qualities, the same moral qualities, are not in Massachusetts regarded as they would be if they were white men."[53] Other New Englanders were not always so honest about the status of Negroes in the North, particularly when they were talking to Southerners.

As the debate on Kansas dragged on, Senator Hammond of South Carolina helped Wilson's bid for re-election by making his "King Cotton" speech. With memories of his own bondage as an indentured servant still vivid he intended to reply to Hammond at the first moment he could secure the floor. He told Sumner that he meant "to vindicate the 'Northern slaves' and show up the condition of the 'poor whites' of the South."[54] His opportunity came on March 20, 1858 in connection with the bill to admit Kansas under the Lecompton Constitution. It was a long speech entitled, "Are Working Men 'Slaves?' "

Hammond regarded the Northerners as mere factors for the South; he made a general defense of slavery, and assumed that there would always be a need for mudsills to tend to the mean duties of life. In reply, Wilson made a general defense of the North and compared it to the South economically and culturally. He claimed that Free State farms cultivated by 2,500,000 persons yielded a production of nearly $8 an acre, and more than $300 per head to each person. Slave States tilled by more than 3,250,000 persons yielded a production of less than $4 per acre and less than $200 per head to each person. Wages to women were higher in the cotton mills of Massachusetts than the wages of men in iron works of South Carolina. In 1855 the

North had 4,250,000 tons of shipping; the South had 855,000 tons of shipping. Massachusetts had $55 million invested in railroads within the state, and many millions more invested in other states. The North had more bank capital and more manufacturing. The North encouraged education. The South forbad education of nearly four million people. More libraries were in the North, and nine-tenths of the books were published and written in the free states. The poor houses in the North would be in rebellion in three days if the inmates had to subsist on the quantity and quality of food that Senator Hammond estimated as ample compensation for slave labor.

Wilson continued, "Go home, say to your privileged class which you vauntingly say 'leads progress, civilization, and refinement,' that in the opinion of the 'hireling laborers' of Massachusetts, if you have no sympathy for your African bondmen, in whose veins flow so much of your own blood, you should at least sympathize with the millions of your own race, whose labor you have dishonored and degraded by slavery." The battle in Kansas was between free labor which elevates, and servile labor which degrades. "Fealty to the Administration, to the Democratic Party, is now fealty to human slavery, to violence, to trickery, and to fraud." Wilson believed that the time had come to take the reins of power by using the ballot box against the slave-holding aristocracy of the South and their allies in the North. Then statesmen would put the Republic "in harmony with the sacred and inalienable rights of mankind."[55]

In Massachusetts Wilson's speech was considered one of his best efforts and he seemed sure of being reelected by the new legislature which would be chosen in the Fall. But neither Hammond's nor Wilson's oration influenced the vote at hand. The vote in the Senate carried the Lecompton Constitution 33 to 25 and the fight moved to the House. It would be a long time before there was a real settlement of the Kansas question.

*   *   *   *   *

Building a railroad to the Pacific coast was one more ramification of the slavery question. Should the route go through the North, South, or central part of the country? Congress had gathered in December to debate the issue, and the subject carried into the next year. President Buchanan had recommended a railroad route in a temperate zone to avoid extreme weather conditions. But the rivalry among men in various sections of the country intensified since great rewards would presumably fall to the winning area. Politicians and businessmen in Illinois and Minnesota opposed the Southern route proposed by Jefferson Davis, and their counterparts in Louisiana and Tennessee opposed a Northern route. The people of St. Louis favored a central route, but this simply aroused opposition from both North and South.

The measure pending before the Senate, which had been held over from the previous session, provided that the western terminal should be in San Francisco and the eastern starting point somewhere between the Big Sioux and Kansas Rivers as they entered the Missouri. The government was to grant alternate sections of land twenty miles wide on each side, and to lend $12,500 a mile for every section of twenty-five miles completed. The loan would be paid back with interest in mail service and military transportation. The plan satisfied Senators Douglas and James Harlan of Illinois, and Senator William Gwin of California no friend of Wilson's.

Southerners opposed the bill because they thought that the road favored the North and would tax the whole nation. Some slave state Senators thought they might win an El Paso to San Diego line because government surveys indicated that it was the shortest and cheapest route. Wilson, Fessenden of Maine, and some other New Englanders opposed the plan too. They criticized the projected financial arrangements and favored a north-central route. It seemed to them that unscrupulous contractors could raise half a million dollars as security, start work at Sioux City or Council Bluffs, build the line through six hundred miles of easy country and then stop short when they reached the rattle-snake and prairie dog belt. Wilson had been convinced of the need for a road for twenty years, but he thought this measure should be entitled, "An Act to facilitate the schemes of speculators in the public land."[56] He wanted the government to build the railroad itself as a great national enterprise and reserve all the adjacent lands as a sinking fund to pay off the bonds sold for construction. If Northerners and Southerners wished to build their route, he would give them land grants, but at a later date. The central route would be first and serve the needs of the country. Commercial roads could wait. Wilson felt certain that in thirty or forty years a nation with seventy or eighty million people would be only lightly taxed when they redeemed the necessary bonds.

Although without foundation, Wilson claimed that the South had a secret plan to locate the western terminal at Guaymos on the Gulf of California where it would be useful to a future Southern Confederacy. This was denied, but Wilson quoted Senator Iverson of Georgia as saying, "It is because I believe that separation is not far distant; because the signs of the times point too plainly to the early triumph of the Abolitionists, and their complete possession and control of every department of the Federal Government, and because I firmly believe that when such an event occurs the Union will be dissolved, that I am unwilling to vote so much land and so much money as this bill proposes, to build a railroad to the Pacific, which, in my judgment, will be erected outside of a southern confederacy and will be exclusively to the North."[57]

Wilson would have preferred a northern railroad, but he was willing to give it up for a central road that would accommodate both North and South. There was merit in his plan for a national railroad, particularly in retrospect when Credit Mobilier revealed itself. But more ironic, Wilson would be tarred by that scandal. On January 27, 1859 the bill failed by a vote of 38 to 20 and it would be some time before the problem of the Pacific Railroad was solved.

The Pacific railroad debate forecast the formation of a Southern Confederacy, but Wilson never translated these threats into a need for expanding the army to preserve the Union. On the contrary, as a member of the Military Affairs Committee, he actively sought curtailment of expenses. At the start of 1859, reelected for a six year term, he was of the opinion that the army expenses could be reduced at least thirty percent, possibly from $19 million to $13 million. The reduction of expenditures generally were very much on his mind and he seemed to set himself up as a kind of watchdog, even to the extent of wanting to reduce the mileage allowance for Senators from forty cents to twenty cents, and opposing an increase in salary for members of Congress from $3,000 a year which he believed was adequate. The entire operation of the government, he thought, could be carried on for $50 million annually. "We are very much in the condition," he said, "that Macaulay said the people of England

were, when Byron left that country for the continent under the
burden of popular condemnation. He said that they had spasms
of virtue; and we have spasms of retrenchment. We have been
talking retrenchment this whole session and still we have no
plans."[58]

In Massachusetts the departure of Henry Gardner from the
Governor's chair did not eliminate the nativist problem. The
General Court submitted an amendment to the state constitution to the people in 1859 which would require a naturalized
citizen to wait for two years before being allowed to vote. Many
of the proponents of the measure had never been members of
the American party; they simply feared the growing power of the
Roman Catholic church throughout the state.

Wilson's contemporary and long standing adversary, Amasa
Walker, was in the forefront of those favoring the amendment.
Although Walker's position was the popular one, Wilson publicly
opposed him. Some newspapers claimed with some logic that he
was inconsistent and recalled his membership in the American
party, but this did not deter him. He took a battering from
some quarters, but his concern about nativism went beyond the
borders of the state. He saw the proposal as an affront to foreign elements that could strengthen the Republican Party. This
was especially true of the antislavery Germans in Iowa.

To counter the nativist tide, Wilson and Edward L. Pierce
conceived the notion of bringing Carl Schurz of Wisconsin to
Boston as a spokesman for antislavery Germans of the Northwest. Wilson attended a dinner with Schurz, ostensibly to cele-
brate Thomas Jefferson's birthday, but actually to rally prominent antislavery forces. And on April 19, 1859, Wilson presided
at a public reception in Faneuil Hall where Schurz decried
nativism. The object was to look at the issue as Republicans in
their capacity as a national party.[59]

Once again, the Boston correspondent for *The New York Daily
Tribune* seemed to appraise Wilson's actions realistically. To
show that he was a member of the Know Nothing party and gave
general approbation to the doctrines of that party, proves nothing," wrote the newspaperman:

> He is a man of expedients, like most politicians, but not
> by any means less honest than men who look further than he.
> He acts for and in the present day, rather than for five years

or one year hence. His leading purpose is and has been for twenty years to overthrow the Pro-Slavery Democracy. In pursuit of this object he has traversed the Free State, helped to organize new parties and break down old ones, formed combinations here with Americans, there with Democrats, yonder with Germans, and is no doubt ready to cooperate with Irishmen for the same purpose. Such a man will never be known as a philosophic statesman, he is simply a worker, and an organizer for the time being, and of great ability in this line. The intimations that he professed American opinions for the sake of office, and that now he has secured office he is ready to abandon such opinions, is grossly unjust. He loves to be in office—not because he loves power or profit, but because he is a born politician, and cannot keep out of politics if he would. Perhaps I should say he loves to be in politics rather than in office, for I think he enjoys the "rapture of the strife" quite as much as the fruiticn of the victory. Nothing can harm him so long as he remains faithful to the Antislavery cause."[60]

It was quite true. Wilson was "in politics," not "in morals." But his activities did not convince enough citizens in 1859 about the Two Years Amendment which became a part of the Massachusetts Constitution by popular vote.

Nativism was not the only threat to the Republican Party that Wilson feared. Another extreme movement made him apprehensive. It was the activities of "old Brown." Wilson had heard early in May that John Brown, as agent for the Massachusetts State Kansas Committee, had been given custody of arms for use in Kansas. Wilson had never met Brown, but he was aware of his lack of balance when he wrote a worried letter to Samuel Gridley Howe who was closely associated with the committee.

You had better talk with some few of our friends who contributed money to aid old Brown to organize and arm some force in Kansas for defence, about the policy of getting those arms out of his hands and putting them in the hands of some reliable man in that territory.

If they should be used for other purposes, as rumor says they may be, it might be of disadvantage to the men who were induced to contribute to that very foolish movement. If it can be done, get the arms out of his control and keep clear of him at least for the present. This is in confidence.[61]

In response to Wilson's concern, both Howe and George L.

Stearns, chairman of the committee, took steps to comply with his wishes about the arms. On May 9 Howe reassured Wilson that no countenance had been given to Brown for any operations outside of Kansas. On May 14 Stearns wrote to Brown, enclosing a copy of a letter from Wilson, and warning him not to use the arms for any purpose other than the defense of Kansas.[62]

On May 28, Wilson met Brown for the first time at a dinner at the Parker House. According to Wilson, John Brown said, "Senator Wilson, I understand you do not approve my course." Wilson replied, "I am opposed to all violations of law, and to violence, believing that they lay a burden on the anti-slavery cause." Brown answered, "I do not agree with you, sir."[63] There is no reason to doubt Wilson's account which illustrates the vast gap between the politician and the fanatic. The man who Thoreau described as possessing "rare common sense," who Emerson admired for his courage, and who Amos Lawrence believed possessed "deep religious faith," only frightened Henry Wilson.

When John Brown led his small band of armed troops into Virginia and seized the federal arsenal at Harper's Ferry, killed the mayor and took some prisoners, the news enraged Wilson. Wendell Phillips was sure that the act of butchering was committed by an "angel of light", and Sumner could not help admire the man in whom he found "much of the Covenanter, the Puritan and even the early Christian martyr."[64] But Wilson felt that he had been grossly deceived and claimed that he did not care if Howe and Stearns were hanged for the crime along with Brown. Immediately he thought of the Republican party. He did not realize that in the future John Brown would help elect Abraham Lincoln. Instead, he was sure, as he told Amos Lawrence, that Harper's Ferry would have a bad influence on the Republicans.[65] As another Presidential campaign drew near he wanted unity, not interference from disunionists. For all his close association with abolitionists, he did not talk out of two sides of his mouth on this subject. The Thirty-Sixth Congress devoted many words to the John Brown raid and Wilson contributed his share. He believed that the sober judgment of the people of Massachusetts was against Brown and he declared, "if there be any Republican in Massachusetts, who upholds or justifies that act, he has my unqualified opposition and condemnation."[66]

To Henry Wright, Wilson let it be known that he had no sympathy for either the John Brown raid or any other cause designed to incite slaves to resistance, a position which the fierce abolitionist upheld. Wilson maintained only one stand—that of peaceful, legal, and constitutional opposition to the extension of slavery where the national government held responsibility. "I shall not cease to remember," he told Wright, "that slavery in the States is local, not national, and that our appeals must be addressed, not to 'the slaves to resist their masters,' not to armed invasions, but to the reason, the heart and conscience of our countrymen of the South, upon whom rests the fearful responsibility of the slavery system." When Massachusetts required him to uphold Wright's policy of insurrection there would be "a vacant chair for her to fill in the Senate of the United States."[67]

Henry Wilson's distaste for the barbarous activities of John Brown was natural and humane. But his fear that Harper's Ferry would disrupt the Republican party was wrong. He misjudged the tide of public opinion because of his own instincts. Perhaps, too, because he was not an intellectual who wanted to idealize John Brown as a symbol of moral order. Reasonable people might denounce the fanatical raid, but unreasonably it crystallized anti-slavery reactions in the North and became a favorable factor in the national election.

NOTES

[1] By his children, *Francis William Bird—A Biographical Sketch* (Boston: Privately Printed, 1897), p. 47.

[2] *Cong. Globe,* 34 Cong., 1 Sess., pp. 89-95.

[3] H. A. Wise to Edward Everett, February 20, 1856, Everett MSS, MHS.

[4] John Palfrey to Charles Sumner, March 1, 1856, Palfrey MSS, HL; *NYDT,* March 8, 1856.

[5] Glyndon Van Deusen, *William Henry Seward* (New York: Oxford University Press, 1967), pp. 168, 169.

[6] See Donald, *Sumner,* pp. 278-311.

[7] *Ibid.*

[8] Van Deusen, *Seward,* p. 170; Donald, *Sumner,* pp. 288, 289.

[9] *NYDT,* May 23, 1856.

[10] *Cong. Globe,* 33 Cong., 2 Sess., pp. 1279, 1317; Frederick W. Seward, *William Henry Seward* (3 vols., New York: Derby and Miller, 1891), II, 272, 273.

[11] Joshua Giddings to daughter, May 28, 1856, Julian-Giddings MSS, LC; *Evening Post,* New York, May 26, 1856.

[12] *Cong. Globe,* 34 Cong., 1 Sess., p. 1306, and *Appendix,* p. 631.

[13] Wilson, *Rise and Fall,* II, 486, 487.

[14] *Ibid.*

15 Wilson to Rev. Samuel Hunt, May 29, 1856, Brown University Library; Pierce, *Memoir,* III, 476n; Lydia Maria Child, *Letters* (Boston: Houghton Mifflin & Co., 1882), p. 88.

16 Wilson, *Rise and Fall,* II, 487.

17 *NYDT,* June 3, 1856.

18 CFA, *Diary,* June 4, 1856.

19 *NYDT,* June 11, 1856.

20 *Ibid.,* June 7, 1856.

21 *National Anti-Slavery Standard,* June 21, 1856. Reprinted from *Richmond Enquirer,* June 4, 1856.

22 *Cong. Globe,* 34 Cong., 1 Sess., pp. 1399-1405; *New York Evening Post,* June 17, 1856.

23 Wilson to Seth Webb, March 10, 1856, Boston Public Library; Allan Nevins, *Fremont—Pathmaker of the West* (New York: D. Appleton-Century Co., 1939), p. 425.

24 *NYDT,* June 18, 1856; A. W. Crandall, *The Early History of the Republican Party* (Boston: R. G. Badger, 1930), p. 182.

25 Francis P. Weisenberger, *The Life of John McLean* (Columbus: The Ohio University Press, 1937), p. 152.

26 Merriam, *Samuel Bowles,* pp. 155, 174; Mrs. Robinson, ed., *Pen Portraits,* p. 437.

27 Bean, "Transformation of Parties," p. 349.

28 *Cong. Globe,* 34 Cong., 1 Sess., p. 13; William Lawrence, *Life of Amos A. Lawrence* (Boston: Houghton Mifflin & Co., 1888), p. 105.

29 *NYDT,* October 6, 1856.

30 *The Works of Charles Sumner* (20 vols., Boston: Lee and Shepherd, 1870-83), IV, 380.

31 McClure, *Recollections,* p. 46.

32 Wilson to Charles Sumner, January 6, 1857, Sumner MSS, HL.

33 Wilson to Charles Sumner, January 27, 1857, Sumner MSS, HL.

34 T. W. Higginson to John Palfrey, January 17, 1857, Palfrey MSS, HL.

35 Wilson to Charles Sumner, January 19, 1857, Sumner MSS, HL.

36 Wilson to Charles Sumner, January 29, 1857, Sumner MSS, HL.

37 Wilson to F. P. Blair, Jr., May 31, 1857, Wilson to Edwin D. Morgan, July 22, September 9, 1857, Edwin D. Morgan MSS, New York State Library; *NYDT,* June 4, October 31, 1857; Laura E. Richards (ed.), *Letters and Journals of Samuel Gridley Howe,* I, 431n.

38 Wilson to Charles Robinson, June 15, 1857, Kansas State Historical Society.

39 Wilson to Charles Sumner, January 13, 19, 1857, Sumner MSS, HL; Wilson to William Claflin, 1857, Claflin MSS, RBH.

40 Wilson to Charles Sumner, August 26, 1857, Sumner MSS, HL.

41 Allan Nevins, *The Emergence of Lincoln* (2 vols., New York: Charles Scribner's Sons, 1951), I, 254.

42 Richards (ed.), *Letters and Journals,* I, 431n.

43 See Nevins, *Emergence of Lincoln,* I.

44 *Cong. Globe,* 35 Cong., 1 Sess., p. 112.

45 Nevins, *Emergence of Lincoln,* I, 367.

46 Wilson to William Schouler, February 19, 1858, Schouler MSS, MHS.

47 Horace White, *The Life of John Trumbull* (Boston: Houghton Mifflin & Co., 1913), p. 78.

48 Merriam, *Samuel Bowles,* pp. 232, 233.

49 Nevins, Emergence of Lincoln, I, 367, 368.

[50] CFA, *Diary*, January 13, 1858.

[51] Wilson, *Rise and Fall*, II, 577.

[52] Wilson to William Claflin, February 1, 1858, Claflin MSS, RBH.

[53] *Cong. Globe*, 35 Cong., 1 Sess., p. 1966.

[54] Wilson to Charles Sumner, March 8, 1858, Sumner MSS, HL.

[55] Henry Wilson, "Are Working Men Slaves?" March 20, 1858, printed speech, New York Public Library.

[56] *Cong. Globe*, 35 Cong., 2 Sess., 72, 156, 304, 307, 310; *Appendix*, 293; *The Pacific Railroad*, Printed Speech, New York Public Library, January 11, 1859; Nevins, *Emergence of Lincoln*, I, 427-444.

[57] *Cong. Globe*, 35 Cong., 2 Sess., pp. 993, 994, 1034, 1222, 1585.

[58] *Ibid.*, p. 993.

[59] E. L. Pierce to Chase, April 28, 1859, Chase MSS, LC; Schurz, *Reminiscences*, II, 118, 119; Mrs. Robinson, ed., *Pen Portraits*, 544.

[60] *NYDT*, May 2, 13, 26, 1859.

[61] Frank B. Stearns, *The Life and Public Services of George Luther Stearns* (Philadelphia: J. P. Lippincott & Co., 1907), p. 168.

[62] *Ibid.*, 169, 170, 171.

[63] Wilson, *Rise and Fall*, II, 592, 593.

[64] Bartlett, *Phillips*, 208-218; Donald, *Sumner*, 350, 351.

[65] W. Lawrence, *Life of Amos A. Lawrence*, 131.

[66] *Cong. Globe*, 36 Cong., 1 Sess., p. 128.

[67] Wilson to Henry C. Wright, December 27, 1859, HL.

[1] Mrs. Robinson, ed., *Pen Portraits*, p. 425.

[2] Wilson to Amos Lawrence, Nov. 25, 1858, A. A. Lawrence MSS, MHS.

[3] Wilson to Salmon P. Chase, 1859; Wilson to Salmon P. Chase, Oct. 14, 1859, Salmon P. Chase MSS, HSP.

6

Presidential Year

The Bird Club, named for Francis Bird, met every Saturday for lunch at the Parker House in Boston around 1860 and has become fairly well publicized in history as an elite antislavery group. Among its members were Charles Sumner, Samuel Gridley Howe, and John A. Andrew, and they and their friends generally appeared to be anti-Banks and pro-Seward in sentiment. Less radical, and less well known was another Saturday eating club at Parker's which remained nameless although some have referred to it as the Banks Club. Each faction developed considerable political influence, but Wilson, resisting clannish confinement and exclusive connections, ate at both tables.[1] Typically, he refused to cut himself off from the broadest base for the latest news and gossip, particularly in a presidential year, and he had no qualms about where and with whom he was seen.

Since 1855 many Republicans had been eagerly looking forward to the next national election and they had started early to explore possible nominees. From time to time someone would sound out Wilson about his preferences, but he remained uncommitted. He did know whom he did not want, however. Seward, he told Amos Lawrence in 1858, was not the man to produce unity and victory. But this was not flat opposition. At that premature date he did not want to start a movement for him or any other man. Instead, he wanted to organize the opponents of the administration and let the question of a candidate alone for at least a year.[2]

As time passed Wilson continued to give reservations about Seward. He would say kind things about him, and then back off. He kept in touch with Salmon Chase and in 1859 went so far as to tell him, "Were it in my power you would be in the White House on the 4th of March 1861." But this was hardly unqualified support, and he was sufficiently frank to tell Chase that he found the feeling to be in favor of the strongest man "whether it be Seward, yourself, or some new man."[3]

There was a host of minor candidates in the field, Banks, Fessenden, Hale, McLean, Wade, Cassius Clay, Lincoln, Caleb Smith. Even Wilson's name cropped up now and then, but there is no evidence that he ever considered himself a serious contender. He must have known that he could not produce the unity that he so desperately desired for the Republican Party any more than Seward and he did not have any consequential following. In 1860 he seemed more convinced than ever that the Republicans could not win without the votes of moderates. "I hope therefore that every effort will be made to so shape affairs that our cause will not be sacrificed to men or to the interests of any class of men," he told Henry Carey, the Philadelphia economist. "We must have men fully committed to our principles and policy, but we want men not so mixed up in the conflicts as to have the support of the more moderate men." He told George Julian much the same without making any predictions as to who the candidate might be.[4] And he remained conscious of the Middle and Western states too.

Wilson's talk of moderation infuriated the abolitionists. He did not like to be called timid or lacking in love for the cause, but as a matter of practice he never replied to their denunciations. Upon reflection he was sure that he had made mistakes, but he was also sure that for over twenty years he had tried to help the antislavery cause. "And now," he wrote James Freeman Clarke in a letter rare for its length and effusiveness, "looking over the not inactive years I cannot see a single day of my life when I failed to be in the strongest position that I could be in to do the most practical work for the cause. When censured, as I have been I have worked on and trusted to time and events to vindicate my action. I shall so continue to act, for I have no time to turn the

little ability God has given me from the support of the cause of
the slave to assailing the action of other men who are fighting for
the cause of the bondmen in their own way. I feel that I have
been hardly dealt with by some, but I have not and I do not mean
to retaliate upon them.

"Little do some of our Anti-Slavery friends know what some
of us here have borne for a few years. They speak at home surrounded by sympathizing throngs—we stand here in the face
of the majorities, led by men of great talent, with the galleries,
the streets, the hotels filled with throngs of men who pour upon
our heads bitter caresses—we stand around and ready for anything that may come, and often compelled to be silent or moderate
our words because men who stand by us are representative of
portions of the country like parts of Pa., N.J., Indiana, Ill. and
we want to spread our sentiments in the dark sections of the
country where people are growing up to our position but doing
it slowly. . . . This my dear Sir, is rather hard to bear, but then
we must bear it as best we can, but I assure you it is anything
but gratifying to men who are hourly subjected to reproach
here."[5]

Wilson must have irritated extremists too when he talked
about the equality of races. In April 1860 he wanted to appropriate $25,000 for the education of all children in the District of
Columbia. He wrangled bitterly in the Senate with his friendly
enemy, Jefferson Davis, but he declared that it was not a matter
of equality of races. "I do not believe in the mental or the intellectual equality of the African race with this proud and domineering
white race of ours." Explaining his position further, he continued,
"I believe in the equality of rights of all mankind. I do not believe
in the equality of the African race with the white race, mentally or
physically, and I do not think morally. I do not believe in the
equality of the Indian race with us, but upon the question simply
of equality of rights, I believe in the equality of all men of every
race, blood, and kindred."[6] His words spoke more softly than his
actions.

At the same time Wilson espoused his theory of equal rights he
clashed with Mason over the condition of the colored people. He
had a real feeling for the underdog that could never be smothered.
"It is the practice here to denounce West Indian emancipation as
a failure and to represent the condition of the colored free people

as degraded. "I intend," he told J. Freeman Clarke in another letter, "to say a few words on this topic, and I do so not for the interest of party, but for the cause of a despised race."[7]

As convention time approached, Seward, confident of the nomination, told Wilson in the Senate Chamber, "considering your antecedents, and your relations with me here, you ought to have given me your support, but you have done more against my nomination than any member of the Senate." Wilson claimed that he replied that if he could elect a President it would have been Seward or Chase, but that the cause was superior to personal considerations. "Like Mr. Chase, you have, by your ability and long devotion to the anti-slavery cause, excited prejudices and awakened fears in the great states of Pennsylvania, Indiana, Illinois, New Jersey, and Connecticut which are to be the battleground of the contest, and whose votes must be secured to give success; their votes in the convention will decide the nomination; and as necessity must rule at Chicago." According to Wilson, Seward reiterated his own confidence and left the Chamber with Sumner sure of his eventual election to the Presidency.[8]

The Radicals controlled the Massachusetts delegation to the Republican National Convention and supported Seward for President. John Andrew was in charge of the state convention that chose a radical delegation and gave instructions to support Seward. In the meantime, however, Seward became too moderate for Andrew who privately resolved to defeat his nomination. So, for reasons opposed to Wilson's, the Massachusetts delegation's backing of Seward faded. There is no indication that Wilson influenced the outcome of Lincoln's nomination, but he was right in believing that a moderate would have the broadest appeal. Such states as Indiana, Pennsylvania, and New Jersey would play a key role in naming the candidate and they were not attracted to radical thought. Unlike John A. Andrew or Charles Francis Adams, Wilson wasted no time in misgivings about Lincoln. And unlike others, he was the last man to look upon Lincoln snobbishly or dismiss him as a "simple Susan." Instead, he rejoiced in the nomination of a "son of toil," and predicted that the masses would rally around the ticket.[9]

When Seward returned to the Senate after his defeat at the convention he saw himself "in the character of a leader deposed by my own party," and he was sensitive about his new role.

Seward's description of his return to the Chamber reveals something of the character and natural instincts of Wilson which Seward appreciated. "The scene was entirely changed from my entrance into the Chamber last winter. Cameron greeted me kindly; Wilkinson of Minnesota, and Sumner cordially and manfully. Other Republican Senators came to me, but in a manner that showed a consciousness of embarrassment, which made the courtesy a conventional one; only Wilson came half a dozen times, and sat down by me, waiting for me to open a conversation on transactions at Chicago."[10] With a total lack of self consciousness he could show that he understood the feelings of others.

Wilson took to the stump and campaigned incessantly. His exhausting schedule took him around the country, Brooklyn, Boston, upstate New York, Maine. Appearances before military drills, choral groups, Wide Awake parades, and packed auditoriums became standard diet, but this was the atmosphere he loved. The crowds, the noise, the challenge made him vibrant. He said that he attended nearly one hundred public meetings, saw hundreds of thousands of people, and endured speeches by hordes of others who shared the platform with him during the canvas.[11]

He shared too in the hard, discouraging work of raising money. The previous fall he had raised funds for the young state of Minnesota and complained that the moneyed men in Massachusetts could raise $80,000 to get a tariff through Congress, but they would not give a dollar for the cause of the Republican Party in a new state. "Indeed most of them might give money to defeat us."[12] In 1860 businessmen in the East worried about the loss of Southern trade if Lincoln might be elected and they did not part with money freely.

The fragmentation of the Democrats probably helped the Republicans as much as any single element in the campaign. When Stephen Douglas received the presidential nomination at Baltimore, Southern delegations formed to name John C. Breckinridge for President. A fourth party had also been formed for the benefit of old Whig remnants, former Know Nothings, and a variety of other conservatives. John Bell was their candidate and headed the Constitutional Union Party, with Edward Everett as the Vice-Presidential nominee.

Initial optimism diminished as Wilson moved among the people. In August he informed Lincoln that he had traveled 4,000 miles in the previous four weeks in New York and New England. The turn outs were good, but he stressed the importance of organization, work, system. Never afraid to put in a full day, he felt that others were neglecting work and suffering from over-confidence. He realized that Lincoln was under pressure from many quarters, but he feared that they would lose the House through indifference. "Press action," he urged, "upon our National Committee. They ought to have their eyes upon every Congressional district, and work, as men never worked before for the next 70 days."[13] In accordance with the custom of the time, Lincoln did not campaign and the national organization should have been more effective. Edwin Morgan headed the national committee, but he was busy running for re-election as Governor of New York and did not provide the leadership the party needed. Wilson knew this and he tried to reach beyond the borders of his own state as much as possible.

Earlier in the year, as Wilson searched for unity, Sumner's provocative remarks, as in his speech on "The Barbarism of Slavery," must have exasperated Wilson. But now, these sentiments grew in popularity and he asked Sumner, always the reluctant campaigner, to enter the contest and speak in New Jersey, New York, and Boston. "I say to you that there is danger that we are lost."[14]

The labor vote was important in the election, and perhaps Wilson contributed most to victory by his appeals to working men. As the bound out boy, mudsill, and "Natick Cobbler," he was well cast for the assignment and could talk to these audiences as one of them. At East Boston he delivered a long speech, "How Ought Workingmen to Vote in the Coming Election." He saw slavery as the unappeasable enemy of free laboring men and this was his argument, particularly among the Boston Irish, who feared the competition of free Negroes and exhibited little sympathy for the slave. He quoted Senator James Hammond, " 'The man who lives by daily labor—in short, your whole class of hireling manual laborers, and operatives, as you call them, are slaves. . . . The difference between us is that our slaves are hired for life—yours are hired by the day—your slaves are white—of your own race!' " He also quoted Herschel Johnson, candidate for Vice President on the Douglas ticket as saying, " We believe capital should own labor.' " To Wilson, Johnson was an insolent flesh jobber. He also cited instances of the South silencing free speech and free press. The Republican Party, in contrast, accepted as its living faith the creed of equality of all mankind and recognized the poor and humble. He did not claim power to abolish slavery in states by Congressional legislation, but he did claim power to exclude slavery from the territories. As he reached his conclusion, he knew how to rouse an audience with appropriate platitudes:

> Born in the ranks of the toiling masses, reared in the bosom of the people, trained in the hard school of manual labor, Abraham Lincoln, and Hannibal Hamlin are true to the rights, the interests, and the dignity of the workingmen of the Republic—worthy to lead their advancing hosts to victory for vindication of rights as old as creation, as wide as humanity.[15]

As the campaign progressed, Douglas visited New England, and at the time, told Wilson that Lincoln would be elected. He said that he would go South and urge everyone to submit to the verdict of the people.[16]

When victory materialized, Wilson, at a Jubilee at the Boston Music Hall, felt the glow of success that stimulated strong talk. "We have won power; we are to take possession of the Federal Government. I have the most undoubting confidence in the capacity, honor, integrity and devotion of Abraham Lincoln . . . I say to the men of the South, who have been threatening the dissolution of the Union, who are calling conventions, who are calling blue blockades, Go on if you dare! We intend to stand by the constitution and by the Union at any and every hazard, come what may."[17]

Upon returning to Washington, all signs pointed to disunion. Wilson appreciated Lincoln's firmness, but he thought that many of their political friends were weak. "We need all the aid that fidelity to principle, firmness, and good sense, can give us. I hope more from the folly and rashness of the secessionists than I do from the wisdom and courage of our friends."[18] With war threatening, Wilson, as a member of the Military Affairs Committee, finally related the administration of the Army to the possibilities for treason. On the last day of the year he submitted a resolution asking the Secretary of War for information concerning the disposition of arms during the past year. But it made little difference. It was too late and it was laid over anyway.[19]

Wilson did not seem to exhibit great interest in political appointments. He urged Chase to accept the Secretaryship of State if offered because he thought it would give confidence to their antislavery friends. "They will feel that we shall not be sold out."[20] By letter he introduced a state delegation to Lincoln to discuss a cabinet appointment for New England, and in another letter recommended Adams specifically for such an assignment. But he expressed some doubts about his propriety in doing so and made it clear that he did not wish to press or embarrass the President-elect. He understood that Adams and Gideon Welles were the leading candidates, and he spoke well of both of them.[21] Since Lincoln heeded the recommendations of members of Congress when making appointments, Wilson's sudden sensitivity over propriety must have made its meaning clear. There had been too many snubs, too many lectures, too many expressions of disapproval over the years for Wilson to become too enamored of the idea of Adams receiving his enthusiastic endorsement for a Cabinet post. What could be more devastating than faint praise?

When there was a flurry of interest for Sumner to go to England as Minister, friends wrote to Wilson to press his nomination on Lincoln. Wilson replied to the poet Henry Wadsworth Longfellow that he had learned from the highest source that either Adams or William Dayton, who had run on the national ticket with Fremont in 1856, would receive the post. "Seward is for Adams and the President is for Dayton."[22]

The New Year brought intense anxiety to Washington. Rumors of invasion and insurrection circulated throughout the town, and numerous fires broke out each night. Wilson and his wife lived at the Washington House and they heard that threats had been made to burn the place down because so many Republicans lived there. Many wives had left for home, but Mrs. Wilson hoped to remain as long as possible even though their young son lived in Massachusetts with the Claflins. She had not been well for months and she was sure that she would be happier with her husband.[23]

Wilson felt that they were all drifting and no one knew where.[24] In February he submitted a resolution requesting information from the President concerning the unlawful seizure of forts, arms, or munitions belonging to the United States in Louisiana, and whether or not the mint at New Orleans had been taken, but again one of his resolutions was laid over.[25] Mainly, it seemed to him that everyone was waiting for the fourth of March to see what would happen. If a rebellion occurred, Wilson knew that New York and New England would have to bear a heavy share of the cost. When a bill for a higher tariff came up for a vote early in 1861 he voted for it against the wishes of an influential portion of his state because he wanted to increase government revenue.[26]

Wilson wanted to preserve the union and hoped that they could pass through these critical times with the government intact. But he resisted compromises which he thought would destroy the constitution and gave no help to those who wanted to halt secession by conciliating the upper South. With talk of compromise measures in the air, Governor John Andrew hastened to Washington to confer on Christmas Eve with Senators James Doolittle of Wisconsin, Lyman Trumbull of Illinois, Sumner and Wilson. They all agreed that the integrity of the Union must be preserved even if it "cost a million lives."[27]

In the debate on the Crittenden Compromise Wilson cried out that treason held its carnival in the nation's capitol and on two occasions moved to put aside the resolutions. He argued that there had been no oppressions, no invasion of public liberties, no ruin of private happiness, no rights violated, no wrongs unredressed, to justify the assault upon the constitution by the proponents of compromise. The folly and madness, he thought, came from the desire of some to command the bodies and souls of their fellow man. This was not the work of a day. It was the work of thirty years since Andrew Jackson had put down the threat of nullification.[28]

During the last presidential campaign, Wilson claimed, Republican speakers had expressed their determination to use all their constitutional and legal means to arrest the extension of slavery, but they did not express any hostility towards the people of the South. "Had Massachusetts proposed, either by State or Federal action, to interfere directly or indirectly with slavery in the States?" Virginia searched the ships of Massachusetts, South Carolina imprisoned her colored seamen, but the North had not retaliated. He conceded the bravery of the men of the South, but he also tired of their boastful vaunting of chivalric courage. Crittenden's motives were pure, but his proposals did not sustain the

Constitution, the Union, or law enforcement. Wilson saw them as demands to incorporate the dark spirit of slavery into the organic law of the nation.

At the inauguration of Lincoln, extremists of both sides exhibited the utmost cordiality, and Wilson hobnobbed with all in the friendliest manner.[29] But it meant nothing as he must have known. With the secession of Mississippi, and the departure of Jefferson Davis, Wilson became Chairman of the Military Affairs Committee. For the next four years his fight against slavery would become a legislative struggle to build an efficient military organization that would devour the enemy.

NOTES

[4] Wilson to Henry C. Carey, April 16, 1860, Edward Carey Gardner MSS, HSP; Wilson to Lysander Spooner, March 15, 1860, Boston Public Library; Wilson to G. W. Julian, June 20, 1860, Julian-Giddings MSS, LC; Emerson Fite, *The Presidential Campaign of 1860* (New York: The Macmillan Co., 1911), p. 122.

[5] Wilson to Rev. J. Freeman Clarke, Jan. 29, 1860, Misc. MSS, HL.

[6] *Cong. Globe,* 36 Cong., 1 Sess., p. 1684.

[7] Wilson to Rev. J. Freeman Clarke, January 29, 1860, Misc. MSS, HL.

[8] Wilson, *Rise and Fall,* II, 694.

[9] *NYDT,* May 28, 1860.

[10] Frederick Seward, *Seward,* II, 454, 55.

[11] Wilson to Caleb Cushing, Dec. 15, 1860, MHS: *Cong. Globe,* 36 Cong., 2 Sess., p. 1090.

[12] Wilson to D. Robner, Sept. 10, 1859, Minnesota Historical Society.

[13] Wilson to Abraham Lincoln, Aug. 25, 1860, R. T. Lincoln MSS, LC.

[14] Wilson to Charles Sumner, Sept. 25, Oct. 24, 1860, Sumner MSS, HL.

[15] Henry Wilson, "How Ought Workingmen to Vote in the Coming Election?" Speech at East Boston, Oct. 15, 1860, New York Public Library.

[16] Wilson, *Rise and Fall,* II, 699.

[17] *NYDT,* Nov. 10, 1860.

[18] Mrs. Robinson, ed., *Pen Portraits,* p. 93.

[19] *Cong. Globe,* 36 Cong., 2 Sess., p. 210.

[20] Wilson to Salmon P. Chase, Dec. 15, 1860, Salmon P. Chase MSS, HSP.

[21] Wilson to Abraham Lincoln, Jan. 4, 5, 19, 1861, Robert T. Lincoln MSS, LC.

[22] Wilson to Henry Longfellow, March 14, 1861, HL; Duberman, *Adams,* p. 256.

[23] Mrs. Wilson to Mrs. William Claflin,, Jan. 14, 1861, Claflin MSS, RBH.

[24] Wilson to William Schouler, Feb. 1, 1861, Schouler MSS, MHS.

[25] *Cong. Globe,* 36 Cong., 2 Sess., p. 720.

[26] *Ibid.,* p. 992.

[27] William B. Hesseltine, *Lincoln and the War Governors* (New York: A. A. Knopf, 1948), p. 110.

[28] *Cong. Globe,* 36 Cong., 2 Sess., pp. 289, 290, 305, 308, 1088, 1090; Albert D. Kirwen, *John J. Crittenden* (Louisville: University of Kentucky Press, 1962), pp. 392, 393, 396.

[29] *NYDT,* March 5, 1861.

7
Military Affairs

The regular army was nothing more than a skeleton force when war started. In a land of three million square miles, with a population of thirty-one million, there were fewer than 18,000 officers and men listed on the rolls. The line organization consisted of 198 companies; 183 were stationed on the frontier or enroute to posts west of the Mississippi River. The remaining fifteen companies were stationed along the Atlantic coast from Maine to the Gulf of Mexico.

The militia offered no real support. It was a paper organization of three million untrained and inexperienced men who occasionally held musters on village greens and acted in social or political capacities. Moreover, Congress had failed to provide for its strength and growth, they appropriating the same amount of money for it in 1860 as in 1808. But increased appropriations would not have solved the militia's problems. The history of militia proved it was possible to waste money notoriously and still remain notoriously inefficient. When in June 1860 an appropriation bill came up for consideration to increase the amount of arming the militia from $200,000 to $600,000, Wilson, speaking for the majority, favored equipping them with old weapons. "These arms were good enough to fight the Mexican War with, they have been good enough to fight the battles of the country in the past, and, I think, are as good to be distributed among the militia of the country, for the purpose for which the militia need to use them, as improved arms are now being made."[1] In retrospect, this sounds like shocking neglect, but better arms would not have made better soldiers. Obsolete firearms were good enough for Sunday drills, and no amount of traditional training would have conditioned men for the trials they would face in the next four years.

But even the regular army was not prepared to face this crisis in the nation's life, and the blame rested largely with Congress. It had refused to expand the forces and continually reflected the citizen's inherent fear of the military. In 1860 the only positive indication of congressional interest in the army was an act to increase the rations of sugar and coffee for enlisted men. Shortages in the early part of the war were not seriously affected by Secretary of War John Floyd's storing arms in the South, or issuing that part of the country more than its share of weapons. They were caused by Congress failing to make adequate provisions, and Wilson, as a member of the Military Affairs Committee, must share the blame.[2]

But Wilson's neglect of the army in the past did not mean neglect in crisis. As the new committee chairman he set to work at the furious pace that he sustained throughout the war. Within four months the army would increase twenty-seven times to a strength of 485,640 three-year-men under arms. This rapid increase was not matched in either World War I or World War II.[3] Lincoln had taken the first steps with his call for troops, but when Congress convened on July 4, 1861 there was need for additional legislation that would not only increase the numbers of men, but also increase the efficiency of organization. Troops had to eat, be clothed, and sheltered and machinery had to be created for the task. Wilson spearheaded the passage of required legislation which was not always accepted with unanimity in either the Senate or the House. Criticism and amendments were endless. In disgust, Wilson once said, "I believe if we introduced the Lord's Prayer here, there would be a large number of amendments proposed to it."[4]

In the weeks before Congress convened Wilson engaged in a variety of war activities. In April he went to New York by steamer at the request of General Butler to buy some heavy guns to defend Annapolis from armed men in the neighborhood.[5] In May he met with the President and Secretary of the Treasury to discuss the credit of the government, and he urged Governor Andrew to have Massachusetts banks take about five million at par of a fourteen million dollar six percent loan.[6] And before the appointment of a Massachusetts agent he helped in all kinds of business relations between the Federal Government and his state.[7] At this point there were no clearly defined jurisdictions or organizations. It was a matter of pitching in, and Wilson pitched in.

Wilson considered himself well versed in military matters since he had a long association in the Massachusetts militia and had risen to the rank of Brigadier General. Actually, he knew more than most politicians, but by itself this meant very little. One thing he did exhibit was a concern for the men. On April 18, 1861 five hundred Pennsylvania troops arrived in Washington. The next day they were joined by the Sixth Massachusetts Regiment, and a few days later New York's Seventh Regiment appeared. Wilson mingled with the troops and observed their needs. The condition of the Massachusetts militia mortified him. They lacked equipment, and compared with the troops of other states, he did not think that they were well fitted out. Immediately he complained to Governor Andrew. "It is of more importance to equip and dress the men we now have than to get more in the field. The condition of the field is disgraceful in point of equipment and uniform. Not a regiment here is so badly off, and the men feel this deeply. Do for the good name of our state see to it that our men in the field are fitted out well, for we are getting more men than we wanted." The men who supplied the wagons for the First Regiment, he thought, simply cheated the government in its time of trial.[8]

Wilson worried about the quality of men too. He wanted talented young men for officers; leaders who would come from those who had a reputation to make rather than a reputation to preserve. He did not think militia generals should cast around among their family relations, as they seemed to do, when they wished to fill officer vacancies. As an example, he considered Colonel Cowden's regiment a disgrace to the state. Men fired muskets out of train windows, killed hogs, endangered life, and the commanding Colonel lost control. He told Governor Andrew his only hope for efficient leadership was to obtain the service of some experienced officers from the army. Colonel Joseph Hooker, a native son, was one possibility to head up a regiment.[9]

Wilson frequently felt that Lincoln did not move fast enough in the war effort, but on all critical matters he gave the President full support. When Congress convened he endorsed Lincoln's suspension of habeas corpus without any doubts.[10] And he did his best to give the War Department the backing it needed. He did not think that the war would be over quickly, and generally believed that officers paralyzed by age should be weeded out and placed on a retired list, that the comfort of the men in ranks was a major consideration whatever the cost, and that the efficiency of the volunteer forces had to be improved. He knew that many of the officers were unfit for command and he believed that the President should have authority to discharge from the service those who were incompetent, or neglected their duty. Walking around the city he saw troops standing in the burning sun for hours while their leaders drank champagne and ate good dinners at the best hotels and it gnawed his insides.

In four and a half weeks of the special session Congress enacted a series of acts to build and strengthen the forces. The Act of July 22 authorized the President to accept 500,000 volunteers for service not exceeding three years nor less than three months. The Act of July 25 recognized that short term enlistments would not answer their problems, so they permitted the President to call out an additional 500,000 men for enlistment for the duration of the war. An Act of July 29 provided an increase in the Regular Army on the condition that within one year after termination of the war it might be reduced to 25,000. And another Act of July 29 authorized employment of militia to continue in service until discharged on condition that such term was not prolonged more than sixty days after the beginning of the next regular session of Congress. Acts of August 3 and 5 related to staffs and created an Assistant Secretary of War. On August 6 four measures increased the Engineer and Topographical Corps, stopped the election of volunteer officers, increased the pay of privates from $12 to $13 a month, and most important, sanctioned all actions of President Lincoln before Congress met. In a short time, Congress provided for a military system to fight one of the greatest wars of modern times. Whatever the defects of the system, it was a gigantic undertaking with few precedents to guide actions.[11]

Wilson was an excellent Chairman of the Military Affairs Committee during this period of stress because he possessed a combination of useful qualities and experience. At a time when staffs of experts were small or non-existent in either the executive or legislative branches, the burden fell on Wilson to prepare and introduce bills for Congressional approval. The great energy that he lent to the job was, in itself, no small matter and created a sense of urgency. He appreciated the value of time when a vast amount of military problems awaited legislation before the War Department could move their antiquated organization into action. Never a man to cross t's and dot i's, he was willing to listen to the needs of the army and to give them what they wanted as a rule without becoming either a rubber stamp or a petty obstructionist. He maintained friendly relations with War Secretary Cameron, and his successor Stanton, when it would have been easy to have fallen prey to bickering and personal jealousies. As a common sense legislator he knew how to get things done and to cope with his difficult colleagues without ruffling too many feathers. Sometimes he moved too quickly, sometimes he made mistakes, but he was neither afraid to act nor to accept responsibility, and he could be counted on to take the pressure and avoid the temptations of corruption.

On the morning of July 21 columns of men in blue moved to Bull Run field on the plains of Manassas, and Wilson, like many Washingtonians, went out to see the action. One soldier saw Wilson in an open barouche with a large hamper of sandwiches which an attendant freely handed out to the troops.[12] Wilson joined the Illinois Congressman, Elihu Washburne, and they looked up General McDowell who was sitting in a tent on dry ground. McDowell, in a depressed mood, lacked confidence in the outcome. He spoke of the rebel forces, the poor Union position, and the rebel knowledge of the country. Any optimism that Wilson and Washburne may have had vanished, and they returned to their buggy feeling like a wet blanket had been thrown over them. Washburne said to Wilson, "I don't know how you feel Wilson, but I feel the same as I have often felt the day before an election when our party has been awfully licked." Wilson answered, "Upon my word, that is precisely the way I feel."[13]

Garrett Davis, Senator from Kentucky, and others claimed that Wilson fled from the scene when the enemy attacked. But according to Wilson, and witnesses, he was under the impression that the Union Army had the situation under control until he arrived at Centreville where rumors were rampant that the Northerners were falling back. This seemed incredible to Wilson, and after lingering a while at Centreville, he started on foot for Washington. Later he was given a lift by a gentleman from Pennsylvania, but he did not hurry back because he saw no fighting at Centreville or on the road back to Washington.[14]

The defeat worked Wilson up to a fever pitch, and he made a nuisance of himself. In the middle of August he visited Boston in a state of great alarm, and, according to Governor Andrew's secretary, "on every street [he] comes scaring everybody, and making everybody feel d--d miserable. Swears Washington will probably be taken and he is going right on there tonight so he *says.*"[15]

Not content with playing a purely legislative role in the midst of wartime excitement, and yet not wanting to relinquish the power of his office, Wilson turned down a commission as Brigadier General from Abraham Lincoln, but accepted a place as a Massachusetts Colonel. For a brief time between sessions Wilson served on the staff of General McClellan. Both he and Secretary of War Stanton believed that he could obtain some knowledge of the organization and condition of the army while serving there. But his chief purpose was to encourage recruiting. Since the start of hostilities, the practice of individuals raising regiments on their own initiative, and thus quickly becoming Colonels or Brigadier Generals, had grown up. The system had many evils, and in Massachusetts Ben Butler caused no end of trouble for Governor Andrew when he got permission to raise six regiments in New England. But Wilson's case was somewhat different. It was not a matter of self aggrandizement because he had nothing to gain except an outlet for his energy and a sense of achievement. With the manpower needs of the Army in mind Wilson returned home to organize a regiment. He had about a hundred days before the next meeting of Congress and he thought that he could use the time to step up volunteering which had slowed down. In this effort he had Stanton's complete support.[16]

Looking for healthy men twenty years old and older, Wilson declared at a Union War Meeting at Faneuil Hall that 150,000 men were needed in the field, General McClellan, he said, needed 50,000 men that night on the Potomac, and General Fremont needed 100,000 men in Missouri to carry the flag to the banks of the Rio Grande. He thought that Massachusetts ought to have ten more regiments in the field in the next thirty days.[17]

Wilson, with his usual frenetic energy, made an ideal recruiter in his appeal for three year men. The early enthusiasm which had produced short term enlistments had evaporated, and the idea of bounties had not yet been conceived. The reverse at Bull Run had also shown the less glorious side of war and increased the difficulty in obtaining long term enlistments. Nevertheless, traveling around the state at his own expense, he raised and organized nineteen companies of infantry, two batteries of artillery, and a company of sharpshooters. In six weeks he had signed up 2,300 men. On September 28, 1861 the Twenty-Second Regiment of Massachusetts Volunteers, with Wilson in command, was born at a race track in Lynnfield, twelve miles from Boston. The Third Battery of Light Artillery and the Second Company of Sharpshooters were also attached to the regiment.

Wilson took pride in supporting his men with good equipment. There were no gaudy uniforms, no scarlet clothes, gold lace, or gay caparisons. Dressed in sober, sensible uniforms, the sharpshooters carried heavy muzzle loaders with telescopic sights and the rest of the men had Enfield rifles. There were Sibley tents for the men, wall tents for the officers, a hospital wagon and two ambulances. On October 8 the regiment moved to Boston for departure to Washington. Riding up State Street on a fine Morgan horse presented to him by his friends, the stout, florid Wilson proudly led the regiment to the Boston Common where the men stacked arms, partook of a collation provided by the citizens of Boston, and received a stand of colors from Robert E. Winthrop.

In his gentlemanly way, Winthrop made a pleasant little speech that buried his political differences with Wilson and expressed the hope that his appearance manifested the unified determination of all the people of Massachusetts. Wilson replied in kind and modestly remarked that their regiment had nothing to boast about yet, but that they hoped to do their duty.

From Boston the troops moved by rail to New York where extensive preparations had been made for their reception. The main body of the regiment arrived in a train of twenty-six cars drawn by two locomotives of the Boston and Worcester Railroad. Flowers and flags draped one of the engines and the other had a striped smokestack and a steam calliope. Marching through the streets of New York, observers remarked that Wilson looked well in his uniform and had no want of military self-possession. Hand clapping and scarf waving greeted them from almost every window. The officers paraded to the Fifth Avenue Hotel where they had a substantial breakfast provided by the "Sons of Massachusetts." Among the dignitaries present were Governor Morgan of New York, Thurlow Weed, George Bancroft, and Henry Bellows, President of the Sanitary Commission. In reply to the welcoming speeches, Wilson thanked the New Yorkers for their warm reception and paid tribute to the men who controlled the moneyed institutions for their support of the Union. Their backing, he said, showed England, a nation of shopkeepers, that the United States intended to fight the battle to a successful conclusion.

After breakfast officers and men marched to Madison Square Garden where the Honorable James T. Brady, on behalf of a committee of New York ladies, presented the regiment with a flag and delivered a highly patriotic speech with references to his Irish ancestry. Again Wilson replied. He noted that the men under his command had been recruited within thirty days and that they came from the toiling masses. Some had the blood of Puritans, but many were born on the "Green Isle of the Sea." And, said the ex-Know Nothing, "the history of the world shows that no men more bravely do their duty than those in whose veins courses the blood of the men of Ireland."

When the officers finished supper at the Fifth Avenue Hotel, the regiment embarked on a boat at the Battery for South Amboy, New Jersey. Unhappily two men were lost overboard—possibly they had imbibed too much at New York—but the troops continued their trip by train from Amboy to Camden, then ferry to Philadelphia. The next day they took a train to Baltimore where they switched to the Baltimore and Ohio Railroad and arrived in Washington, Friday, October 11. Parading down Pennsylvania Avenue, the regiment met the President who was out for a drive and he acknowledged their salute.

The next day the Twenty-Second pitched tents at Falls Church, Virginia. Under order of October 15, 1861, the regiment became a part of General Fitz-John Porter's Division and General J. H. Martindale's brigade. On October 27, Wilson made a formal farewell and returned to the Senate. The Twenty-Second Massachusetts Volunteers, known as "Henry Wilson's Regiment," would see much action at Antietam, Shepherdstown, Chancellorsville, Gettysburg, the Battle of the Wilderness, Spottsylvania, and Petersburg. At Gettysburg fifty-nine percent of the men were casualties.

Henry Wilson was a Sunday soldier with a moment or two of glory. He saw no action, but he served a real purpose in raising the troops, and nearing the age of fifty, there was no reason for him to be conscience-stricken in returning to the Senate. One of the officers who served under Wilson wrote him a fond note. "You have chidden (sic) only when it was for our good, and have exhibited a kindness and benevolence of heart which no man shall ever dare to deny to you before me."[18]

In the midst of all this activity, a story that Wilson had a government contract for a million pairs of shoes which would give him a quarter of a million dollars profit disturbed him sufficiently for him to write a denial to *The New York Daily Tribune.* He stated that he had no contract with the government directly or indirectly for anything, and that the government made no contract with anyone as a result of his influence. He had spent hundreds of dollars of his own money, and he pointed out that his pay as Colonel of the Twenty-Second had been directed to go to the regiment hospital, and that he received no pay as a member of McClellan's staff. There is no question that he was in an excellent position to make a personal fortune, but there is not the slightest indication that he made a penny by selling or using his influence.

Back in the Senate, his days of command over, Wilson handled a continual flow of complaints, requests for appointments, promotions, transfers, and a raft of other favor-seeking letters, as well as major proposals for reorganization. He kept in close touch with the War Department, asking their opinion on proposed bills and referring many incidental matters to them.[19]

Wilson also had hopes of keeping army expenses down wherever possible, and asked the Paymaster General for his recommendations. Benjamin F. Larned replied with a number of suggestions which included abolishing regimental bands, reducing the number of volunteer cavalry regiments, eliminating the payment of forty cents a day to cavalry officers for the use and risk of their horses, careful scrutiny of forage pay, and a closer look at chaplains.

There was an unconfirmed report that one regiment employed a French cook, and mustered him as chaplain to meet the expenses. The Paymaster General also mentioned the demoralizing influence of sutlers.[20]

In the past year Wilson had visited most of the camps of the regiments in the Army of the Potomac, and had seen the damaging effects of the sutler system which charged the men exorbitant amounts of money, and made monthly profits of one to two thousand dollars a month. In December 1861, Wilson introduced a resolution that the Inspector General, Quartermaster General, and Commissary General of Subsistence be directed to inform the Senate what articles, in their opinion, should be sold by sutlers to volunteers as necessary for their comfort, and which were best adapted to promotion of interests of the military service. The sutlers resented these attacks, formed a "Sutlers Defense Fund," and according to Wilson, told him defiantly that his project to eliminate them would be defeated.[21]

Late in the year, Wilson also introduced a resolution, which was adopted, for the Military Affairs Committee to consider whether or not any legislation was necessary to correct existing evils in the management of army hospitals. General McClellan had asked Dr. Henry Bellows, head of the Sanitary Commission, to draft a bill for the reorganization of the medical bureau and both Abraham Lincoln and Thomas A. Scott, Assistant Secretary of War, advised that Wilson present the measure to the Senate.[22]

Wilson also badgered John Andrew about the Massachusetts regiments, and at times, must have been a source of annoyance to the hard working Governor. But Wilson tried to consider Andrew's feelings. In expressing shock over the drinking of a Seventh Regiment Colonel, he was quick to add, "In what I have said I hope you will not feel that I wish to find fault with you. I know you have toiled with fidelity, zeal, and ability. It would be strange if you did not sometimes make some mistakes in your selection of officers." And Wilson was also quick to do favors for Andrew, such as following up appointments of particular interest to him.[23]

The war had just begun. It was a war run by a President without the greatest regard for Congress. But the problems of the country were mammoth, and Congress had its work to do, which even when minimized, was still important to the running of the government. Wilson's part was not small, and in the next three years of war he served the Executive well in formulating legislation for the expansion of the fighting force and following its course through Congress.

*   *   *   *   *

Always willing to listen to the worst about Wilson, Edward Everett entered two items of interest in his diary in October 1861 that must have delighted him. The first, October 30, noted that a letter of twelve pages from Rose Greenhow to General Pierre G. T. Beauregard had been intercepted and had caused her arrest.[24] The second, October 31, 1861 read:

> In Mrs. Greenhow's letter referred to yesterday, there is a passage to the effect that General Wilson had been appointed on Gen'l. McClellans Staff. If he accepts (Says Mrs. G.) I shall be able to tell you more of McClellan's secrets. Information of this strange statement was communicated to Governor Andrew. There is no reason to suppose that W. is disloyal but Dalilah ensnared a wiser and more valiant than the General.[25]

Rose Greenhow, about forty-four, tall, well formed, graceful carriage, olive complexion, black eyes, and black hair turning gray, had, it is said, a commanding personality.[26] She was an aunt of Stephen Douglas, and well acquainted with many members of Washington society, including James Buchanan, William Seward, Charles Francis Adams, and Henry Wilson.

Many years later in May 1870, another diarist, Hamilton Fish, wrote that James Watson Webb had told him that day of a recent conversation with General Thomas Jordan, who in 1861 had been adjutant-general of the Confederate forces at Manassas and chief of staff under Beauregard. The Southern officer claimed that he had found at the outbreak of the war that an intimacy existed between Mrs. Greenhow and Wilson and that he, Jordan, had established the same kind of intimacy with her. He then prevailed upon her to gain from Wilson all of the official news that she could get and gave her a cipher to communicate with Confederate authorities. Jordan said that she obtained word from Wilson that McDowell had been ordered to advance upon Manassas which she passed along. The Confederates thus knew about McDowell's plans within a few hours after the orders were given, and in this way were able to concentrate their troops and win the Battle of Bull Run. Fish entered the story without comment.[27]

Popular historians have made much of this intriguing tale, and of ten love letters that are deposited in the National Archives which Wilson is presumed to have written to Mrs. Greenhow. Most of the letters are simply signed "H." Writers state that the evidence against Wilson is not complete, but then seem to proceed as if he were guilty. It makes a good story even though the stout, middle aged Wilson does not make the most romantic figure.

There are grave doubts that there is any substance to the story beyond the fact that Wilson knew Mrs. Greenhow. He was certainly capable of speaking carelessly in a less security conscious age than ours, and with a sickly wife, it is even possible that Wilson might have had an affair with Mrs. Greenhow. But it all seems most improbable. Though Everett said that the report about Mrs. Greenhow came to him from Governor Andrew, there is nothing in the John Andrew papers to give additional support to the episode. Andrew, moreover, continued to work with Wilson throughout the war without any apparent reservations. Conscious disloyalty, even as Everett admitted, seems completely out of the question.

The ten love letters in the National Archives are not in the handwriting of Wilson, nor are they written in his distinctive style. None of the letters give away any military secrets or even military gossip. One letter that sounds most like Wilson reads:

> I am happy to say that I feel particularly well this morning; and can well account for the favorable change. We are in the act of entering on the consideration of the Pacific RR Bill. I will not fail you tonight and will bring with me the thing of which we spoke last night. Bless you always. Yours.

Another letter written on a letterhead of the Thirty-Sixth Congress, dated January 30, 1861 reads:

> Your note is read. Believe me or not you cannot be more wretched than I am. I cannot now explain. Let it suffice until we meet that for the last few days every movement and act of mine have been watched with hawkeyed vigilance. For your sake more than my own I have been compelled to be cautious. But tomorrow at 10 A.M. I will see you at all hazzards [*sic.*] Yours ever. H.[28]

Rose Greenhow wrote of her experiences as a spy in a book called, "My Imprisonment," which does nothing more than speak bitterly of Wilson as a Radical Republican and relate some of his idle chatter. One example being that he thought they would lead Senator Crittenden into believing that he was a possible candidate for Chief Justice of the United States until they had him allied with the Union. She said that young Doolittle, the son of the Senator and a clerk on the Military Affairs Committee, was an occasional and useful visitor at her home. She thoroughly enjoyed playing the part of a spy, and like most of them, exaggerated her importance far out of proportion. It is difficult to understand how she could have been effective when she loudly announced her Southern sympathies to all.[29]

If Rose Greenhow entertained clerks and found them helpful, it might be well to point out that in 1861 the official clerk of the Military Affairs Committee had the initials "H. W." and his handwriting strongly resembles the penmanship in the ten love letters in the National Archives. Comparing his writing in a committee record book with the letters one can see a number of similarities. The young clerk's name was Horace White, and it may be as unfair to malign him as Henry Wilson. But the similarity is there and it may be taken for what it is worth. Horace White became a prominent journalist and publisher, and like Wilson, never seemed tainted by any breath of scandal.[30]

With the fingers of accusation pointed, perhaps unfairly, it also seems that if anything of an espionage nature occurred, it was for little good. Although the emotional Mrs. Greenhow liked to think that her deeds caused the sending of more troops to Manassas, it was McDowell's actual advance that made Beauregard send for help. According to Mrs. Greenhow, she received a copy of the order to McDowell, but there is no such order in the records, and the general seems to have been under orders to move when practical.[31]

Romance and espionage are intriguing, but this time it seems like much ado about nothing. Mrs. Greenhow gained notoriety, but the episode, true or false, did not disturb Wilson's career. The gossip that Edward Everett enjoyed must have received very narrow circulation. Untarnished, in the public eye or with his colleagues as a result of this tale, Wilson continued his wartime activities.

*   *   *   *   *

Over his head in the administrative intricacies of the War Department, and suspected of playing fast and loose with government funds in the purchase of military supplies, Simon Cameron resigned as Secretary to become Minister to Moscow. Whatever the failings of this slick political manipulator from Pennsylvania, he had also been the victim of haste and outmoded procurement procedures. Before leaving he generously thanked Wilson for his energetic support. No man, he thought, had done more to help organize the army. By preparing bills for clothing, arming, and supplies, and for assisting in obtaining appropriations, he had become a mainstay in the early days of the struggle. "At the first call for troops, you came here," he noted, "and up to the meeting of Congress, a period of more than six months, your labors were incessant."[32]

In Cameron's place came abrasive Edwin Stanton. One of his first acts was to meet with the military committees of both Houses. He asked for frequent advice and constant cooperation, and throughout the war he had little cause to complain about Henry Wilson.[33] There were occasional differences, but for the most part Wilson sought the professional views of the Department and kept in close touch with Stanton.

Armies rarely enter a war with proper organization and equipment, and the Civil War was no exception. There were antique remnants in policies, procedures, tables of organization, and equipment from previous wars that needed overhauling. Many officers had lingered in the service nourishing old ideas, and they required replacement too. To make matters worse many officers and men had departed with the South and these defections severely aggravated the inadequacies of the Union Army.

There was a steady stream of legislation to modernize the army, and almost all of it passed through Wilson's hands. Among the many problems that immediately faced Congress were the condition of hospitals, effectiveness of medical doctors, the sutler system, the size and staffing of corps and divisions, and whether or not cavalry regiments were as useful as infantry. Early in 1862 the management of government hospitals occupied much of Wilson's time. Part of his interest probably came from the pressures created by the Sanitary Commission, his good friend, Clara Barton, who would become founder of the American Red Cross, and the mass of complaints that reached his desk from private citizens. But it was a natural subject given his instinct for reform and his innate kindness. He found that a large number of the doctors on the medical board had been in the army for many years and had seen little or no practice for sometime. In his opinion, they acted like they knew everything, but really knew very little. Wilson wanted them retired and vigorous young men brought into the service.

There was a desperate need for military doctors. Wilson had heard that recently wounded men had not been tended for the first time until a week had lapsed. He introduced a bill to increase the efficiency of the medical corps by increasing the number of surgeons and establishing a merit system. Most of the men who had been in the medical corps opposed the merit system because they preferred the easy route of seniority, but the bill passed.[34]

Wilson had already expressed his low regard for sutlers, but he found them a difficult enemy to conquer. He told members of the Senate that his careful estimates indicated that the sutler sales in the Army of the Potomac exceeded the rate of ten million dollars a year, and that the profits were more than one half of sales. He originally wanted to abolish the system and adopt the Navy small stores system, but the Quartermaster's Corps objected because they would have to supply clerks. He would have settled for restricting the number of articles sold by sutlers and for defining their duties. This would have curtailed the distribution of liquor, the greatest source of trouble. But he met with no success. It seemed to him that he had never met with so much personal abuse, misrepresentation, and coarse, unqualified slander. He claimed that men had defiantly said to him, "I have got thousands invested in goods for sutlers, and you cannot pass your bill through Congress."[35]

The effectiveness of cavalry was also a question that engaged Wilson's attention. Their cost was frightful and Wilson suspected that they had too many regiments. Forage payments, frequently extended to officers who did not have horses, ran into millions of dollars. He submitted a resolution directing the Secretary of War to report to the Senate the number of cavalry regiments authorized, mustered into service, where stationed, condition of equipment, and asked about the possibility of converting some cavalry regiments not yet mustered into service into infantry regiments.[36]

The Senate learned that there were seventy-seven cavalry regiments authorized and thirty to forty of them were in the field armed, equipped, and in service. Several regiments had men, but no mounts. Wilson thought that some of the new cavalrymen were in more danger of stampeding themselves than injuring the enemy. A well armed, well trained, well mounted cavalry outfit was a powerful striking force, but without training they were far less efficient than the infantry. He wanted to reduce the total force to fifty regiments, and turn the excess into infantry. Senator William P. Fessenden, for reasons of economy, would have preferred a deeper cut to thirty regiments. Finally, Wilson moved to reduce the number of volunteer units to forty regiments with forty-eight thousand men. The measure passed the Senate in February 1862, but House amendments forced Wilson to move to lay the bill on the table. As the war continued, however, Wilson became convinced that the cavalry contributed little. They were helpful on the Western plains, but of little service in the areas of heavy fighting.[37]

As in every war, it was difficult to attain both efficiency and economy. Politician generals, Ben Butler for one, cried out for more men and Wilson found himself criticized for blocking the expansion of the army. One newspaper account held him personally responsible for not having more troops in the field. It reported that he had maintained that they had more men in the field than they needed. Actually, he had said that the government had overestimated the number of troops on hand by about a hundred and fifty thousand, and if there were that many soldiers on duty it was more than enough. It was easy for misunderstandings to develop, but Wilson never claimed the army had too many effective men. And yet Wilson did continually talk economy. Earlier in the year he was told that the army of the Potomac cost a million and a quarter dollars a day, and he thought this astronomical sum should be cut by mustering some of the men out of the service.[38]

The need for new military legislation never ceased. There were pay rates to define, pensions to set, militia acts to amend, investigations to make, and army corps to establish. There was much detail to handle and the Congressional committees were small with only a clerk to serve as staff. Wilson also carried on a regular flow of military business with Governor Andrew. In the Spring of 1862, Wilson had been chagrined to learn that Andrew held unkind thoughts toward him which arose over some relatively minor matter. Still, Wilson went out of his way to calm Andrew. "I supposed that you were my friend for I knew that I had been and was your friend. You have been active and earnest since the war opened, so have I. You will now see that you have made a few mistakes, I know I have."[39]

Wilson also tried to quiet tempers when the irascible behavior of Stanton stirred protests. He pictured the Secretary of War to the public as a man of great zeal and determination who wished to end the war as soon as possible. In reply to reports that Stanton habitually indulged in disparaging remarks about General McClellan, Wilson answered that the Secretary probably censured some movements of generals whom he regarded as slow and dilatory, and that perhaps he was too impetuous, but day by day and week by week he upheld McClellan and all other generals in the field.[40]

During the year most people thought that the war could be won by a voluntary force and many believed that the war would come to an end soon. In July, Abraham Lincoln issued a call for three hundred thousand volunteers and the states exceeded their quotas by thirty-three percent. But in August the President took a step towards a draft under authorization of a bill introduced by Wilson which revised an Act of 1795. Its strength rested in a clause which stated, "If by reason or defects in existing laws, or in the execution of them, in the several states, or any of them, it shall be found necessary to provide for enrolling the militia and otherwise putting this act into execution, the President is authorized in such cases to make all necessary rules and regulations."[41] Lincoln issued an order for three hundred thousand men to serve for nine months and directed that if any state failed to furnish its quota of men the deficiency should be made up by a special draft from the militia by August 15. In September the President called another three hundred thousand men and drafted about eighty-seven thousand. This was the final call by the general government for men before conscription. The country had reached the stage where every citizen owed the nation miiltary service.[42] The governors did not question the legality of the President's action, but the draft was a heavy burden upon them. Many wondered, too, why Lincoln resisted the use of Negroes in the army. Governor Andrew appealed to Heaven's judgment on this subject, but

Governor Kirkwood of Iowa said plainly that he wanted some dead black as well as white men at the end of the war.

When times permitted, Wilson liked to escape from the capital and visit with the troops, particularly Massachusetts troops. It had been a year of military failure and disappointment and contact with the men seemed to give him new vitality. In September he returned to Hall's Hill to visit his old regiment and their appearance shocked him. Instead of the well clothed unit that he had left in the Spring, he saw ragged, dirty, broken up companies. There were odd hats of all shapes, buttonless blouses and trousers, some without shoes, others without socks. They had been through fire and the only consolation might be that they were now of stronger fiber.[43]

In December, General Ambrose Burnside met defeat at Fredericksburg from Lee's well entrenched army. He retreated across the Rappahannock River with a loss of about 13,000 men. The *Tribune* correspondent, Henry Villard, had been at the scene of action and sent his report by special messenger to New York on the night train since the government censor at the main telegraph had been ordered by the Secretary of War not to allow any news from Fredericksburg.

After Villard filed his story, he returned to Washington and ran into Wilson at the entrance of the Willard Hotel. Known to local correspondents as the most persistent news hunter in Washington, Wilson asked, "Have you come from the army? What is the news? Have we won the fight?" Villard answered, "Senator, you know whatever news I have belongs to my paper, but for the sake of the cause, I will tell you in strict confidence that Burnside is defeated, and in such bad plight that I think you can render no greater service to the country than to go at once to the White House and tell the President, if he does not know what has happened on the Rappahannock, to make an immediate demand for the truth. You can state further to him that, as I believe he knows me to be a truthful man, I do not hesitate to say to him, through you, that in my deliberate judgment, he ought not to wait for information, but instantly order the army back to the north bank."

Later in the evening, perhaps after some checking of reports, Wilson took Villard to the White House where they found Lincoln in the old reception room on the second floor. Lincoln greeted Villard with a hearty handshake saying, "I am much obliged to you for coming, for we are very anxious and have heard very little." Villard related his story and Lincoln asked questions for about a half an hour. He wanted to know about the defenses of the rebels on the right front, their command of the town and river, the physical and moral condition of the troops, the chances of success of another attack from either of their wings, the extent of the losses, and the feeling among the general officers. When Villard told Lincoln that he should order Burnside to withdraw from the south back immediately, the President took no offense, but said, "I hope it is not so bad as all that."[44]

Impressed by the danger, Wilson rushed to Fredericksburg and spent two days there to determine the condition of the troops for himself. One member of the Twenty-Second Regiment wounded at Fredericksburg called on Wilson in Washington. According to the soldier there was not a paymaster in the town who had funds and the army was six months in arrears. Wilson loaned him enough money to take care of his needs.[45]

Wilson also took an interest that winter in the condition of the troops at Alexandria who a correspondent for the *Detroit News* reported were suffering in convalescent camps. At Lincoln's request, Wilson visited the camp to examine the situation. He brought two ambulances loaded with blankets and provisions and quietly inspected the camp, making notes about the worst cases. When he left, he said, "We'll be here again, boys, Monday, and will have a different state of things." When Monday arrived, Wilson returned with a board of surgeons with orders to discharge or furlough every man who was not ready for immediate active duty. New barracks were built, and camp "Misery Hill," was put out of business permanently.[46]

At another time, Wilson visited another camp in New Hampshire where he learned that there were some dishonest surgeons who had discharged men for illegal compensation. On the other hand, there were thousands of men who remained in the hospitals who should have been discharged. Wilson said that there were about one hundred and fifty general hospitals with sixty thousand patients. He estimated that ten thousand of these patients would never again render service to the government and the cost of maintaining them was exorbitant. He moved to consider a bill to discharge disabled soldiers from the army that proposed two medical inspector generals, and eight medical inspectors to designate fit subjects for discharge. There were somewhere between four and five thousand surgeons in service and about fifteen hundred civilian surgeons temporarily employed which seemed sufficient to Fessenden who complained that he was tired of trying to solve problems by increasing rank and pay. Still, Wilson had his way and the bill passed.[47]

For all Wilson's visits to camps, and occasional intervention into minor military operations, he seemed to have a clear idea of his correct role in the total situation. Sometimes suspicions arose about his influence in conducting army affairs and the placement of generals. In reply to Senator Lane of Kansas he once said that, as Chairman of the Military Affairs Committee, he had something to do with shaping policy, but nothing to do with its administration or the command of generals in the field.

> I have never, in my place in this Senate, uttered a word of criticism in regard to the military operations of any general in the field. I have never before the people uttered a sentence of criticism of the military operations of any general in the field. I have never written a line, even to my own wife, criticizing the military operations of any general. I early made up my mind that it was not my duty, as Chairman of the Committee on Military Affairs to make such criticisms. I entertain opinions—and I have expressed them, as I am accustomed to do, in private conversation—in regard to military operations and in regard to military men; but I have never publicly made, nor written, nor printed criticisms upon military operations or men; nor have I ever advised the President, or the Secretary of War, or those holding authority, to give any man a command. I have ever felt that it was not my duty, as Chairman of the Military Committee, or as a member of the Senate, to engage in putting this man in place or that man out of place. Before the Senate and the country I declare that I am in no degree responsible for any changes of commanders in the field; nor have I attempted to influence the action of the Government in regard to its designation of commanders on sea or land.[48]

Given the difficulty of finding a successful general to lead the Union army, Wilson was probably quite happy to disown any part in the naming of men who moved from one defeat to another. Still, he appears to have given careful consideration to the part that he played and the restrictions that he should place upon himself. Wilson also denied that party affiliations carried any weight in obtaining commissions. In the fall of 1863 he said that more than two hundred officers had entered the service bearing commissions secured by his influence, but he always forgot to ask about their political sentiments. Since the start of the war, 6,725 military nominations had passed through the Military Affairs Committee composed of four Republicans and three Democrats and they never gave a divided political vote on a single nomination.[49]

Estimates indicate that there would be an annual saving of forty-five to fifty million dollars a year by reducing the number of regiments from eleven or twelve hundred to two or three hundred. Many new regiments had been created instead of filling up the old units, many of which were depleted. Despite the insufficient number of enlisted men there was always a full complement of officers. A *New York Times* editorial declared, "A regimental Chaplain is ready to preach and pray whenever fifty of the old guard can be got together. And no Colonel, Lt. Col., or Major will be lacking so long as any one of the ten Captains or twenty Lieutenants is willing to exchange his small salary for the much larger one of a field officer."[50] Many regiments existed in name only, but continued on the payroll, and others, with thinned ranks, only drained the remaining members physically and emotionally. But there were political objections by governors who felt that they would be deprived of their rights to officer the regiments. Wilson introduced a bill to consolidate the regiments and, at the same time, secured the governors' rights by providing that the officers of the new regiments would be taken from the commissioned officers of the state from which the regiments came. But this did not convince enough members of the Senate and the bill had to be laid over for further consideration.[51]

Wilson also introduced a bill to promote the comfort of wounded and sick soldiers, and brought up a resolution for the prompt payment of troops. Thousands of soldiers received letters from their families telling of their troubles because the army had not forwarded their pay. Some men deserted because of anxiety for their families. Wilson looked upon prompt payment as a necessity for securing discipline and engendering good feeling in the army. Over and over again he called for information about payments only to receive assurances that the Government was doing everything possible with the means available.[52]

In February 1863 another of Wilson's bills for the health and comfort of soldiers came before the Committee of the Whole for consideration. Its main purpose was to unite the medical department with line officers to supervise cooking and improve sanitary methods, but there was also a provision to furnish tobacco to enlisted men which Sumner opposed. His attitude, undoubtedly the most virtuous, was that if the men had to have tobacco, let them get it for themselves. But Wilson, more sympathetic to human failings even though he had never smoked a day in his life, recognized the strong desire of the men for tobacco and he wanted to prevent them from paying sky high prices to sutlers. Sumner lost the argument, and the bill passed.[53]

In March 1863 Wilson sponsored acts to provide additional Major Generals and Brigadier Generals to be selected from those who had been conspicuous for gallant or meritorious conduct in the line of duty. He also proposed measures to promote the efficiency of the Corps of Engineers, and the Ordinance Department, and to prescribe the organization of the Signal Corps. But the major piece of legislation that became law on March 1863 was national conscription. For months there had been heated discussion about the need for such a bill. Copperheads were particularly bitter. The proposal, the work of Henry Wilson more than any other single person, was far from perfect, but it became the first federal law which created an army without the intervention of states. For months volunteering had declined and desertions had increased. Lincoln knew that the volunteer system was inadequate and urged legislation to strengthen the deficiency. Something had to be done. Governors, jealous of their powers, resisted pressures of the federal government, but they failed to raise sufficient men, and, of necessity, eventually surrendered states rights in military matters.

The chief objectives of the measure, called, "An Act for enrolling and calling out the national forces, and for other purposes," were first, to enroll and hold liable to military duty all citizens capable of bearing arms, with certain exemptions; second, to call the national forces by draft when required; and third, to arrest deserters and return them to their proper commands. The national force to be formed would consist of male citizens between the ages of twenty and forty-five with three exemptions: first, the physically and mentally unfit, and persons convicted of a felony; second, a restricted number of officials such as the Vice President, federal judges, cabinet members, and Governors; and, third, sole supporters of aged or infirm parents or of orphaned children. Among the men who were not exempted there were two classes: first, all men, married or single, between twenty and thirty-five, and all single men from thirty-five to forty-five; second, married men from thirty-five to forty-five who were not to be called until the first group was exhausted. The law was to be administered by a provost marshal general who became head of a separate bureau in the War Department, and a corps of provost marshals all appointed by the President. There was also to be a provost marshal in charge of each enrollment district which was to correspond to a congressional district. The most troublesome part of the Act permitted substitutes or the payment of three hundred dollars in lieu of a substitute. Those who evaded service by illegal methods became deserters, subject to trial by court martial.

Wilson was not happy about becoming the proponent of a draft. It was an unpleasant piece of business for a politician which aroused strong opposition in the North. The draft of the militia the previous year had caused riots in Wisconsin and threatening moves in Pennsylvania. But the ranks of wasted regiments could not be filled by the old system. The militia who had enlisted under Lincoln's August call for nine months men would start going home in May, and before long the three year regiments of three year volunteers would dissolve as enlistments expired. Introducing the bill on his fifty-first birthday, he referred to the constitutional authority to raise and support armies and stated that the unqualified grant of power carried with it, in the language of *The Federalist,* "all the powers requisite to the complete execution of trust." He claimed that the bill bore as lightly as possible upon the toiling masses, but he was aware of the difficulties of substitutes, and payment in lieu of a substitute. His main argument rested upon a choice between a dismembered Union or a war fought until the rebellion collapsed. "If we accept peace, disunion, death, then we may speedily summon home again our armies; if we accept war . . . then we must see to it that the ranks of our armies, broken by toil, disease, and death, are filled again with the health and vigor of life."[54]

In presenting his case, Wilson reviewed each section of the bill, and emphasized that it was enrollment of the population of the country that was needed, not of the militia. All kinds of objections arose, and many made sense. Senator William Richardson of Illinois suggested that the states that had not furnished their quotas should have conscription. Senator Edgar Cowan, who had no faith in a draft, wanted members of Congress exempted. The ultra conservative Pennsylvanian went so far as to say that he opposed saving the country if they had to use men who would only support the government under the threat of a provost marshal's baton. He wanted willing soldiers. Senator Lazarus W. Powell of Kentucky wanted to exempt teachers and professors, and Sumner wanted to exempt clergymen.

Wilson argued for as few exemptions as possible. "I want the masses of our people, the men who till our farms, who labor in our workshops, who support their families by their daily toil, to feel that the more fortunate and favored of the sons of men are liable to this draft as well as themselves." But this was an inadequate reply since Wilson also objected to a move by Powell to reduce the fee for substitutes which seemed to negate his words about helping the masses. He claimed that there was a humane purpose for substitutes to help out in situations of real need. Apparently he believed that if the fee were too low it would be used too freely, and if it were too high it would aid only the rich. In response to Cowan, he blandly stated that it was not necessary to exempt Congressmen because they could furnish substitutes if they must. But he thought that a flat exemption of members of Congress would weaken the moral force of the bill.

There were contradictions and inconsistencies in Wilson's position which probably reflect his inner reservations and uncertainty about the proper way to organize a draft. His own background had been closely associated with the state militia and in the early days of the war he had been friendly to state rather than national control of recruiting. As a longtime spokesman for the working-man it is strange that he did not completely oppose payment for substitutes. But his genuine sympathy for the masses never took the form of hostility to business. It may be reasonable to assume that he felt there was a reason for leeway to help men of responsibility out of their predicament. At any rate, he talked around the subject without being completely convincing about his viewpoint and his conflicting opinions confused the preparation of the bill. He had become a proponent of the draft only by sheer necessity and he moved into an area where no one could speak with any authority. He did believe, however, that the draft would produce recruits. He said that he had often heard the remark, " 'I do not like to volunteer; I think I can hardly afford to do it; but if I am drafted I will go willingly.' " He accepted that statement as the general sentiment of the public, but he was wrong in his estimate and did not anticipate future difficulties. Enrollment turned out to be far more complex than he had realized.

The bill passed the Senate in one day, but it came up again later in the month with amendments from the House. James Bayard of Delaware moved for an indefinite postponement because he did not believe that the bill was constitutional, and even if it were, he was sure that it was inexpedient and a dangerous disregard of the liberty of citizens and the security of states. To him it was a bill to increase the regular army which utterly abandoned and subverted the militia system. The whole male population could be enrolled at the mere will of the Executive. He said:

> I have at least this authority, that from the foundation of the Government to this day no attempt has ever been made in this country to pass a bill of this character by any Congress of the United States. . . . Heretofore it has always been held that the reserved force of the nation is the militia of the several states, which can be called into its service by the President of the United States under the provisions that Congress may adopt for that purpose; but when you call that militia into service, you call them in, not as individuals, but as organized bodies of men, to be commanded under the express provision of the Constitution, by officers appointed by the States, and to be disciplined under the discipline that Congress prescribes, by State authorities alone.

Despotic governments had large standing armies, but it was neither necessary nor consistent with a Government founded on the consent of the governed. Bayard left no doubt where he stood. He favored peace and restoration of the union if possible, but certainly peace even if the states had to separate. He would not have given George Washington the power that Wilson's bill conveyed.

Senator David Turpie of Indiana suspected that the supporters

of the bill, and especially Wilson, would use it to harass political
opponents, gratify party malice, and avenge political defeats and
fancied wrongs. "The Senator from Massachusetts has adopted
the most ingenious method yet offered in this body for the crushing out of insurrectionary forces. His plan is merely this: to reiter-
ate, day after day, his own loyalty, and disparage the loyalty of
others, his superiors here and elsewhere. . . . If the rebellion can
be crushed out by stale, vapid, vociferation in regard to the merits
of Massachusetts, or the Senators who happen to represent her,
it will disappear most speedily." He said that Wilson had advised
him in a friendly manner not to butt his head against Plymouth
Rock. "I tell the Senator he is butting his head against that which
is just as capable of resisting and overthrowing its assailants. He
is butting his head against the voluntary (not compelled) patriot-
ism of his country."

Turpie's feelings ran so deeply he cried out that if Wilson had
lived in the days of Luther he would have stood by the Pope and
Vatican. If he had lived in the times of Jesus, "He would have
followed him from the garden of Gethesemane through the streets
of Jerusalem to the judgment seat of Pilate, and there his voice
would have been heard: 'Release us unto Barrabas: as for this
Jesus, let him be crucified!' "

Wilson replied to these harsh words with restraint. "Mr. President, self respect, regard for the character of the Senate of the
United States, the priceless value of these passing hours, alike
forbid that I should pause for a moment to reply to the personal
allusions of the Senator from Indiana. I am not so lost to all sense
of personal character, or to what belongs to this presence, so as
to descend so far as to notice this voluble tirade of vituperative
epithets. I know not what I might have been had I lived in other
ages and in other lands, but I happen to live in this age and in
this land, rife with treasons and conspiracies, and sympathizers
with traitors and conspirators; and I now know that I am not a
traitor or conspirator nor a sympathizer with traitors and conspirators."

Others joined in the debate and expressed the fear of despotism.
Powell of Kentucky declared that they had plenty of volunteers
when men thought they were fighting to preserve the Union; but
the passage of unconstitutional confiscation bills, the Negro
becoming the avowed object of the war, and the encroachment

upon State's rights, dimmed interest in volunteering. Apparently confident that he had the votes, Wilson did not debate much with the opposing Senators. The bill became law, and Senator Willard Saulsbury of Delaware exclaimed, "I regard it as the crowning act in a series of acts of legislation which surrender all that is dear to the private citizen into the keeping and at the mercy of the Executive of this nation."[55]

Almost as soon as the draft became law, trouble started with enrollment. The Provost Marshal had to obtain the names of those liable to the draft, but no one had to submit his name freely. The enrollers faced all kinds of problems from simple deception to outright violence; and some were injured and others killed in the line of duty. In some regions organized opposition required troops to overcome disruption. In other areas secret societies, newspapers, and politicians cultivated an opposition public opinion. Even governors developed a protective attitude towards their people and tried to reduce quotas. In July drafting in New York City led to rioting which required thousands of troops to quell. New York's Governor Horatio Seymour, regarded the draft as unconstitutional and did everything in his power to obstruct enrollment. But even John Andrew had his troubles in Massachusetts. The Governor had to move three hundred troops into Boston to maintain order. A mob gathered at the Cooper Street Arsenal and some threw stones at the men. The soldiers fired into the crowd and killed several persons.

As sponsor of the draft, Wilson found himself forced to defend the unpopular measure. The Copperheads and draft dodgers were beneath his contempt, and he scorned men like the Mozart Hall leader, Fernando Wood, and Governor Seymour. In a letter to Wood, Wilson noted that the New Yorker's denunciation of the Conscription Law could only fire the hearts and nerve the arms of traitors.[56] Later he said that, "The very presses and persons who are denouncing the draft, a year ago were denouncing me and the government for not giving the country such a measure. The *Illinois State Register,* for one demanded the drafting of a million men, and the *New York World,* and the Albany organ of the Democracy called on the government for a draft. And in obedience to their demand, we passed the act, and in doing so, we tried to make it lay as lightly as possible on the poor man and placed within its power all the classes that were before exempted from draft by state and national laws. I insisted on putting into the act a provision that should exempt immature young men—those under twenty—for I had seen them perishing by thousands in our hospitals, overborne by hardships. The $300 clause has been denounced, and into the credulous ear of ignorance has been hissed its injustice. But I tell you there is not an honest and intelligent poor man who would vote it out of the bill." He emphasized that National and State militia laws had favored the rich and that they had exempted nearly a million Negroes.[57] There was much to criticize about the Enrollment Act, and the portions that Wilson defended the most heatedly appear to have been the weakest parts. Under the law a drafted man might furnish a substitute or pay $300 for total exemption. For all his talk about protecting the workingman, these provisions seemed to favor the financially secure and hurt the poor. Even worse, the system bred bounty jumpers, substitute brokers, and corrupt doctors who would pass mentally and physically unfit men for service. Substitutes frequently accepted payments and bounties, deserted, and then enlisted some place else. Even with a costly array of provost marshals the hope of raising a half million men faded.

Wilson argued chiefly that the price of substitutes would go up to twelve or thirteen hundred dollars each if the three hundred dollar commutation were repealed. Perhaps this was the best explanation that he could offer on this delicate matter. He knew that the bill was imperfect, but he probably felt that he had produced the best piece of legislation that he could under the circumstances. It is possible that he had to settle for the latter figure in his struggles to get a draft bill through Congress. Stanton had opposed the commutation fee, and Wilson was usually ready to accommodate his views. The precedents of old militia practices certainly affected many members in the House and Senate as well as himself. Wilson admitted that insufficient men were raised under the act, and amendments were made the following year which eliminated the three hundred dollar payment. Still, Wilson never became a wholehearted advocate of a total forced draft. When he received reminders of the effective conscription in the Confederacy, he replied that in the process they had destroyed everything but a bare subsistence. "They have no commerce, no mechanic arts, no agriculture, nothing but a bankrupt treasury, a ruined people, and an absolute military despotism."[58] He did not wish to follow that example.

For all its faults, the Enrollment Act broke new ground, served as a precedent in establishing the power of the national government, and illustrated mistakes to avoid in the future. It was a basic change in the life of the nation. The drafts of 1863-1864 brought 170,000 men into the army, and stimulated volunteering. The national force had increased from a total strength of 556,000 officers and men at the end of 1862 to about 918,000 men a year later. Not all of this increase can be attributed to the draft. Part of the increase came from re-enlistments which resulted from an improved morale aided by improved arms, equipment, commissary, and medical care. Much of the credit for improved conditions belongs to men like the industrious Montgomery Meigs, the Quartermaster General. But credit also belonged to Henry Wilson for the thankless task of steering massive amounts of legislation for the care and equipping of the army. From this legislation evolved a modern military system to take the place of antiquated ways and total confusion.

Meanwhile, the administration gave up the idea of a national army raised by Congress alone, and used the draft as a threat to governors to renew their efforts to enlist troops. On October 17, 1863 Lincoln issued another call to Governors for 300,000 men, and the War Department assigned quotas by states. If a state failed to raise its quota by January 1, 1864, it was stated that a draft would be ordered. It seemed as though states rights and the national government had fought to a stand-off, but it was an illusion. The trend to a strong government in Washington had started.

Henry Wilson, always a respecter of states rights, had no interest in promoting a philosophy of centralization with his draft bill. He had become its exponent simply because the desperate manpower situation called for greater control and strength at the head of the government to raise more men for the army. Before the end of the war, Abraham Lincoln had determined that the nation, not the states, was supreme, and Henry Wilson had helped him accomplish the feat in one major area, but it was an area that he would have preferred to avoid.

Wilson, and other Radical Republicans, continued to work closely with the workingmen who, despite their grievances against the draft, did not rush into the Democratic party. By 1865 the labor movement would join with middle class reformers to make a united front. In the next few years, especially in the Grant administration, Republicans, and Wilson in particular, eagerly sought and often gained labor's support. Radicals, in their pursuit of equality for all by using the government for the common good made a strong appeal that minimized much of the draft trouble.[59]

Except for the draft and the use of Negro soldiers, most military legislation concerned non-political subjects, so Wilson did not face a public battle every time he introduced a bill. But, in many ways, the task that confronted him throughout the war was even more demanding. It required an enormous amount of hard work and a capacity for sheer drudgery to prepare and shepherd through the Senate the large number of bills to expand and modernize the Union army. The struggles were often more subtle and complex because they dealt with professionals, professional soldiers, professional bureaucrats, and professional politicians, all capable infighters with special axes to grind; and accomplishments counted more than headlines. There were human differences, too, that had to be overcome for the sake of progress, and in the Senate this called for a man who had the respect of his colleagues. Every Senator is a prima donna, and during the Civil War, as in every other period of American history, their personal characteristics had to be considered. Some had sense, some did not, some were co-operative, others were not, some worked, others were lazy. The art of moving legislation off dead center in a time of emergency in a Congress that was far from unified in the objectives of the war required an understanding of men and the assumption of responsibility for measures sponsored.

As in most politicians' lives, Wilson received credit, as well as blame, for many things that he did not do. Easily overlooked is the mass of work that Wilson, and others, have done in the day to day life of the Senate. This work required the sure hand of a legislative technician, but lacking drama it is generally ignored by the public. Wilson's energy, toughness, and long legislative experience, which started at the State House in Boston, paid off for the people in his years as Chairman of Military Affairs.

NOTES

[1] *Cong. Globe,* 36 Cong., 1 Sess., p. 2794.

[2] Frederic L. Huidekoper, *The Military Unpreparedness of the United States* (New York: The Macmillan Co., 1915), pp. 94, 99, 101; See A. Howard Meneely, *The War Department, 1861* (New York: Columbia University Press, 1928).

[3] Russell F. Weigley, *Quartermaster General of the Union Army* (New York: Columbia University Press, 1959), p. 204.

[4] *Cong. Globe,* 37 Cong., 1 Sess., p. 82.

[5] *Ibid.,* 38 Cong., 1 Sess., p. 1571.

[6] Wilson, E. R. Hoar, Dwight Foster to John A. Andrew, May 2, 1861, John Andrew MSS, MHS.

[7] E. R. Hoar to John Andrew, May 7, 1861, John Andrew MSS, MHS.

[8] Wilson to John Andrew, May 8, 1861, John A. Andrew MSS, MHS: *NYDT,* May 27, 1861.

[9] Wilson to John Andrew, June 25, 27, 1861, John Andrew MSS, MHS; *Cong. Globe,* 37 Cong., 1 Sess., pp. 78-80.

[10] *Cong. Globe,* 37 Cong., 1 Sess., p. 43.

[11] Huidekoper, *Military Unpreparedness,* pp. 94-101; *Cong. Globe,* 37 Cong., 1 Sess., pp. 84, 110, 162, 163, 182, 219, 310.

[12] Edwin C. Bennett, *Musket and Sword—The Army of the Potomac* (Boston: Coburn Publishing Co., 1900), p. 16.

[13] Elihu Washburne to Wilson, Sept. 7, 1874, Wilson MSS, LC.

[14] *Cong. Globe,* 38 Cong., 1 Sess., p. 183.

[15] A. G. B. Jr. to John A. Andrew, Aug. 17, 1861, John Andrew MSS, MHS.

[16] *Cong. Globe,* 38 Cong., 1 Sess., p. 183; *Boston Journal,* Aug. 23, 1861; *NYDT,* Aug. 29, Sept. 1, 2, 1861.

[17] *NYDT,* Sept. 10, 1861.

[18] See John L. Parker and Robert G. Carter, *Henry Wilson's Regiment, History of the Twenty-Second Massachusetts Infantry—The Second Company Sharpshooters and the Third Light Battery in the War of the Rebellion* (Boston: The Regimental Association, 1887).

[19] Letters received by the War Department, 1861, 1862, National Archives.

[20] Letter from Benjamin F. Larned, Paymaster General to Wilson, Dec. 5, 1861. *War of the Rebellion,* Series III, I.

[21] *Cong. Globe,* 37 Cong., 2 Sess., p. 68.

[22] *Ibid.,* p. 125; Samuel H. Kamm, *The Civil War Career of Thomas A. Scott* (Philadelphia: University of Pennsylvania, 1940), p. 54.

[23] Wilson to John Andrew, Dec. 15, 1861, John Andrew MSS, MHS.

[24] Edward Everett, *Diary,* Oct. 30, 1861, MHS.

[25] *Ibid.,* Oct. 31, 1861.

[26] Louis A. Sigaud, "Mrs. Greenhow and the Rebel Spy Ring," *Maryland Historical Society Magazine,* XLI, No. 3, Sept. 1946; Margaret Leech, *Reveille in Washington—1860-1865* (New York: Harper & Bros., 1941), pp. 22, 95, 137, 138; Ishbel Ross, *Rebel Rose* (New York: Harper & Bros., 1954), pp. 77-81, 105, 113, 118, 128, 147, 207, 208, 225, 227, 255, 256.

[27] Allan Nevins, *Hamilton Fish—The Inner History of the Grant Administration* (New York: Dodd, Mead & Co., 1936), p. 609.

[28] Letters attributed to Henry Wilson and allegedly written to Rose Greenhow, National Archives.

[29] See Rose Greenhow, *My Imprisonment* (London: Richard Bentley, 1863).

[30] Military Affairs Committee Record Book, 1861, National Archives; *Dic-*

tionary of American Biography, 104, 105. In 1861 the *Chicago Tribune* made White its Washington correspondent and also permitted him to serve as clerk of the Senate Military Affairs Committee. In 1864, with Henry Villard and Adams Sherman Hill, he founded the first news agency to compete with the Associated Press. Later he worked for *The Nation* which Villard purchased, and in 1899 became editor-in-chief of the *Evening Post.* A Greek Scholar, he published *The Roman History of Appian of Alexandria,* translated from the Greek, and in his retirement wrote, *The Life of Lyman Trumbull.*

[31] Kenneth P. Williams, *Lincoln Finds a General* (2 vols., New York: The Macmillan Co., 1949), I, 85, 86.

[32] Simon Cameron to Wilson, Jan. 27, 1862, Huntington Library.

[33] *NYDT,* January 23, 1862.

[34] *Cong. Globe,* 37 Cong., 2 Sess., pp. 696, 697, 2656, 2722.

[35] *Ibid.,* pp. 272, 289, 377.

[36] *Ibid.,* p. 182.

[37] *Ibid.,* pp. 843-848, 877, 1164.

[38] *Ibid.,* pp. 505, 1189, 3202.

[39] Wilson to John Andrew, April 12, 1862, John Andrew MSS, MHS.

[40] *Cong. Globe,* 37 Cong., 2 Sess., p. 3226.

[41] Fred A. Shannon, *Organization and Administration of the Union Army* (2 vols., Cleveland: Arthur Clark Co., 1928), I, 275. Cites U.S. Statutes at Large, vol. 12, 597.

[42] Huidekoper, *Military Unpreparedness,* p. 105.

[43] Parker and Carter, *Henry Wilson's Regiment,* pp. 162, 63; *NYDT,* Nov. 19, 1862.

[44] Henry Villard, *Memoirs of Henry Villard—Journalist and Financier* (2 vols., Boston: Houghton, Mifflin & Co., 1904), I, 388-390.

[45] Bennett, *Musket and Sword,* p. 120.

[46] *Natick Bulletin,* Dec. 10, 1875.

[47] *Cong. Globe,* 37 Cong., 3 Sess., pp. 5, 16, 185, 357, 358.

[48] *Ibid.,* p. 328.

[49] *NYT,* Oct. 18, 1863.

[50] *Ibid.,* Jan. 17, 1863.

[51] *Cong. Globe,* 37 Cong., 3 Sess., pp. 5, 16, 185, 357, 358.

[52] *Ibid.,* pp. 185, 197, 200, 468, 476.

[53] *Ibid.,* p. 1276.

[54] *Ibid.,* p. 976.

[55] *Ibid.,* pp. 976-979, 982, 988, 994-996, 1001, 1002, 1363-1370, 1382-1390.

[56] *NYT,* April 2, 1863.

[57] *NYT,* Aug. 9, 1863; *War of the Rebellion,* Series III, v. 3, 570; Henry Wilson, "The Draft," speech delivered at Goshen, New York, Aug. 22, 1863.

[58] *Cong. Globe,* 38 Cong., 1 Sess., pp. 2804-2806, 3197.

[59] David Montgomery, *Beyond Equality—Labor and the Radical Republicans —1862-1872* (New York: Alfred A. Knopf, 1967), pp. 46, 102, 109, 125, 134.

8

Antislavery

Henry Wilson was always able to make nice distinctions. He could damn Democrats and join them in coalitions, condemn abolitionists and praise their character, criticize nativists and become a member of their party. He could applaud and abhor the same subject at the same time with an adeptness that brought envy to the eyes of his fellow politicians. But he made no nice distinctions about the cause of the war. There was only one evil cause and that was slavery.

For all his military concerns, Wilson did not forget the Negro. He wanted them to gain their freedom quickly. The question was how could it be accomplished. The power of slavery lingered as the nation broke in two. Certainly no general emancipation was possible in the early days of the war. Lincoln had to keep the border states in the Union by every means at his command, and in his inaugural address he had made it clear that he did not intend to interfere with slavery in the states where it existed. His annulment of Fremont's proclamation of emancipation in Missouri also demonstrated his deep concern for preserving the Union despite slavery. Antagonizing reluctant loyalists made no sense. Wilson fretted about Lincoln's ability to move faster, but their position was much the same. Both had subscribed to the Republican platform of 1860, which declared that the states should control their own domestic institutions. Both realized the difference between the practical and impractical.

As he had always done, Wilson looked for a first step that might reasonably meet with success. It seemed so senseless that the government would take rebel lives, and rebel property, and yet refrain from touching slavery. Radicals demanded immediate abolition, but he knew that the adoption of a sweeping change was a drastic and problematical act. Achievement, he found, usually came after an inch by inch struggle. Henry Ward Beecher might preach Sunday sermons, Wendell Phillips might lecture at the Smithsonian, and the YMCA might schedule an antislavery program, but the slave would have to find his freedom in the labyrinth of Congress where he had strong enemies. Antislavery proposals horrified many Senators, particularly those from Kentucky, Maryland, and Delaware. They considered an attack upon the institution of slavery as unconstitutional, revolutionary, and a criminal violation of faith.

Despite their reaction, public opinion increasingly favored antislavery. Republicans and Northern Senators started to move the first of a long series of legislative acts that would bring freedom to the slave. In July 1861 Senator Lyman Trumbull of Illinois, Chairman of the Judiciary Committee, reported a bill to confiscate property used for insurrectionary purposes. Wilson supported the measure which became known as the First Confiscation Act. It provided that owners' rights to slaves engaged in hostile military service would be forfeited. The law, as cautiously interpreted by Attorney General Edward Bates, did not cancel the fugitive slave law, but it was a beginning.

Late in 1861, a commotion over the frightening condition of the Washington jail, the "Blue Jug," which Wilson had previously railed against, stirred a number of notables in town. Designed to hold no more than a hundred prisoners, it now contained more than two hundred assorted criminals and fugitive slaves. One man was a free Negro who had been in confinement for more than six months for no good reason, and others had been sent there by disloyal masters for safekeeping until the war was over. One piece of property, an old woman, belonged to a former Senator from Florida. Incensed by these conditions, Wilson introduced a resolution that all laws relating to the arrest of fugitives from services, and all other laws relating to the colored people in the District be referred to the Committee on the District of Columbia and that they be instructed to consider the expediency of abolishing slavery in the District with compensation to loyal owners of slaves. It did not pass, but the shocking publicity enabled Secretary of State Seward to issue an order to the marshal which forbade holding persons not charged with any crime or misdemeanor.[1]

The furor over "the Washington slave pen" also set the stage for Wilson to introduce a bill to abolish slavery in the District, and he did not lose any time in making the move. In a different time and setting, Abraham Lincoln had tried to gain gradual abolition in Washington and failed. Now, twelve years later, December, 1861, Wilson also tried. The introduction of the bill excited intense reactions from some of the best people, men who believed that it would make the town a "hell on earth for the white man." The Board of Aldermen passed a resolution which urged Congress "to provide safeguards against converting this city—into an asylum for free negroes, a population undesirable in every American community."[2] Other Washingtonians protected their human property by shipping them into Maryland.

Similar objections were raised in Congress. Senator Anthony Kennedy of Maryland wondered what earthly good could come from a bill that would bring so much corresponding evil. Senator Willard Saulsbury of Delaware moved an amendment that he thought would answer the problems that would arise from freeing the Negro. Within thirty days of passage of the bill, he suggested, all liberated people be transported to New England, New York, Pennsylvania, and the West. It was not accepted, but there was much bitter and loose talk about mixed marriages, and miscegenation. Garrett Davis asked, "Why do you not go out into this city and hunt up the blackest, greasiest, fattest old negro wench you can find and lead her to the altar of Hymen?" In the course of the debate the Kentucky Senator, ever an anathema to Wilson, noticed some Negroes in the gallery and was sure that soon they would be crowding out white ladies. He was equally certain that freedom for Negroes meant freedom to become worthless beggars. It was an old and preposterous argument.[3]

Senator James Harlan of Iowa, infuriated by the hypocrisy, reminded his Southern colleagues of some of their own transgressions. He referred to a former Vice President, clearly Richard Johnson, who lived with a Negro woman and raised a family by her without a whisper from any member of the Senate, and a recent Senator from a slave state who currently had mulato children attending school in Ohio.[4]

Slavery in the District of Columbia, as in all the South, had a cruel past. There were many brutal laws for punishment of the slave which did not fit the crime. A slave's ear could be cropped for striking a white man, and breaking street lamps or setting off fire crackers near a house called for whipping on the bare back. Wilson cited these travesties of justice as he defended his bill which would eliminate these unfair laws.[5] Sumner eloquently supported his colleague, too, but his remarks only prompted Garrett Davis to say that he did not know of any political, religious, or social mischievousness and noxious "ism" that did not have its origin in Massachusetts.

The management of this bill through the Senate demonstrated the difference between Wilson and Sumner. Wilson was hardworking, genial, and conciliatory. Sumner was aloof, unbending, and certain that any opposing party was guilty of moral delinquency. In the give and take of the Chamber, Wilson could do battle, sometimes furiously, and still retain a sense of fellowship. Sumner simply became irritated, and did badly in debate. Wilson had the respect of the Senate. Sumner had a favorable public image in Massachusetts, at least, and little, if any, respect among the working members of the Senate. Wilson was a lawmaker. Sumner was an orator. Senator James Grimes of Iowa said that Sumner originated no measures, but simply made sophomoric set speeches. Rigid and doctrinaire, vain and egotistical, he lacked insight concerning his associates and their politics. In contrast, Wilson seemed to be completely lacking in vanity and his ego was subordinated to the issues for which he fought to an extent that he seemed to get outside himself. Yet, Sumner, blind to his own shortcomings, was sensitive and jealous. When a news item appeared praising Wilson as the most efficient practical leader of thought and action in the Senate, Sumner was quick to consider such remarks disparaging to himself.

Personalities aside, moderate thinkers were of the opinion that a system of gradual emancipation similar to Lincoln's proposal in 1849 would have been more acceptable than Wilson's measure, and many Democrats declared that abolition had nothing to do with the preservation of the Union. But the bill had strong support. Fessenden, Wilmot, Doolittle, Hale, among many others, gave their backing, and on April 3, 1862 it passed with twenty-nine yeas and fourteen nays. President Lincoln signed the bill on April 16. Three thousand humans were immediately freed by a law sponsored by Henry Wilson, the man who had been called a political harlot.

Eventually about a thousand owners made claims for 3,128 slaves at three hundred dollars a head. On the rare occasions that history has taken notice of Wilson he has been classified as a Radical, but in his plan to free slaves he had taken a moderate approach which Lincoln fully appreciated. Extremists had objected to paying for a human being's freedom, but Wilson saw no objection to buying off slave owners. He even favored taxing the people of his state if it would accomplish the job of emancipation quickly. He also voted for a joint resolution which stated that the United States government should cooperate with any state which might adopt the gradual abolition of slavery. Pecuniary aid was to be given to such a state to use at its discretion to compensate for the inconvenience, public or private, produced by the change in system. Lincoln had a particular interest in this method and had originally proposed the idea in a special message to Congress in March.

As the year progressed Wilson also utilized his position as Chairman of the Military Affairs Committee to further the cause of the Negro. He realized that military measures frequently presented an opportunity to incorporate clauses for freedom and greater rights to the enslaved or recently unchained. He was not the only practitioner of such tactics, but it was a legislative technique that appealed to him. A bill introduced by him the previous December, which called for the dismissal of Army officers who surrendered fugitive slaves to their owners, became law in March 1862. It was passed to protect slaves in rebel states who gaves themselves up to the Union Army. Wilson said that while it was death for a Union soldier to steal a "secession chicken," a Massachusetts colonel had returned a fugitive slave to his owners without condemnation.[6]

Although not a military measure, Wilson offered an amendment in May to Senator Grimes' bill providing for the education of colored children in Washington which made Negroes subject to the same laws and ordinances as white people. They were to be tried in the same manner, and subject to the same punishment. With this amendment black codes were abolished in the Nation's capital.[7] Wilson could have received all the accolades that he required from the antislavery people for some time to come with his bill freeing slaves in the District, but he was not satisfied. He believed in equal rights for all, and he did not intend to stop before the job was finished.

In June Wilson voted for a long time dream, the prohibition of slavery in the territories, in the form of a bill introduced by Isaac Arnold of Illinois, a good friend of Lincoln's. Wilson also used the Navy, as well as the Army, by adding an amendment to the Naval Appropriations Bill which prevented the employment of slaves in any capacity in any naval installation.[8] Lincoln tread lightly on the status of the Negro because of its political sensitivity. In the early days of the war Negroes were used as laborers in the army, but were refused enlistment. Secretary of War Cameron had talked about enlisting Negroes, but it only served to annoy Lincoln. With the accession of Stanton as head of the War Department there was a slowdown in the idea of using Negro soldiers because the new Secretary was anxious to reflect the President's views. General McClellan also offered similar conservative advice. A declaration of radical views, especially upon slavery, the general told Lincoln, "will rapidly disintegrate our present armies."[9] But time favored extending a helping hand to the slave. Wherever the Union army moved into slaveholding states, loyal or disloyal, they disturbed established patterns. Northern soldiers were prone to look upon slaveholding and loyalty as one and the same thing. As relations between Stanton and McClellan deteriorated, the Secretary supported the Negro more strongly and in a short time was in advance of Lincoln in his thinking on the subject.

In the Militia Act of July 17, 1862, which Wilson introduced, Negroes could be drafted into the service for the first time, and slave soldiers of enemy ownership, together with their families, were freed. Peace Democrats had opposed the enlistment of Negroes with great zeal. They looked upon such an act as an attempt to excite a servile war. On the same day, July 17, the Second Confiscation Act became law and provided that if anyone committed treason his slaves were free, and that the slaves of all persons supporting the rebellion should be forever free of their servitude. Now the President could employ Negroes for the suppression of the war in the numbers and manner that he considered necessary. Wilson did not expect the North to acquire any large amount of property by confiscation, he simply wanted to emancipate slaves. Slavery to him was the great rebel, the giant criminal, and he wanted to free the bondsmen of every rebel in the country.[10]

Wilson had shown that he could gladly support moderate measures, such as gradual or compensated emancipation, but he grew impatient when they did not produce results. He had wanted to cooperate with the President, but as time passed he believed that there should be a general emancipation proclamation. Lincoln's cautious attitude until mid-1862 did not please Wilson and he commenced to press him for greater action. The President complained to Senator John B. Henderson of Missouri that, "Stevens, Sumner, and Wilson haunt me with their importunities for a Proclamation of Emancipation. Where I go and whatever way I turn, they are on my trail, and still in my heart, I have a deep conviction the hour has not yet come."[11]

Lincoln told another visitor much the same thing about Sumner, Stevens, and Wilson, and as he looked out the window he saw the three approaching the White House. He said he was reminded of the boy in Sunday School who, chosen to read the story of the three Hebrew children in the fiery furnace, stumbled miserably over the names of Shadrack, Meshack, and Abednego. Pained and embarrassed, the boy read on, when his eye, looking down the page, noticed the three names again, he cried out in anguish: "Look! Look there! Here comes the same three damn fellers again.[12]

Impetuous by nature, Wilson fumed over Lincoln's patience, and since he always wore his heart on his sleeve, he made many rash statements around town. It seemed to him that he was always pressing the President on military, antislavery, and party matters that he believed required immediate attention, and when the action was not forthcoming he would fret over the lackadaisical ways of the administration. Many of his complaints were genuinely felt, but they were of short duration.

When Congress gathered in December 1862, Lincoln proposed a system of gradual, compensated abolition once again. In his annual message he recommended a constitutional amendment that would provide compensation in federal bonds for every state which would eliminate slavery before 1900, and guarantee freedom to slaves who had gained it by the events of the war, with compensation to loyal owners. It also authorized the colonization of freedom overseas. It was a reasonable plan to produce harmony in the country, but neither the North nor the South seemed interested in reason. White workers feared the loss of their jobs to competing Negroes; white homeowners feared the destruction of their neighborhoods by Negro homeowners. The proposal should have been preferable to continued bloodshed, but both sections were at a point of no return, and both conservatives and radicals found objections. Orville Browning of Illinois regarded the whole idea a dream; Charles Sumner thought it was something to ignore, and radical Ben Wade and conservative Horatio Seymour, for totally different reasons, opposed Lincoln. Henry Wilson had already demonstrated that compensation emancipation was acceptable to him, and would have found some areas for agreement if there had been any hope for the plan to pass Congress and gain public support. He had always adopted an attitude of forgiving and forgetting the sins of the South, but at the moment there was no way to get a toehold on reconciliation.

Lincoln finally announced the Emancipation Proclamation and there was no one more jubilant than Wilson. Upon hearing the news, he told one of the White House secretaries, "he has struck another great blow. Tell him for me, God bless him."[13] Sumner and Andrew, among others, picked at the Proclamation and thought that the language was insufficiently elegant. But with Wilson there were no misgivings, no minimizing, no fault-finding of the President's act, and he considered it, then and later, the great historic event of the war.

Wilson proved to be a good friend of Lincoln's and a strong supporter of his administration when the chips were down and events called for considered judgment. In 1863 Senator Powell of Kentucky read a statement in the Senate condemning the President. He referred to "repeated injuries and usurpations tending directly to the overthrow of State authority and State institutions and a consolidation in the Federal Government of all political power and the erection upon their ruins of a great military despotism as tyrannical and despotic as the worst Governments of Europe." To prove his case he listed the President's suspension of the writ of habeas corpus, the arrest of citizens without charge, denial of trial by jury, and attempts to destroy the freedom of the press, speech, and right to petition. He considered the Emancipation Proclamation completely unwarranted, and on behalf of his fellow Kentuckians he wanted a speedy end to the war.

This was too much for Wilson. He replied that "never in the history of mankind has it happened that any government has been so charitable, so forgiving to traitors in arms, or to men in sympathy with traitors in arms." He portrayed Lincoln as a man with a heart as soft and tender as that of a mother sitting beside the cradle of her sick baby. "Throughout this fraticidal war, the President oppressed by day and night with anxieties and labors enough to break down any man in America, has ever been charitable, kind, forgiving to men who are striving to destroy this splendid fabric of free government." As he continued his defense of Lincoln he humanly aired his own sentiments and frustrations when he said, "As I have witnessed his tender mercy, his charity, his considerable kindness towards these men whose hands are dripping with blood of our loyal countrymen, I have prayed for one hour of Andrew Jackson." Nevertheless, he strongly defended Lincoln's suspension of the writ of habeas corpus. "The Executive should be clothed with that power; and I am among those who believe our fathers made a Constitution and endowed it with power enough to carry the country through sunshine or storm, victory or defeat, peace or war."[14]

Political differences had never been a legitimate excuse for Wilson to upset personal relationships. While he followed his own course in Congress and may have held some reservations about Lincoln's ways, he never held any personal animosity towards him. At least once he cautioned Lincoln to take care of himself and remonstrated with him about the pressures of office. Lincoln knew, too, that Wilson worked long hours, particularly in reorganizing and modernizing the new army, and as the war progressed he gained confidence in Wilson's handling of legislation.

The President must have also appreciated Wilson's support when southern military victories only made the mood of Congress more irascible. Democrats and border Republicans wanted only the restoration of the Union and a strict interpretation of the Constitution. But more extreme Republicans wanted stepped up military activity, increased confiscation of Confederate property, more slaves freed, and greater use of Negro soldiers. No one was more adamant about the use of Negro soldiers than Thaddeus Stevens. He wanted Negroes armed, particularly the slaves of rebels, so that their owners could be obliterated. There was only one way to treat disloyal states, and that was as conquered provinces. Wilson did not share Thaddeus Stevens' extreme views about conquering the South, but he approved the use of Negro soldiers and wanted to improve their lot when they enlisted. His friend, Stanton, now wished to accelerate Negro enlistments and urged Congress to remove wage and bounty discriminations.[15] Ben Butler also called upon Congress to place Negroes upon an equal basis with other troops.[16] Wilson shared their views and did all that he could to equalize the status of the Negro soldier.

Not every Northerner had altruistic motives about the use of Negroes in the army. Many felt that it was a good way to fill difficult quotas for manpower, and the Negro substitute could do the dirty work of the war. Stumping in New York in the Fall of 1863, Wilson reported to Lincoln that the President's call for more men would give Horatio Seymour several thousand more votes in the Governorship race. "Everybody wants to know why we do not raise more black soldiers." But the responsibilities of soldiering also created opportunities for the Negro, whatever the hardships or hazards. Through military service the Negro found emancipation and increased rights.

In February 1864 Wilson reported a Joint Resolution to pay soldiers the same amount regardless of race. It directed that all persons of color who had been or would be mustered into military service would receive the same clothing, arms, equipment, rations, and medical attention. In the future Negroes were also to receive the same bounty.[17] Up to then white soldiers received thirteen dollars a month and an allowance of three and a half dollars for clothing. Black soldiers received ten dollars a month and had three dollars deducted from their pay for clothing. In addition, families of white soldiers received allowances and Negroes received none. Senator James Lane of Kansas said that the first colored regiment of Kansas, which he claimed was the first colored regiment in the United States, was not paid for the first six months of their service because the government did not think that they had any authority to pay them.[18]

This simple act of justice, which Wilson presented on the basis of promoting enlistments, was not a simple matter to pass through Congress. Discussion centered on when the equal pay would become effective, and even a respected Northerner like Fessenden of Maine disagreed with Wilson who wanted retroactive payments. Thinking of the drain on the Treasury, Fessenden favored equal payments to commence with the passage of the Act. Wilson also wanted to free the wife and children of a Negro mustered into service and at this late date would have agreed to pay masters a proper value for their property. But such ideas worried the financially conservative. Rather than cause delay, Wilson offered an amendment to start payment March 1, 1864, but another Northerner, Grimes of Iowa, countered by moving to recommit the measure because he wanted the effective date of January 1, 1864. Anxious for action, Wilson introduced a new bill in March as a substitute for the Joint Resolution and he pressed the proposal at every opportunity. It included a provision to free wives and children of Negro soldiers, but this added to the delicacy of the situation. The recognition of a wife of a slave was a ticklish one since the slave states had not recognized marriage among Negroes. Wilson defined a wife for this purpose on a common law basis as a woman regarded and treated as such. Still another Northerner, James Doolittle of Wisconsin, slowed progress by declaring that he preferred to wait for a constitutional amendment. Wilson answered that he wanted to strike now, not wait for the future. "I say it is sound policy to strike this system of slavery whenever and wherever you can get a blow at it."[19] Trying to furnish a practical basis for passage, he argued that the bill would fill up the armies. The enlistment of Negroes had caused much suffering because the wives and children left behind could be sold or abused. "How can you go to a man and ask him to enlist to fight the battles of his country when he knows that the moment his back is turned his wife and children will be sold to strangers?"[20] The spending of a few million dollars to hurry the end of slavery that caused and continued the war would be, in his eyes, true economy. But the measure did not pass then. After many conferences and amendments the bill was transformed into a piece of legislation for general increases of pay in the army. In June colored troops received the same pay as white men.[21]

Ironically, for a politician who made it a practice not to make personal enemies over political differences, Wilson found himself leading a movement against Garrett Davis early in 1864. The Kentuckian had offered a series of resolutions which declared that the people of the North ought to revolt against their war leaders. Wilson considered this treason and on his own responsibility submitted a resolution moving the expulsion of Davis. This led to a number of bitter personal exchanges between the two Senators. Davis, taking off his neckerchief and unbuttoning his waistcoat, waded into Wilson. He considered the "jaundiced, narrow mind of the Senator from Massachusetts" incompetent to make such an attack, and claimed that Wilson tried to make himself the overseer of the Senate. "I have been amused," he said, "at the important, authoritative, and dictatorial manner with which he bustles about the Senate, and administers his lectures and rebukes to everybody, to use a fashionable term, whether they are on his side or the other side of the Chamber. He is very frequent in, and exceedingly pleased with, his use of the term 'Government.' He has persuaded himself that the President, the Secretary of War, and the Chairman of the Committee on Military Affairs of the Senate constitute the *Government*." Davis wanted to stop the war and he looked upon Wilson as a bloody minded Senator prolonging the war to destroy slavery, more concerned with abolition than the Constitution and the laws of the United States. Davis also made a number of charges about Wilson running from the scene of battle at Bull Run, about his activities raising a regiment, and charged that he had sought graft. He repeated a story that he had heard that Wilson would appoint a sutler for his regiment if he could share in half the profits.

Wilson did not think that Davis' exhibition in the Senate would do credit to a Kentucky barbecue, but he took pains to retrace his steps at Bull Run, with the Twenty-Second Regiment, and with sutlers. He denied each and every charge. In the fray, Wilson spoke up strongly for the administration, but he received no help from his fellow Senators in his efforts to oust Davis. After about two weeks, Davis retracted and modified some of his language and disclaimed the idea of "revolt" and Wilson withdrew his resolution. He summed up the hectic affair by saying that Davis had launched some vulgar flings at him, "but I feel very much as did the man who said when his fractious wife was berating him, that he did not care much about it, for it did not hurt him, and seemed to do the little thing a great deal of good." The truce between the two men did not last long. Not too many days passed before Davis declared that Wilson was a sort of whip, not only of the Black Republicans, but of the whole Senate, and that he should have inscribed on his chest, "The self constituted gagger of the Senate."[22]

There were other issues of varying degrees of importance to the Negro that the Senators debated. Sumner was as exercised about the exclusion of Negroes from railroad cars in the District of Columbia as any rights measure and offered an amendment to prevent this type of discrimination. In the same month, June 1864, the fugitive slave law met its death, and in July a civil appropriations bill stated that no witness should be excluded from the courts of the United States on account of color. Wilson had been in favor of this for a long time. The same bill also prohibited the coastal slave trade forever.[23] Wilson and other fighters against slavery in Congress made real progress. They accomplished much during the war years, but it was done step by step. Slavery did not collapse quickly, and increased rights for the Negro did not arrive with any single sweeping gesture. While hostilities raged, and men of the North and South gave their lives, old institutions remained, and each move forward had to be pried out of the Congress in ways that were most readily available to the anti-slavery legislators. It was not an easy or simple struggle, and they were never completely sure of public support in the North where there were many degrees of enthusiasm and animosity to their cause.

*   *   *   *   *

Life consists of many strands, and Wilson could never enjoy the simple luxury of concentrating on a single task at one time. The fight against slavery was a major objective in his life, but it competed for attention throughout the war not only with the problems of military affairs, but also with party politics. The days never seemed long enough to give sufficient priority to each subject, but somehow he juggled each phase of his public life with great dexterity. Concurrently he contended with the broad questions of national survival with the narrow difficulties of a parochial politician.

As the national conventions approached, there was much dissatisfaction with Lincoln and much plotting to remove him from the Republican ticket. The fears, tensions, and opposition stirring within the party were frequently more troublesome to the administration than the obstacles created by the Democratic Party. Francis Bird seemed anxious to start a movement to convince Lincoln that he should withdraw, and he conferred with sympathetic, although hesitating, Charles Sumner and John Andrew. Bird's attitude was defeatist since he aimed to preserve a compact opposition party for the future. But he thought it best not to tell Wilson of his plans just yet because he did not trust him and suspected that he would let the cat out of the bag.[24] Many other party leaders regarded Lincoln's candidacy as a lost cause and the opposition was especially strong in New York and Massachusetts. Thurlow Weed looked upon Lincoln's re-election as an impossibility, and Horace Greeley thought that they must have another ticket to save the country from utter revolution.[25]

Most Radical Republicans preferred a new candidate for President. By 1864 their relations with Lincoln had been severely tried, at least, so they thought. The ever ambitious Chase was always a contender for the White House, and a friend of most Radicals. Other Presidential hopefuls were Ben Butler and John Fremont, and some politicians were attracted to Grant. But Wilson did not give up so easily and for all of his private criticism of the President he remained loyal to him. He knew that Lincoln was popular with the men of the army as well as the general public, and he had no desire to shift to another candidate despite his reservations. Vice President Hannibal Hamlin believed that Wilson was among the few leading Radicals who had pursued an independent course in Congress, and yet had used his influence for Lincoln's renomination when he needed it most.[26]

Hamlin also related later that Wilson called at the White House just before the convention to obtain the Presidential authority to support the renomination of the Vice President. A. J. Waterman, a delegate, and later Attorney General of Massachusetts, recalled that on the night before the convention met, Henry Wilson showed up at the headquarters of the Massachusetts delegation and convinced him to support Hamlin. "He explained the necessity of President Lincoln's abstaining from any public declaration of his preference for the second office, but assured me that he had full authority to represent the views of President Lincoln privately, and that it was the earnest desire of Mr. Lincoln that Hamlin should be renominated."[27]

Once the ticket of Lincoln and Johnson was settled, Wilson went to work like an old warhorse. But he was quite blunt in his remarks to Lincoln. Ever the optimist, he thought that the Chicago convention roused the people, and he hoped that in a few weeks their friends would start hard campaigning. But, he told Lincoln:

> They have been very much cast down, and I must say to you they have been finding great fault with their candidate. One scolds about the Cabinet, another finds fault with something else. Our merchants are down on Welles. Stanton is not loved, not I am sure at all appreciated. Blair everyone hates,—tens of thousands of men will be lost to you or will give a reluctant vote on account of the Blairs. There is in circulation a story on the authority of a Major General that we came very near being defeated near Atlanta by the drunkenness and incapacity of Frank Blair. This hurts us among our most intelligent men. They say you gave him a position in violation of law, under the influence of the Blairs at Washington, and that McPherson lost his life on account of his blundering. Major Generals are given as authority. A friend of mine and yours told me Saturday that one of General Grant's staff states to a friend of your, Mr. Bates of Chicago, that you was [sic.] every day losing in the Army of the Potomac because you tried to hold Grant back from promoting young officers. He said that the opinion in the Army was that you did not want to make promotions in place of some incompetent officers on account of the election. I hope you will look to this. If the Army of the Potomac goes against you we are defeated. We ought to carry all the States but New Jersey and Kentucky, and I hope we shall fight for all but those states and leave our friends in those states to do their best alone. Missouri ought to be seen to at once. Wade ought to be in the field to brake the force as far as he can of his manifesto. Chase should speak to the country for you. Winter Davis, Kennedy, and Johnson of Maryland should be brought in if possible. Dix, Rosecrans, Grant, Logan, and all the generals should be induced to come out for you. No man should be passed over nor neglected. We are to have a terrible contest. Let us not throw away any help. If we are beaten our friends will cast the blame wholly on you for they believe they can carry the country easy with another candidate. You must lose no time in the work of putting all our friends in the fight. You

will think I have written you a very strange letter. I have written it as a friend of our cause and a friend of your election. Read it and then *destroy it*.[28]

During the campaign Wilson thought that Andrew Johnson would lose more votes than he could gain and so advised Lincoln.[29] But he kept his faith and worked hard for the President, and other Radicals followed his example. After the election, Wilson plainly stated his views to Lincoln about members of the Cabinet. He regarded Stanton, Fessenden, and Seward as able men, and thought the public looked upon them in the same light. There were all kinds of rumors afloat about Stanton, but Wilson hoped that he would finish the war. "He is sometimes hasty and rough, but he is honest, patriotic, and energetic. This country owes him a debt for his labors." He believed that the appointment of Chase as Chief Justice would strengthen the administration and prove that the President was liberal and generous. "With you at the head of the nation and Chase Chief Justice and with Seward, Fessenden, and Stanton and some great lawyer of antislavery sentiments and deep convictions as Attorney General, and Congress true we shall soon have no state out of the Union and no slave in the Union."[30]

In the previous four years much progress had been made against slavery, but Wilson was of the opinion that many citizens were unaware of the advances. To help publicize the actions that had been taken, Wilson compiled, with the aid of Reverend Samuel Hunt, a book entitled *History of Anti-Slavery Measures of the Thirty-Seventh and Thirty-Eighth Congresses*. It is a dull book, but it recites the antislavery legislation passed to that time. Wilson told the historian, Benson Lossing, "I thought our friends did not realize how much had been done, and I wished to encourage them to further efforts, for the final extinction of slavery." He was right. Much had been done. Much still remained to be done.[31]

Wilson had good reason to want to portray the progress that he and other fighters against slavery in Congress had made. Despite concrete accomplishments, Wilson still received sharp criticism. During the summer, Charles Wright, whom Wilson had befriended more than once, planned to write a pamphlet using him as a bad example of a public man. It seemed to be some part of a vague move to depose the Senator at the next election.

Wilson complained to Henry Dawes that, "No man has ever been —and that wholly without cause—so unjust to me as Mr. Wright. You know that I have not repaid his assaults upon me by neglecting to do an act of kindness to one of his sons. Now he is to come out with a pamphlet to strike at me who never wronged him. . . . Well so goes the world."[32]

Despite such an attack from a party politician in his state, Wilson looked forward to his own re-election without any major difficulty, but, unexpectedly, he had a few tense moments before he received confirmation. A more serious undercurrent against him developed by friends of John Andrew and Ben Butler. Popular as Wilson was, Andrew was also popular, and some thought that he would make a better Senator; and the ambitious Butler was always a threat. A delay in the voting occurred in the state Senate and Wilson made no secret of his disappointment in having his return to Washington held up and he was in a quandary as to the source of opposition. "I have no reproaches to utter against any of its members, but they have by their action touched me in a tender point." In recent months he had received all kinds of assurances from all parts of the state, but now there seemed to be doubts. "The unexpected action of the Senate I confess surprises me." Worriedly, he told his friend William Robinson that he would be glad to hear from him.[33] When he heard talk about Cabinet appointments he made it clear that he was a candidate for the United States Senate and wanted no other offices.[34] Henry Dawes reported to his wife that Wilson was in perfect agony, and Mrs. Wilson was crying over the postponement of the election.[35]

Some of Wilson's friends thought that the delay in the Massachusetts Senate was an effort to strengthen Andrew's hand for a Cabinet post, probably the Treasury, which Fessenden was soon to leave. Others blamed a Butler coterie who thought they could gain the Senate seat. Andrew longed to be Senator, but he gave his personal support to Wilson and was certain that he would be re-elected. "At all events," he commented, "I could not be a candidate against General Wilson."[36]

Francis Bird reassured William Claflin that Andrew was not competing against Wilson. "I daresay the three you name are against Wilson, with a few others who can never breathe freely so long as a shoemaker is in the Senate of the United States. . . .

The worst of it is, that a few gentlemen known as friends of the Governor and supposed to represent him are active in opposition and thus it is feared a contingency may arise w'h will place him in a position of antagonism to W. . . . There is not the slightest foundation for the impression or suspicion that the Governor directly or indirectly encourages the opposition."[37] Bird was correct in his appraisal, and in a few days the air cleared and Wilson gained re-election. Massachusetts politics had never been a simple matter, and the complications still abounded. But Wilson was able to surmount these relatively minor obstacles. The veteran politician had survived one more personal skirmish. Now he could see the end of the war from his place in the Senate and take part in the grave problems of reconstruction. Wilson showed that he knew how to balance the serious business of the federal government with the equally serious business of retaining his political base at home.

NOTES

[1] *Cong. Globe,* 37 Cong., 2 Sess., pp. 10, 12; Henry Wilson, *History of Anti-Slavery Measures of the 37th and 38th Congresses* (Boston: Walker, Fuller & Co., 1865), pp. 348, 356.

[2] Leech, *Reveille In Washington,* p. 242.

[3] Wilson, *Anti-Slavery Measures,* pp. 52-55.

[4] *Ibid.,* p. 53.

[5] Henry Wilson, "On Bill to Abolish Slavery in D.C., "March 27, 1862, speech in Senate, New York Public Library; *Cong. Globe,* 37 Cong., 2 Sess., p. 1350.

[6] Wilson, *Anti-Slavery Measures,* p. 30.

[7] *Ibid.,* p. 185.

[8] *Cong. Globe,* 37 Cong., 2 Sess., pp. 1862, 2721.

[9] Benjamin P. Thomas and Harold M. Hyman, *Stanton: The Life and Times of Lincoln's Secretary of War* (New York: Alfred A. Knopf, 1962), p. 210.

[10] *Cong. Globe,* 37 Cong., 2 Sess., p. 1895; Wilson, *Anti-Slavery Measures,* pp. 203, 223.

[11] Ralph Korngold, *Thaddeus Stevens* (New York: Harcourt, Brace and Co., 1955), p. 181.

[12] Benjamin P. Thomas, *Abraham Lincoln* (New York: Alfred A. Knopf, 1954), p. 343.

[13] Wilson to Abraham Lincoln, Sept. 3, 1863, R. T. Lincoln MSS, LC; John G. Nicolay and John Hay, *Abraham Lincoln—A History* (10 vols., New York: The Century Co., 1914), IX, 109; Wilson, *Rise and Fall,* III, 380.

[14] *Cong. Globe,* 37 Cong., 3 Sess., pp. 1161-1164.

[15] Thomas and Hyman, *Stanton,* p. 264.

[16] Wilson to Abraham Lincoln, Oct. 25, 1863, R. T. Lincoln MSS, LC.

[17] *Cong. Globe,* 38 Cong., 1 Sess., p. 466.

[18] *Ibid.,* pp. 482, 483, 562, 565.

[19] *Ibid.,* pp. 770, 873, 896, 991, 1181.

20 *Ibid.*, pp. 1178, 1805; Wilson, *Anti-Slavery Measures*, p. 319.

21 Huidekoper, *Military Unpreparedness*, p. 130.

22 *Cong. Globe*, 38 Cong., 1 Sess., pp. 139, 177, 178, 182, 183, 194.

23 Wilson, *Anti-Slavery Measures*, pp. 292, 361, 365.

24 Francis Bird to John Andrew, Aug. 26, 1864, John Andrew MSS, MHS.

25 Sherwin, *Prophet of Liberty*, pp. 499, 500.

26 Charles E. Hamlin, *The Life and Times of Hannibal Hamlin* (Cambridge: The Riverside Press, 1899), pp. 462-471.

27 *Ibid.*

28 Wilson to Abraham Lincoln, Sept. 5, 1864, R. T. Lincoln MSS, LC.

29 Wilson to Abraham Lincoln, Oct. 13, 1864, R. T. Lincoln MSS, LC.

30 Wilson to Abraham Lincoln, Nov. 12, 1864, R. T. Lincoln MSS, LC.

31 Wilson to Benson J. Lossing, Nov. 12, 1864, MSS Division, New York Public Library.

32 Wilson to Henry Dawes, Aug. 23, 1864, H. L. Dawes MSS, LC.

33 Wilson to William Robinson, Jan. 12, 1865, Simon Gratz Autograph Coll., HSP; Oakes Ames to John Andrew, Jan. 14, 1865, John Andrew MSS, MHS.

34 Wilson to William Claflin, Jan. 13, 1865, Claflin MSS, RBH.

35 Henry Dawes to wife, n.d., H. L. Dawes MSS, LC.

36 John Andrew to George B. Blake, Jan. 16, 1865, H. Woodman MSS, MHS.

37 H. G. Pearson, *Life of John A. Andrew*, II, 177, 183, 184.

9

Radical Republican

No man had exerted more energy for the Northern cause, but as the war clouds dissolved Henry Wilson eagerly looked forward to the return of the Southern states. For all his military and anti-slavery activity, Wilson showed no ill feelings towards anyone in the rebel states. As George Hear, a close associate, noted, Wilson had had many fierce political battles, but never bore malice or seemed to remain angry overnight. Secure in the Senate after his reelection in January 1865, this was the man who now looked for peace and brotherhood between the North and South. In the early months following the war he saw one obstacle to this goal, the harsh treatment of the Negro in the South.[1] Despite this apprehension he gave a friendly hand to petitioners from the South who looked for favors, pardons, and restoration of privileges. In August 1865 he spent two hours in Alexander H. Stephens' damp prison room, and then reported to President Johnson that Stephens thought he could "exert a good influence for the Union" if he were home.[2] Wilson also requested a better room for the former Vice President of the Confederacy. One ex-General, H. R. Jackson of Savannah, Georgia, claimed as early as June 1865 that Wilson had urged upon the President a policy of restoring "those in our position."[3] In the fall, Wilson, said, "Some think we are pardoning rebels too fast. I don't. I would have selected some two hundred or three hundred of the more principal leaders and would not have pardoned them. The rest should have gone free."[4] The next year he visited Jefferson Davis at Fortress Monroe and expressed a desire to help him regain his freedom.[5] And when Clement Claiborne Clay, former Senator from Alabama, was accused of participating in Lincoln's assassination, Wilson voluntarily called upon Mrs. Clay to assure her of his belief in her husband's innocence and wrote a recommendation for him. This was done at a frenzied time when Mrs. Clay had already held a futile interview with Edwin Stanton.[6]

Wilson did not wish to degrade the white Southerner, but at the same time he did not wish them to degrade the Negro. In June 1865 he begged Secretary of State William H. Seward, in a private letter, to try to stop the abuses of the freedom in the rebel regions. "I hope our government is not to abandon these poor creatures that have been so true to us to the cruelties of the defeated rebels. . . . I know you are true to liberty and humanity, and I beg you to look to this matter."[7]

While Wilson cautioned Seward in one direction, he cautioned his colleague, Charles Sumner, in another. He did not want his fellow Senator to go to extremes that would damage practical efforts to help the Negro. Sumner pushed for Negro suffrage against the President's plan and Wilson advised a more conciliatory approach. By the end of the summer he warned Sumner:

> I fear our friends in Minnesota have harmed us by voting down a resolution of support of the administration. We are in a critical position and must commit no false step. While we stand firm as a rock for suffrage of the Negro, we must not weaken our cause—the cause of the poor and oppressed by saying or doing imprudent things. [sic.] We have a President who does not go as far as we do in the right direction, but we have him and cannot change him, and we had better stand by the administration and endeavor to bring it right. If it finally turns against our course than we must follow where our principles lead whether to victory or to temporary defeat.[8]

This was good advice from a fellow politician experienced in the ways of party organization. Even a man less interested in keeping his ear to the ground would have known that there were plans afoot among the conservatives to reshape the parties, gain political control, and destroy the Radicals. Newspapers frequently reported rumors of reorganization, and the Weed-Seward faction in New York had been especially active in promoting a new party formation since the re-election of Lincoln. There were also signs of political realignment in connection with the passage of the Thirteenth Amendment. Many men believed that the abolition of slavery would reduce the strength of Northern abolitionists and Southern fire-eaters and build up a new Union party which would support President Johnson and a generous reconstruction policy toward the South. Wilson knew too, that Mississippi had held a convention the previous month under the President's plan of restoration, and that they had passed the responsibility of protecting Negro rights to the legislature which had not yet convened.[9]

Wilson told Sumner that he intended to see President Johnson and to deal plainly with him. On September 14, 1865, Wilson called at the White House and had a free interchange of opinions concerning reconstruction policies. He later remarked to a friend, according to the *New York Herald,* that however he might differ from the President on questions of expediency, he respected him for his honesty in trying to perpetuate the Union by conciliating the South.[10] Henry J. Raymond reported to Thurlow Weed that Johnson regarded Wilson's manner dictatorial and insolent, but he too, wished to avoid a clash.[11] The *New York Herald* disparaged Wilson's remarks as patronizing condescension, but its hostile attitude was already established. During the summer this newspaper had asked sarcastically why Wilson did not do something about equal rights for Eskimos, Fejees, Indians, and women.[12] Wilson would have been glad to oblige and in time he would have something to say about the treatment of most, if not all, of these underprivileged classes of people.

Wilson's opinions may have irritated, the conservative James Gordon Bennett, the *Herald's* editor, but they were also a far cry from Sumner's. On the same day Wilson visited President Johnson, Sumner delivered a tirade at the Massachusetts Republican State Convention held at Worcester. Sumner made a strong Negro suffrage speech in which he claimed that others might seek a temporary favor by a temporary surrender, but he would not. He eloquently pictured a drifting administration, yet his harsh remarks were not reflected in the resolutions that the delegates passed. One stated that Massachusetts "extends a cordial welcome and confidence to his (Abraham Lincoln's) suc-

cessor and the representative of his ideas—Andrew Johnson."[13]
The convention, however, noted that restoration of order in the
South was of primary importance and that Congress should
maintain faith toward the freedom and rectify abuses. It seems
reasonable to believe that beneath the surface the moderating
views of Wilson made themselves felt upon the gathering, particularly since his very close personal and political friend, William Claflin, received the nomination for Lieutenant Governor.

Despite Wilson's conciliatory position, the *New York Herald*
classified him, along with Sumner, Thaddeus Stevens, and Wendell Phillips, as one of the "New Barbarians"[14] who planned to
exterminate the whites of the South. This must have been surprising news to Wendell Phillips. In the long fight against slavery the
two men rarely shared the same opinions, and within the year
Phillips would charge that Wilson was guilty of "cowardly Re-
publicanism," because of his readiness to compromise on the
issue of Negro suffrage.[15]

In October Wilson stated in a speech at Yonkers, New York,
that the President had told him very recently that he did not
consider advocacy of Negro suffrage, in itself, a hostile action.
Johnson, he said, wanted free discussion from which would
eventually come the truth. Wilson believed that there would be
candid discussion in Congress, and that "there will be no trouble
between us and the President." At the close of the rebellion,
Wilson added, he would have secured the right of suffrage for
some of the Negroes, and especially those who had fought the
battles of the Union. In his opinion the South, if the President
had insisted, would have adopted a provision to give suffrage to
soldiers, to all who could read and write, and to all who paid
taxes.[16]

For all the name calling, Wilson's viewpoint was surprisingly
similar to that of the *Herald*. In August the newspaper had urged
the Mississippi Convention to consider the Negro suffrage question seriously upon the basis of a property qualification, as in
New York, or upon a test of reading and writing as in Massachusetts. It was felt that this would be sufficient to open the doors
of Congress to the State and that there was no need for universal
Negro suffrage. This concession would disarm the abolition
radicals, and make way for the transfer of the political power of
the country into the hands of a new conservative national party.[17]

Completely different motivations could have produced a meeting of the minds on suffrage.

Wilson's desire for compromise did not keep him calm when he read of legislative action in the South against the freedmen. On his return to Boston, after a visit to New York, he found the people upset by a Black Code introduced into the South Carolina legislature which they believed would make the Negroes slaves again. He quickly advised Secretary of State Seward of the New England sentiment:

> I tell you that our best people are mourning over it and other evidences of cruelty to the negroes. Do in God's name stop all this legislation! Say to the States that the slaves are citizens and that they are under the same laws as white people and that they have no right to pass any law in regard to the freedmen that does not apply to their white non-voting people. You can do this and do a great work for liberty and justice. If the Administration does not do it Congress will pass such an act. You at Washington I hope will lead in this matter. Do I pray you act at once.[18]

This was presumptuous, perhaps, but Wilson was frank, friendly, and hopeful of Seward's support; and he did not demand more for the Negro than equality with non-voting whites. Seward informed the President of Wilson's views. A line in a corner of the letter reads: "Submit to Presid't. and ask for return.—W.H.S." A week later Wilson again urged Seward to use his power for the freedmen and expressed apprehension as to the Administration's course:

> We hope that when Congress should meet something for the protection of the freedmen would be enacted but we are surprised to learn that a provision intended to give Congress full power to secure real liberty to negroes is deemed a limitation on the power of Congress. This seems very strange to me. At the opening of Congress the question—not of negro suffrage will be in issue, but the amendment of all laws against the freedmen and their full liberty will be pressed. I hope in the work we are to have the influence of our own administration.[19]

Wilson's reference was to a concession that Seward had made a few days earlier regarding the Thirteenth Amendment. The Southern states resisted ratification because of the provision giving

Congress power of enforcement. To allay the fear that Congress would use this authority to pass legislation affecting the status of the freedmen in the South, Seward sent a message to Provisional Governor Benjamin F. Parry of South Carolina on November 6, 1865. The Secretary of State told the Governor that his objection was unreasonable because the last clause of the amendment actually restrained rather than enlarged the powers of Congress. On this basis South Carolina ratified the amendment with the qualification that any attempt by Congress to legislate on the political status of former slaves, or their civil relations, would be contrary to the Constitution and in conflict with the President's Amnesty Proclamation and restoration of harmony. Alabama, Florida, and Mississippi followed with similar qualifications which left little doubt that the Southern states intended to gain complete control over the freedmen.[20] With Seward's reassurance to South Carolina in mind, Wilson still expressed the hope that the Republican advocates of equal citizenship, short of suffrage, would have the support of their own Administration.

On the day that the Thirty-Ninth Congress, convened, December 4, 1865, Wilson, after consulting six eminent lawyers, introduced a bill to declare invalid all acts, ordinances, rules, and regulations in the states lately in insurrection which established any inequality of civil rights between persons on account of color, race, or previous condition of servitude.[21] Wilson simply did not believe that there could be any peace in the nation while the Black Codes existed and he wanted to sweep them into oblivion. "Let us pass it at once," he said, "as an act of humanity and justice, and then we can proceed to re-organize, re-construct, and bring into the Union these States."[22] He wanted to see that the freedman was really free, and that he could go where he pleased, work where he pleased, could sue and be sued, could lease, buy, sell, own property, real and personal, and could go to school. The South Carolina legislation, in Wilson's view, was a means to make the Negro a degraded serf. It was far better, he thought, to be the slave of one man than the slave of an arbitrary law. He felt that the joy and confidence expressed by the freedman a few months earlier was now slipping away. One moderate listener, Lyman Trumbull, regarded Wilson's speech on December 21 in support of the equal rights measure one of his best, devoid of passion or invective. It made no issue with the President.[23]

In offering this bill Wilson restrained his own radicalism. He did not call for Negro suffrage because he did not wish to jeopardize agreement on more basic civil equality. "Whatever differences of opinion may exist in regard to the right of suffrage, I am sure there can be no difference of opinion among honest and just men in regard to maintaining the civil rights and immunities of these freedmen, they should stand at any rate like the non-voting white population of those States."[24]

Typically, Wilson sought support from all quarters of Congress. At no time was he a member of a coterie or organized voting bloc to put through Radical measures. He seemed to go his own way in promoting his own legislation, and gave support to others, without trying to label them, when he thought that their cause was just. He had been a legislator too long to think that men could be placed into fixed categories. All kinds of attempts have been made to classify Reconstruction Senators, but in the life of the Senate these classifications would have meant little. The shades of difference were always evident from one day to the next, and none of the Senators knew what the future held in store. Wilson appears to have worked as easily, or more easily with moderates like Trumbull, Fessenden, Sherman, and Grimes, than he did with generally accepted Radical types like Wade and Chandler, for whom he never exhibited any special affection. Wilson's voting record was very similar to Sumner's but he was often embarrassed by his colleague's doctrinaire and inflexible attitude.

But Wilson could not resist making a few remarks about the term "conservative." He drew laughter from the chamber when he said, "I have always noticed that when I heard a man prate about being conservative and about conservatism, he was about to do some mean things. I never knew it to fail; in fact, it is about the first word a man utters when he begins to retreat."[25]

Still, Wilson's bill attracted the interest, if not the immediate support, of moderate Republicans. Senators John Sherman and Lyman Trumbull looked upon the measure sympathetically. Sherman questioned the time and manner of introduction, and believed that it would be wiser to postpone action until the Secretary of State announced that the Thirteenth Amendment was the law of the land. Trumbull hoped that the bill would not be necessary when the constitutional amendment was adopted, but he also thought that it might not go far enough if some of the things he had recently heard about the treatment of the freedmen in the South were true.[26]

During the discussion of the bill Wilson again showed that he had no wish to quarrel with the President. He declared that there had been a systematic attempt during the previous few months to separate the President from the party that elected him. Some persons feared these efforts would be successful, but he did not. He would have acted differently in some things, but the President had done nothing to prevent Congress from passing necessary legislation.

> He has made no issue with Congress, and Congress has made no issue with him. He does not undertake to dictate to us; he has pursued his own line of policy. . . . I have an undoubting faith that if we enact the needful legislation to secure the equal liberties of all men and bring back the rebel states into Congress, it will receive the sanction and approval of the executive. . . . I know sir, that it has been the policy of the Democratic party to represent that a great and inevitable conflict is to come between the President and Congress. . . . There are some men who profess to be more devoted to the President than the great mass of men who elected him. It is our duty to give the President a manly, generous, and earnest support; I am sure he wants none other. Let us look with hope and confidence, let us be prudent in speech, but let us be inflexible as destiny itself in the maintenance of the cause of equal, universal and impartial liberty throughout the whole country.[27]

These pacifying remarks followed Johnson's ambiguous message to Congress the same month. Wilson could not have been pleased with the Presidential address which attempted to be all things to all men. But he tried to identify himself, and the Republican party, with Johnson and to minimize the possibility of a clash between Congress and the Executive. Wilson's party was the party of the Administration regardless of Johnson's flirtations elsewhere. Wilson may have been unwanted, but he would not easily be cast aside.

In January Senator William Fessenden of Maine, generally considered a moderate, made very similar comments. He thought Democratic talk about a forthcoming clash between Congress and the President were ridiculous rumors. "The President has done nothing that his friends complain of, and his friends in Congress have done nothing that he can complain of." Like Wilson, Fessenden also said that he might have acted differently had he been President, but that was no reason for a break between the two branches of government.[28]

On January 5, 1866, Lyman Trumbull introduced a Freedmen's Bureau Bill designed to extend the life of that agency and expand its functions. Wilson had a continuing interest in this agency. In early 1865, he had obtained a compromise to establish the Bureau in the War Department thereby helping to rescue the original bill from defeat.[29] Now Wilson thought that the debate in Congress exhibited caste and insensibility on one side, and justice on the other. When Republican Senator Edgar Cowan of Pennsylvania sought to amend the bill so that it would apply only to the states lately in rebellion, Wilson aimed some of his sharpest remarks at him. The legislation, Wilson said, was needed as much in Maryland as in Virginia, as much in Kentucky as in Tennessee. Cowan, who would have preferred to nullify the entire bill, claimed that the Constitution protected free men and provided ample remedy for any wrongs. Wilson agreed that the Constitution protected free men, but added that there was a need for supplementary legislation. His whole philosophy was wrapped up in the belief that no part of the population could be degraded without causing difficulties for the future.

Cowan wondered what Wilson meant by "equal." Did he mean that all men were to be six feet high, weigh two hundred pounds, and have fair hair and red cheeks? This was an insane crusade that was not in the nature of things. Wilson explained that equality meant protection of the law for the poorest man, black or white, as well as the richest man in the land. He showed his longtime sympathy for the workingman too, when he said, "the man who is the enemy of the black laboring man is the enemy of the white laboring man the world over. The same influences that go to keep down and crush down the rights of the poor black man bear down and oppress the poor white laboring man. . . ." The Negro might not have so fine a leg as the Senator from Pennsylvania, but there were many Negroes who had hearts and minds quite as capacious.[30]

Cowan was absent on the final vote, but the bill passed only to be vetoed by the President. On February 19 the return of the

Freedmen's Bureau Bill from the White House created a furor in
Congress and the nation, and marked the beginning of the break
between the Executive and the legislators. The necessary two-
thirds vote for re-passage over the veto was not attained, but
Wilson, like most Republicans, voted against the President.

In January 1866 Senator Trumbull had also introduced what
was to become the first Civil Rights Act, and Wilson's position
was clear on this measure too. He had already spoken freely
about his own civil rights proposal which had failed to pass the
previous December, and he regarded Trumbull's bill substantially
the same as his own, "the grandest act in this series of acts that
have emancipated a race and disenthralled a nation."[31] Both men
believed that securing equal rights for the freedmen would remove
many of the obstacles to an early reconstruction. In the fall
Wilson told a mass meeting at Cooper Institute in New York
that he had informed the President in January that the people
were in favor of exacting additional guarantees from the South
and demanding protection for the former bondsmen. Johnson
replied to Wilson that he was mistaken and that eighteen-
twentieths of the people favored the Presidential policy.[32] At any
rate, the Senate which had originally passed the Civil Rights Bill
by a vote of thirty-three to twelve, dramatically sustained it on
April 6, 1866, against the President's veto.

As resentment against Andrew Johnson mounted, Wilson still
urged moderation. His willingess to compromise distinguished him
from his fellow Senator from Massachusetts. The names Wilson
and Sumner were often coupled together as monomaniacs on the
Negro question. Some regarded Wilson as fanatical as Sumner,
but craftier, and claimed that "the milennium of Sumner and
Wilson will arrive when white men are considered outcasts and
pariahs."[33] Closer observers like John Quincy Adams, Jr., however, realized that there were substantial differences between the
two men. In response to Wilson's moderate approach during
March, Adams proposed a resolution in the Massachusetts House
of Representatives to thank the Senator for his "wise and statesmanlike course in striving to mitigate the asperities of conflicting
theories, and thereby secure the substantial and practical results
which the mass of loyal people have most at heart."[34] This was
not a completely innocent resolution because Adams wanted to
drive a wedge between Wilson and Sumner. It was an unsuccess-

ful attempt, but Wilson continued to be his own man and did not simply follow Sumner's lead.

In moods and manners Wilson and Sumner had always been, and continued to be, a study in contrast. When Senator William Stewart offered his universal amnesty, universal suffrage resolution both of the Massachusetts men immediately favored its adoption. But Sumner had to greet the Senator from Nevada as "a new convert to the necessity of colored suffrage" while Wilson diplomatically, and less pompously, said, "I desire simply to say that I thank the Senator from Nevada for offering this proposition."[35]

There were differences between Sumner and Wilson, however, that were far greater than moods and manners. Unlike Sumner, Wilson had been ready to settle for qualified Negro suffrage. Well aware that the *New York Herald,* "always quick to discern the currents of public opinion," had proposed a limited suffrage plan, he was sure that there had been room for compromise among disparate groups. The Democratic *New York World* and *Boston Post* had been receptive to such ideas too. The great obstacle, he felt, was the President, who avowed qualified suffrage but declined to accept responsibility for doing anything about it. By early March 1866, before the veto of the Civil Rights bill, Wilson feared that the golden opportunity for resolving sectional controversies had passed, perhaps forever. The once humble and penitent Southern states were no longer acquiescent to demands for uplifting the Negro. In the Senate Wilson expressed a not so veiled threat to Johnson that perhaps a liberty loving people would have to turn to the great soldier who had led their armies to victory if they were disappointed in their aspirations.[36]

Yet in April, when Robert Dale Owen presented a moderate plan for a Fourteenth Amendment Wilson gave it support while Sumner opposed it because it contained tacit recognition that ex-slaveholders had a right to withhold suffrage from freedom for ten more years. According to Owen, Wilson approved the proposal and expressed the hope that it would pass for the sake of the country. Sumner, on the other hand, argued, "it is a question of abstract principle, not of expediency."[37]

There were many suggestions for a constitutional amendment and Wilson showed more concern for welding groups together than he did for establishing political theories. In conversation and debate Wilson made it clear that he believed that there should be no discrimination in the right of suffrage because of color. This was the principle that he favored, but he was always ready to listen to a practical solution that might make progress in that direction. He was also politic in not raising the suffrage issue where it would only jeopardize public support for a minimal civil rights program. Senator Willard Saulsbury accused Wilson of misrepresenting issues when he did not say anything about Negro suffrage during a visit to Delaware. Wilson answered that he followed the scriptural principle of giving "milk to babes" and saving his "strong meat" for other sections of the country.[38]

In May, Wilson, however reluctantly, found himself voting with strange company in opposition to an effort to restrict the President's powers of removal during the recess of Congress. As an amendment to the Post Office Appropriation Bill for 1866, Lyman Trumbull vigorously promoted a provision that would hold up salaries of all offices requiring Senate confirmation if appointments were made to them after the Senate adjourned, except in cases where the President had filled vacancies caused by death, resignation, or expiration of term. This was the seed for the Tenure-of-Office Act.

Wilson voted for reconsideration of the amendment with such conservative Senators as Doolittle, Fessenden, and Saulsbury. Seeing no reason for haste, he thought that it was unwise to press the measure at that time even though some action should be taken for the protection of their friends. He did not have any great apprehension concerning the political influence of the appointments which would be made by the President, and believed that "Any attempt to use the offices of this government to control the elections against them will signally and ignominiously fail."[39] The exasperated Trumbull asked Wilson, "Has the Senator from Massachusetts looked around the Senate and seen who is voting with him? He prefers to go with his enemies rather than his friends, does he?"[40]

Wilson replied that there had been men in the Capitol for the past three or four months who had been urging the President to use the corrupt influence of public patronage to build an independent party, "a party that had died before it was born." He named the Blairs who, he claimed, had been picking out a public man here and there and offering them "the kingdoms of the world if they would betray us."[41] But, said Wilson, the executive power to remove had been discussed by some of the most eminent statesmen of the past, and he wanted a careful bill if such a measure were to be passed.

Senator Cowan, who believed that his party would be improved by weeding out the Radicals, charged that Wilson had accused the President of betraying the Republicans. Wilson denied the charge and stated that he had "endeavored at all times and on all occasions, in public and in private, to prevent any disagreement between the President and Congress, any disruption of the ties that brought him into power." But Wilson approached a breaking point as he continued, "I make no assault upon the President of the United States. I say that I believe the policy the President has felt it his duty to pursue, which he has pursued, and which he seems to insist on pursuing, without consulting the views of Congress, this uncertainty, this doubt, this veto of the civil rights bill, has made more sorrowful men and women in this country than were made by any other man that trod the continent."[42]

Despite these sincere sentiments, Wilson knew that his vote on executive patronage supported the President. He exhibited independence in casting his ballot on other key issues too. Sumner opposed Colorado's application for admission into the Union because the proposed State Constitution confined suffrage to "white male citizens," but Wilson, undoubtedly with political considerations in mind, favored admission. And in July 1866, Wilson voted for the joint resolution to admit Tennessee, while Sumner voted against admission.[43]

As the fall elections approached Wilson found that the one thing he had dreaded, the divorce of the President from the party that had elected him, had taken place. The August Philadelphia National Union Convention, the culmination of political activities on behalf of the President's program may not have achieved the goal of establishing a new, clearly defined party, but it divided Johnson from the bulk of the Republicans. To make matters worse, Johnson's "Swing Around the Circle," to defend his Southern policy and help elect conservatives, deepened the split.

As he had often done in the past, Wilson took an active part in the canvass and his criticism of the President increased as he campaigned in New York, Pennsylvania, and Indiana as well as

Massachusetts. When Wilson appeared at a mass meeting in Philadelphia he said that it was hardly necessary for him to speak because, "There is a certain traveller (Andrew Johnson) going over the country making speeches that is doing more for us than all the speakers in the country.[44] The undignified Johnson, he thought, had done more to mortify the pride of the American people than any man who had ever lived. He was certain that Congress would eventually triumph and Johnson would pass out of office.

Wilson spelled out the issues that divided the President from the Republicans. They were the Civil Rights Bill, the Freedmen's Bureau, and the Fourteenth Amendment. Criticizing the President and praising Congress, he told the Massachusetts State Republican Convention that the Civil Rights Bill was one of the grandest in the history of the nation, and that the Freedmen's Bureau and the Constitutional amendment were worthy of a great and free people. Now, too, possibly sensing the tide of local public opinion, he made a particular plea for Negro suffrage by any means that could accomplish the purpose.[45]

Wilson's criticism of the President increased, but during his barnstorming he was careful, as in Indianapolis, to avoid talking about Negro suffrage when it seemed to be too tender a subject.[46] But the election returns reassured him that the Radical Republicans were moving in the right direction. In a discussion of the District Suffrage Bill in December of 1866, he declared that he opposed the qualifications of reading and writing. He admitted that there had been a time when he would have accepted less because he had not thought that he could get anything more. But now it appeared a practical possibility that universal manhood suffrage could be achieved. He even said that he would vote for women suffrage, but he opposed linking it with the pending question of Negro suffrage.[47]

The humane aspects of Wilson's character showed up in other legislation too. In January of 1867, he obtained the abolition of whipping as corporeal punishment in the reconstructed states, after considerable opposition, by inserting it in an Army appropriation bill.[48] He also introduced a bill to abolish forever the system of peonage in the Territory of New Mexico. "I believe," he said, "a white man is as good as a negro; and while I have been against negro slavery, I am also against slavery of this kind for white men."[49] And in March he supported an eight hour day for laborers employed by the government.[50]

As the months passed, and the political bickering continued, Wilson developed a mood of forgive, forget, and unite. The passage of the Reconstruction Act had caused nothing more than confusion and resentment in the South. During the discussion of the Second Reconstruction Act in March 1867, Senator James Nye of Nevada expressed dismay at Wilson's generous attitude towards the rebels and referred to him as "my conservative radical friend from Massachusetts." He objected to Wilson's desire to have the freedmen, the ever loyal men of the South, and those who would now register their loyalty of the Union, to band together, use their franchise, and send representatives to Congress. Nye had little faith in the freedmen, did not believe that the rebels could ever become loyal, and held that the entry of eleven Southern states would shake the foundations of the Senate. The Nevadan claimed that Wilson was willing to have the rebels come back into the Union if they were sandwiched between two black men. "If we are to take poison," he said, "let us take it in small doses."[51]

Wilson denied that he had taken a new position on the reentry of the rebel states. It was time, he thought, to bury the bitter memories of the conflict and cultivate mutual faith and trust. Since the nation had been saved, a race emancipated, and the Negro made a citizen, with civil rights, there was a need for grace in triumph and Christian charity. He reminded Senator Nye that it was easy to appeal to prejudice, passion, and hate, and that he had conferred with Southern men of all shades of opinion during the previous two years. And he had received severe rebukes when he favored the early admission of Tennessee.[52]

In April 1867 Wilson, in a magnanimous mood, started out on a tour of the South. At Petersburg, Virginia he went so far as to say that the Northern people shared the guilt of the war, that it had not been exclusively incited by the South even though slavery was the cause. But he also made it clear that he was a Radical Republican. He told his audience that the President, acting under the malign influence of bad men, had arrayed himself against Congress, and that the Southern people had embraced his policy and stood with him against the party that had rescued the country. The result was that neither the President nor the

Northern Democratic party could fulfill their hopes. Adoption of the policy of Congress was the only solution, and he was certain that the people of the South would accept this view within the next two or three months. He also counseled the colored people to avoid contention, take advantage of freedom, and improve their minds and estates. Three to four thousand people listened to him and received him well.[53] In fact, he was received so well during his tour he soon had many imitators.

At Richmond Wilson spoke at Orange Court House where he claimed that Lincoln had prepared eight conditions for pardon of rebels all of which he approved. Johnson, on the other hand, had prepared fourteen, six too many. Wilson said that he had never favored the twenty thousand dollar clause, and that he wanted the South to be at liberty to go to work, except for a few leaders.[54] Later in the year he said that he did not want an Ireland or a Poland in America.[55]

Wilson's tour did not meet with complete approval in the North. Sickly Thaddeus Stevens, trying to recuperate at his Lancaster home, attacked the Massachusetts Senator, "Who authorized any orator to say there would be no confiscation?" he wrote, "Who is authorized to travel the country and peddle out amnesty."[56] Wilson had other critics too. Gideon Welles thought Wilson was electioneering, "stirring up the blacks, irritating and insulting the whites, promising the people recognition and that they may have their constitutional rights, provided they will submit to the unconstitutional and unwarranted dictation of the Radicals."[57]

No matter how it was regarded, Wilson's travels in the South did not soften his attitude towards the President. When asked about the possible impeachment of Johnson in September, Wilson replied that a few weeks previously most Republicans of the country hoped to accomplish their purpose without resorting to such tactics, but Johnson's "recent course of action," probably referring to the suspension of Stanton from office, carried a great body of the party the other way, "and today the great mass of the Republican party believe that the President will be impeached and that he deserves impeachment." He characterized Johnson as a man who worked in fits and starts because that was his nature. "He acts like a 'fellow on a bust' who goes to sleep and wakes up and breaks things and then goes to sleep again, and so on until he is sober. . . . In my idea he is a foolish man, governed by gusts of passion and temper, and he is a disappointed man because he really believed he was going to succeed."[58]

While these events were transpiring, Wilson suffered a heart breaking tragedy without warning and it is surprising that he conducted any business at all. His only child, Hamilton Wilson, a Second Lieutenant with the 6th United States Cavalry, stationed at Austin, Texas died suddenly, probably of dysentery, while on duty. He had taken sick on Saturday, December 22, 1867, and passed away on Monday. Although only twenty years old, he had considerable military experience. He attended the Highland Cadet Military School in Worcester, and spent one year at the United States Naval Academy. In the winter of 1864 he entered the army as a First Lieutenant with the 31st United States colored troops and was stationed for a few months at Harts Island and Fort Schuyler. Then he moved to the staff of General Ferrero, a Division Commander, and rose to the rank of Lieutenant Colonel with the 104th Regiment. When it was mustered out of service he reverted to Second Lieutenant with the 6th Cavalry.[59]

Wilson returned to work shortly after his loss, but a display of the external mechanics of his job gave no indication of his inner grief. He once said that he knew of no greater joy in life than to be the father of a nice family of children. In January 1868 he lambasted Senator James Doolittle of Wisconsin for upholding the Administration's Reconstruction policy. He was now sure that the treachery of President Johnson had seduced the weak, corrupted the pliant, and demoralized public affairs. He believed, too, that the Congressional policy of Reconstruction had become an accomplished fact. The constitutional conventions, the Negro participants, and the repentent rebels received Wilson's support. "They may not be Madisons and Marshalls in those conventions, they may not have the learned and elaborate discussion that distinguished other conventions . . . but these plain, unlettered men, patriotic, liberty loving, and just are borrowing and incorporating into their constitutions all that is great and grand and glorious of the most liberal and enlightened states."[60] Surprisingly, this view is close to that held by recent scholars.

Wilson's opposition to Johnson continued to grow. On the day that President Johnson gave General Lorenzo Thomas a letter of authority to assume the duties of office of the Secretary of War *ad interim,* Wilson wrote to Stanton a reassuring note, "I trust you will stand firm where you are and we will stand by you."[61] And he did.

Talk of impeaching Johnson had been common for some time. Representative James Ashley, of Ohio an extreme Radical by any count, had tried to instigate proceedings against the President as early as 1866, and he, Boutwell, and Butler had done their best in 1867 to connect Johnson with the assassination of Lincoln. These initial attempts failed, but there was general discontent in Congress and even moderates openly expressed their exasperation and dissatisfaction with the President. Such conversational exchanges bred further discontent and created an atmosphere which seemingly took the participants to a point of no return. Their complaints against the President gained momentum after the Congress had won its own Reconstruction program, and venting their spleen was pointless. But, irrationally, the move to impeach the President had to run its course. The dangers of impeachment, which had been recognized earlier by level heads, were now cast aside. The virtue of patience, which simply called for waiting for the President's term to end, was forgotten.

In 1868 the House precipitously passed the impeachment resolution, followed by articles of impeachment, and the trial of the President. The action centered upon Johnson's removal of Stanton as Secretary of War in violation of the Tenure-of-Office Act. No one seemed to know the exact meaning of the law, but it served its purpose as a basis for making the President a violator of the law. Every member of the Cabinet had regarded the bill as unconstitutional, including Stanton, who had assisted in preparing the President's veto message.

Lacking a firm foundation for their case, the Radicals overstepped their bounds. Emotions held sway, politics ran rampant, but eventually the President's legal defense won.

When Wilson faced the question whether or not to vote for the conviction of the President he decided that he would resolve his perplexing doubts in favor of the country, rather than Johnson. He discarded forms and technicalities, he claimed, and looked only for substance. Wilson believed that the removal of Stanton and the appointment of Thomas in violation of the Tenure-of-Office Act was sufficient reason for voting "guilty." But he also reviewed the President's actions of the previous three years and concluded that Johnson had sought to prevent the enforcement of laws passed over his veto and to prevent the restoration of the Union on the basis of loyalty and equal rights. He admitted that his personal knowledge of Presidential intentions, purposes, and acts influenced his thoughts. "The framers of the Constitution knew, when they gave Senators the power to try an arraigned Chief Magistrate, the country knows, and we know, that personal knowledge and the historic records of the country cannot but influence in some degree the feelings and judgments of men."[62] Still, it was probably a reluctant vote that he cast against the President.

Throughout the struggle for Reconstruction Wilson gained in stature within the Republican party. At the Republican Convention in May his name was placed in nomination for Vice President and strengthened his personal position even though he lost to Schuyler Colfax. With the impeachment effort ended, Wilson let it be known that he was weary of arguments and desirous of speedy restoration. "I would cast aside this cheap legal learning that has so often burdened the debates of Congress and come to the practical consideration of the real questions involved. . . . I would welcome back these States with their reform constitutions with a glad heart, with bonfires, with illuminations." He also said frankly that the seven states then seeking admission, if restored at once, would give their electoral strength in the Presidential election to General Grant.[63]

In December 1868 Wilson exhibited his humanitarian instincts once again by introducing a bill to enfranchise women in the District of Columbia.[64] Practical politician he may have been, but he meant what he said about second class citizenship. He had not done anything about the Eskimos as yet, but before long he would have something to say about the rights of Chinese in the United States.

Henry Wilson was a Radical Republican, but his career is a caution against the easy cataloging of public men. Certainly Wilson does not fit the picture of a Radical Republican riding roughshod over a defeated South and a beleaguered Executive. If Charles Sumner is established as the standard for a Radical, Wilson's record is tarnished by his readiness to compromise. An

ambitious, hard driving, practical politician, he energetically
sought the views of all levels of society and respected popular
opinion. Generous, kind, and impersonal, he lacked the temper
for vindictiveness and had a reputation as a peacemaker in the
Senate. An underdog, friend of the workingman and slave, he held
steadfast to the ideal of first class citizenship for all.

In the postwar years Henry Wilson expressed beliefs and displayed methods, faults, and virtues that were the product of a
lifetime. They were not suddenly adopted for the Reconstruction
period. The "bound out" boy, the struggling shoemaker, the
spokesman for the workingman, the antislavery worker, had
genuine personal and psychological motives for humanitarian
reform. Charles Sumner was not a standard for Radicals any
more than Thaddeus Stevens or Ben Wade. Radicals differed in
background, motives, methods, and shades of policy. They usually,
but not always, worked together for reasons of their own. Senator
Nye's irritated, but apt, description of Henry Wilson as never
more than a "conservative radical" suggests that Radicalism itself
held a measure of moderation with which it has seldom been
credited. The objective of their political battles was, after all,
the advancement of human rights, a far from unworthy cause.
They wanted reforms, and they resisted road blocks, but they were
also politicians accustomed to give and take. They made mistakes,
and the biggest mistake of all was the impeachment proceedings,
but certainly Wilson and most of the other Radicals were not
essentially "hanging judges" ready to string up a political opponent at the slightest provocation.

NOTES

[1] White, *Trumbull*, p. 247.

[2] Wilson to Andrew Johnson, Aug. 14, 1865, Andrew Johnson MSS, LC.

[3] H. R. Jackson to H. L. Dawes, June 16, 1865, Dawes MSS, LC.

[4] *NYT*, Oct. 10, 1865.

[5] Ishbel Ross, *First Lady of the South* (New York: Harper & Bros., 1958),
pp. 283, 292.

[6] Wilson to Andrew Johnson, March 3, 1866, Andrew Johnson MSS, LC.

[7] Wilson to William Seward, June 15, 1865, William H. Seward MSS, University of Rochester.

[8] Wilson to Charles Sumner, Sept. 9, 1865, Sumner MSS, HL: Pierce,
Memoir and Letters, IV, 250.

[9] See La Wanda Cox and John H. Cox, *Politics, Principle and Prejudice
1865-66* (New York: Glencoe Free Press, 1963), esp. pp. 41, 157, 158.

[10] *NYH*, Sept. 16, 1865.

[11] T. W. Barnes, *Life of Thurlow Weed* (Boston: Houghton Mifflin & Co., 1884), p. 451.

[12] *NYH,* July 9, 1865.

[13] *NYH,* Sept. 15, 1865.

[14] *NYH,* Sept. 16, 1865.

[15] Sherwin, *Prophet of Liberty,* p. 539.

[16] *NYT,* Oct. 10, 1865.

[17] *NYH,* Aug. 18, 1865.

[18] Wilson to William Seward, Nov. 13, 1865, Seward MSS, University of Rochester.

[19] Wilson to William Seward, Nov. 20, 1865, Seward MSS, University of Rochester.

[20] Cox, *Politics, Principle and Prejudice,* pp. 169, 170.

[21] *Cong. Globe,* 39 Cong., 1 Sess., p. 39; William H. Barnes, *History of the 39th Congress of the United States* (New York: Harper & Bros., 1868), p. 96.

[22] Henry Wilson, *History of the Reconstruction Measures of the 39th and 40th Congresses—1865-68* (Hartford: Hartford Publishing Co., 1868), pp. 105-115.

[23] White, *Trumbull,* p. 247.

[24] *Cong. Globe,* 39 Cong., 1 Sess., p. 39.

[25] *Ibid.,* p. 114.

[26] *Ibid.,* pp. 41-43.

[27] *Ibid.,* pp. 111, 112.

[28] Eric McKittrick, *Andrew Johnson and Reconstruction* (Chicago: University of Chicago Press, 1960), p. 281.

[29] George R. Bentley, *A History of the Freedmen's Bureau* (Phila.: University of Pa., 1955), p. 48.

[30] *Cong. Globe,* 39 Cong., 1 Sess., pp. 339-44.

[31] Wilson, *Rise and Fall,* III, 689.

[32] *NYT,* Oct. 16, 1866.

[33] *NYH,* Feb. 12, 1865.

[34] Robert Mirak, "John Quincy Adams, Jr. and the Reconstruction Crisis," *The New England Quarterly,* XXXV (June 1962), p. 192.

[35] *Cong. Globe,* 39 Cong., 1 Sess., p. 1438.

[36] *Cong. Globe Appendix,* 39 Cong., 1 Sess., pp. 140-142.

[37] Robert Dale Owen, "Political Results from the Varioloid," *Atlantic Monthly,* XXXV, (June 1875), 662-665.

[38] Wilson, *Reconstruction Measures,* p. 239.

[39] *Cong. Globe,* 39 Cong., 1 Sess., p. 2449.

[40] *Ibid.,* p. 2450.

[41] *Ibid.,* p. 2452.

[42] *Ibid.,* pp. 2452, 2453.

[43] *Ibid.,* p. 4007.

[44] *NYH,* Sept. 6, 1866.

[45] *NYH,* Sept. 14, 1866.

[46] *NYH,* Sept. 24, 1866.

[47] *Cong. Globe,* 39 Cong., 2 Sess., pp. 42, 64.

[48] *Ibid.,* p. 214.

[49] *Ibid.,* p. 1571.

[50] *Ibid.,* 40 Cong., 1 Sess., p. 413.

[51] *Ibid.,* pp. 113-116.

[52] *Ibid.,* pp. 114, 145.

[53] *NYT,* April 7, 1867.

54 *NYT,* April 22, 1867.

55 E. Merton Coulter, *The South During Reconstruction, 1865-1877* (Baton Rouge: Louisiana State University Press, 1947), p. 68.

56 Claude Bowers, *The Tragic Era* (New York: Halcyon House, 1929), p. 159.

57 *The Diary of Gideon Welles* (3 vols., Boston: Houghton Mifflin & Co., 1911), III, 86.

58 *NYT,* Sept. 5, 1867.

59 *Natick Times,* Jan. 12, 1867.

60 *Cong. Globe,* 40 Cong., 2 Sess., pp. 768, 769.

61 Wilson to Edwin Stanton, Feb. 21, 1868, Edwin M. Stanton MSS, LC.

62 *Supplement to Cong. Globe,* 40 Cong., 2 Sess., 1868, Opinion of Henry Wilson re Impeachment of Andrew Johnson, pp. 460, 461.

63 *Cong. Globe,* 40 Cong., 2 Sess., p. 2691.

64 Ida Harper, *Life and Work of Susan B. Anthony* (3 vols., Indianapolis: The Hollenbeck Press, 1908), I, 311.

10

Grant and Wilson

The election of Grant to the presidency stirred much talk about Wilson taking a place in the Cabinet. *The Natick Times,* with a sense of local pride, regarded their townsman as a logical choice. Thinking, perhaps, of Sumner, they editorialized, "He (Wilson) is not so ready and fluent as some others, but when he speaks it is because he has something of vital importance to say, and his words are compact, clear, and forcible, and imbued with that masterly common sense which is so very uncommon in Congress."[1]

In more serious circles, Wilson's name also carried great weight as a possible appointee. Wilson told Grant that either Sumner or Boutwell would be the choice of his friends in Massachusetts. The President-elect replied that William Claflin had added his name when he had talked to him about satisfactory candidates for the Cabinet. But Wilson quickly answered that his name was not to be considered. Such a position might have appealed to him at some time, but this was not the time. Mrs. Wilson advised him not to accept any offers, and aware that his wife was dying of cancer, he had no intention of opposing her wishes. Still, he did not go out of his way to urge the appointment of Sumner or Boutwell. Instead, he reassured Grant that the Republicans of Massachusetts would give him strong support whether or not one of their friends received a cabinet post.[2]

The following Spring, after much suffering, Mrs. Wilson passed away at the age of forty-six. The few bits of information that remain about her indicate that she was a sympathetic wife in complete accord with her husband's career. She left the impression of having been the soul of understanding which could not have been easy with a man like Wilson, immersed in his work and away from home for long periods of time. Elias Nason, an old friend, described her as a model woman, gentle and kind, elegant in speech, patient in tribulation. "She was a 'treasure' which it is given to but few to call their own."[3]

With his wife and only son gone, Wilson turned back to his work, the only way of life that he knew. But, inwardly, he was not quite the same. He rarely gave evidence of inner feelings, but a letter he had written the previous year to his close friends, the Claflins, upon the loss of one of their children, cut into his deeper sentiments. "We who have tasted so much of life, have toiled so long, and won some of its prizes, know how poor and barren are all the possessions of years. Your dear children who have gone before you lessen your hold on this life and make your steps less reluctant towards the life to come."[4]

Early in 1870 the *New York Times* described Wilson as a man of unquestionable integrity and touching generosity. "His face beams with simplicity—a true index of his character in which there is no current of harm or deceit."[5] About this time, Wilson received the credentials of Hiram R. Revells, a Negro elected to the Senate from Mississippi, but he waited a month before he felt that it was safe to present them to the Senate. When the day arrived to swear in the new Senator the packed galleries showed no sign of emotion as Wilson stood by the side of Revells.[6]

Equal rights continued as the major theme in Wilson's philosophy, and they were not idle words. He wanted to secure the rights of Negroes to hold office as well as to vote, and then take the whole question out of politics. He tired of the ten year struggle. "We have had to gather every triumph of human rights step by step, a little at a time; but by the blessings of God the final fruition will come some time, and we will work on for that end."[7] But he did not think of the Negro only. In March 1870 he asked the Senate to enter into a policy of protecting, preserving, and civilizing the remaining Indian tribes. A few months later he spoke out against servile labor contracts and the importation of Chinese coolies at low wages. "I believe," he said, "that God made men in his own image and of one blood. Wherever there is a man throughout God's heritage I recognize him as a man belonging to the brotherhood of humanity and I will protect and defend him. . . . I would meet him like a brother (wherever he comes from) and treat him as a man that God made, and for whom Christ died."[8]

Wilson also disliked the word "class" and objected to its use in a proposed amendment. "We hear a great deal said in our country about "higher classes," and "lower classes," and "my servants." I never hear such an expression without pain; and I do not wish to put in any law that shall recognize classes in this country of any kind. I do not like this idea which is thrown out here about 'rising from the working class' into any other class. I do not believe in classes in this land of equality. . . . It matters not where a man was born, or to what race he belongs, rich or poor, he is in our Republic of no class, but of the great family of equality."[9] This was a naive statement, but it was indicative of his nature and represented his idea of an ideal state.

In the loose political language of the twentieth century, Wilson would be classified as a "liberal." Such a term defies definition, but it is generally associated with the advancement of human rights, and Wilson, a Republican Senator, devoted a good many years to that cause. He was also quite willing to spend government money for human welfare. Money, he thought, was not to hoard, but to do good. This was not only a political view, but a personal characteristic. Money held little interest for him. When there was much higgling in the Senate over a bill for the relief of Chicago after their great fire, Wilson left no doubt where he stood. "I am ready to go as far as we can possibly go under the Constitution of the United States to aid them. . . . The world was made to grow men and women."[10] Since his early days as the "Natick Cobbler," Wilson had also served as a spokesman for workingmen, and since the Civil War his interest in labor had grown. In 1866 a number of Radical Senators took up labor's cause for shorter hours and Wilson was among them. Labor's hopes ran high in Massachusetts, but there was a real risk in losing votes by courting the workingman.

Wilson was a stalwart in money matters, a hard money man who hoped to hasten the day when there would be specie payments in the country. But even then he thought in human terms.

He regarded Western demands for free banking and redistribution as plots against the property of widows and orphans of the East.[11] This was a rationalization of the Northeast pro-business position, but Wilson did not see any basic conflict between business and labor. Each needed the other and was a part of the whole commercial structure. He wanted banking institutions founded upon the needs of business interests in the country.[12] Still, he grew increasingly suspicious about the formation of large conglomerates. This was not his idea of the free enterprise system. He did not like a few men or a few corporations piling up a great amount of money, and he did not like granting vast tracts of land to railroads. He wanted the lands to go to the men who would own and cultivate them. "The railroads have governed legislative bodies quite too much. . . . And if there are agents in the galleries, or in the Capitol, or in the city, interested in these matters I choose for one not to be dictated to by them, nor to have them come here undertaking to influence or direct our action."[13]

In the first session of the Fortieth Congress, Wilson favored a Joint Resolution to protect the interests of the United States in connection with the Union Pacific Railroad. The government had provided five persons to serve as directors to guard the public interest, and three of them asked Congress for protective legislation. Three weeks passed and nothing happened. "As I have listened to the zeal and earnestness with which the question has been discussed here and elsewhere, and especially elsewhere, I have felt sometimes that the Central Pacific railroad had friends, that the Union Pacific railroad had friends, and that the Government had very few. I think our business is to take care of the interests of the country, and not take care of the interests of the Union Pacific railroad or the Central Pacific railroad."[14]

Wilson thought there had been much skullduggery in building the railroads, but he defended his friend, Oakes Ames, against charges that he had used influence to get legislation favorable to the Union Pacific. He claimed that Ames had joined the company when it had substantially broken down, and when the Credit Mobilier was nearly bankrupt. Ames joined the company, he said, with a number of personal associates who put millions of dollars into the road, plus their skill and energy, and pushed the construction. He thought mistakes had been made during their administration, but no favorable legislation had been passed under the Ames regime. Nevertheless, Wilson did not believe that either the Union Pacific or the Central Pacific had yet constructed the road so that the government should accept it. The United States had paid enough for a good road from Omaha to the Pacific Ocean, and no matter what the cost to the parties involved, they should be held liable and complete the road. He did not want to discredit them, but he did want them to be responsible for their work.[15]

There was much talk about corruption in Congress in 1869, and Wilson thought that the press had done great injury to the country by arousing suspicions that almost all public men were corrupt. He had served with more than two hundred Senators, and in his opinion, he did not think ten men among them ever made a dollar directly or indirectly in office. Four or five were probably corrupt, but more often men were weak and sometimes let things pass out of friendship that should have been arrested. To take money for passing or defeating a measure he was sure was very rare.[16]

About this time Wilson placed another burden upon himself. He had an urge to write a history of the antislavery movement and commenced to collect information from participants in the struggle. He had previously hired an unemployed minister, the Reverend Samuel Hunt who had performed his marriage ceremony years ago, to help him with his writing. Wilson had already produced under his own name a *History of Anti-Slavery Measures of the 37th and 38th Congresses,* and a *History of Reconstruction.* Both were dull recitals of measures passed through Congress during these periods, but at least they served as a compilation of legislation in aid of the Negro. Wilson's new project was far more ambitious, particularly for a man who wrote little. His personal correspondence indicates that he wrote the briefest of letters in a hurried fashion. Perhaps he liked the idea of a literary prestige that he felt authordom would bring him. Perhaps he had a secret desire to imitate public men of New England like Charles Francis Adams and John Palfrey. He undoubtedly had a genuine desire to record the events of the days of trial in which he and his friends participated while they were still alive. Never afraid of work, he set out by writing to people like Garrison asking for his confidential estimate of the services of others to the antislavery cause. He hoped, he said, to give the truth and to be impartial

and just. Seward and Weld were other correspondents. He asked
Seward for his recollections of his understanding with Stanton
during the winter of 1860-1861.[17] He proposed three volumes,
and eventually three mammoth volumes were produced which
have taken their place in the historiography of the antislavery
movement. It was a gigantic job, and for sheer effort alone, the
amassing of more than two thousand printed pages demands
respect. While they do not carry much weight among modern
scholars, references to the *Rise and Fall of Slave Power in
America* still find their way into many footnotes, anthologies
print excerpts, and writers on the causes of the Civil War give
Wilson's interpretation of the slave power respectful attention.
He has been presented as a proponent of the conspiracy theory,
but that seems overdrawn. Wilson never claimed that there was
an organized plot by the slave power. He said it simply seemed
that way.

In 1871, Wilson, still working on his project, made a trip to
Europe to see the sights and visit friends. But it was a lonely trip
and one that he did not really enjoy, and he probably worked on
the book to fill the empty gap in his personal life. His heart was
at home and he missed his wife and son. He even missed the
criticism of his friends at the Bird Club, especially the sharp
remarks of Robinson.[18]

Upon returning from Europe, Wilson visited the Claflins where
he found comfort and relaxation among old friends who enjoyed
his company and found his conversation entertaining. More than
once Wilson told them, "Sumner is in agony when I rise to speak
in the Senate, for fear Massachusetts will be disgraced by my bad
grammar." It irritated Sumner and he asked the Claflins before
Wilson went abroad, "Do you think Wilson will murder the
king's English when he is in England as he does here?"

One morning at breakfast the unsophisticated Wilson displayed
some lace that he had bought at Liverpool which was simply
coarse cotton, and this provoked Sumner to discourse for the
next hour on the different qualities of lace; where the finest might
be found, where the choicest bits of old altar-lace were preserved,
what kind of lace Lady So and So wore when he dined with her
at Lord Palmerston's, and the quality of Madame Thier's lace
when he dined with the President of the French Republic. By the
time Sumner finished, Wilson's lace disappeared from sight, and
he made no mention of it again.[19]

Another person distressed by Wilson was the Reverend Samuel Hunt. A graduate of Amherst and a student of theology at Princeton, the minister was happy to find employment with the Senator because he could not find a church and considered himself superannuated at fifty-four. Still, he had misgivings about his chief. His working conditions were fine, but privately he looked down upon Wilson. After two years, it was still a mystery to him how Wilson had gained his influential position. "For though the Senator is very far from my idea of perfection, and I should never choose him as my boon companion, I cannot close my eyes to his great popularity and influence, though it is 'all Greek' to me how he got it or retains it." He told his children that Wilson entrusted the writing of the three volumes to him, but he would never receive proper recognition for the work. It bothered him, but it was not "a part of the plan." Already he had written temperance articles under Wilson's name that had brought much praise to his employer, but none to him. His only hope was that he would receive his reward in eternity.[20]

It is easy to underestimate Henry Wilson. He never seemed to be more than a very ordinary person, and his great self-exertion and persistence could be overlooked. His lack of refinement and refusal to stand on dignity made him an easy prey for criticism from better educated observers. But they lacked his sense of purpose and forgot that he worked while they slept. In a day when ghost writers were not common the Reverend Hunt probably had good cause for complaint, but he did receive credit for completing the final volume after Wilson's death. It seems likely that Hunt did most, or all, of the writing of *Rise and Fall,* but there is evidence that Wilson busily engaged in collecting information and supervising the project.

*   *   *   *   *

General Grant was not one of the more effective statesmen to reside in the White House and before long trouble broke out everywhere. His political appointments, with few exceptions, were undistinguished, and frequently they were made without the advice of the party Senators. This practice, alone, did not please Charles Sumner, and probably annoyed Henry Wilson too. But Wilson was never quick to take offense, and, strangely, for a hard driving politician, he was never a patronage monger. He tired of office seekers pestering him from morning until night and felt that the sooner Senators could be relieved of the responsibility of appointments, the better.[21] But this was not the only difficulty. There was corruption in office, pressure from lobbyists, manipulations of money, and complications in foreign affairs.

By the fall of 1870 Wilson told Hamilton Fish that he had been out stumping for the past two weeks and he had not seen a Republican in Massachusetts, New York, or Delaware who was not more or less dissatisfied. He confided to the Secretary of State that he wished the President would let the matter of the Minister of England drop for the present.[22] It caused profound resentment, particularly with Sumner. Fish knew that Wilson referred to the entire Santo Domingo affair.

Grant had insisted upon annexing Santo Domingo only to run into the firm opposition of Sumner, Chairman of the Foreign Relations Committee. His denunciation of the "deal", which involved Grant's close friend and aide, Orville Babcock, as well as a couple of disreputable friends of Ben Butler's resulted in the defeat of the annexation treaty. Infuriated by such behavior, Grant retaliated by removing Sumner's friend, John Lothrop Motley as Minister to London, and using his influence to have Sumner removed from the chairmanship of the Committee on Foreign Relations.

The bitter ramifications of this battle shook the Republican Party at a time when it desperately needed unity. Wilson knew the dangers of letting the feud continue and did his best to serve as peacemaker between Grant and Sumner. More than once he visited the White House to calm the waters, but made no progress. When he finally gave up trying he referred to the President in language which Edward Pierce said was not worthwhile perpetuating.[23] But Wilson had known Sumner too long not to be aware of his inflexible side.

In March 1871 Wilson spoke in the Senate to retain Sumner as Chairman of his committee, and opposed a resolution that would give Cameron the position. He argued that Sumner should not be removed because there were strained personal and social relations between the President and the Senator. Wilson also blamed the Santo Domingo affair for the removal attempt. Wilson tried to minimize Santo Domingo by saying that he thought it was a small affair when it came up, and a small question now, and he saw no reason for friends to divide over it. Along the way he offered his colleagues some political advice. "I say to my political friends, I do not belong to this party of discipline. You cannot discipline the Republican party. We have a class of politicians who have an idea that if they can show the scalps of their political friends they are mighty war chiefs. . . . Before you attempt this plan of disciplining Senators. . . . my advice to you is to close up your ranks, rectify your mistakes, and stand united before the country. Remember that 'victory clings to unity.' "[24] He disliked petty dictates which he knew were political blunders. But he failed in his efforts to save the chairmanship for Sumner.

Throughout the war and early reconstruction, the Republican Party put on a united face. But under the surface it was, as it had been from birth, an amalgamation of many diverse elements. Within its house a variety of factions held wide differences of opinion on reconstruction, economic, and social problems. Some wanted a progressive party. Others wanted a conservative party. Grant mismanaged the delicate party decisions and missed his opportunity for harmony. He failed to listen to Wilson or any other Republican peacemaker until too late. Near the close of 1871 the President tried, through Wilson, to pacify the Curtin faction in Pennsylvania by offering it a Cabinet post, but the situation had become impossible.[25]

Sumner, like a rejected suitor, used his bitter eloquence to persuade his followers that Grant was unfit for office and could not be reelected. To make matters worse, Ben Butler, no friend of Wilson or Sumner, gained considerable influence over the President and gained a large share of the patronage in the state. Sumner and Wilson, partners in politics for many years, would soon reach a parting of the ways, politically, if not personally. But for all their differences in personality, there was a bond of affection between the two men which made the separation difficult. Each recognized their new roles. Sumner told Wilson that their political paths would soon diverge, and hoped that they would remain friends. Wilson, in turn, reciprocated the sentiment.[26]

The strife that created the Liberal Republicans started in Missouri when Wilson's old associate, Carl Schurz, overthrew the Radical regime and won election to the Senate in 1870. Many Free Soilers and founders of the Republican party with whom Wilson had worked joined the spreading movement. The parting pained Wilson, but he realized that he was now a leading con-

tender for the Vice Presidency, and that Sumner's split with
Grant had only increased his own chances for the nomination.
The man who had walked out of the Whig Party, joined the Free
Soilers, destroyed the Know Nothings, and helped to found the
Republicans, decided to remain with his party.

The Liberal Republicans attracted some idealists and reformers, but they failed miserably in their efforts to become an
ideal progressive party. Too many people joined it for the wrong
reason. While some opposed Radicals like Chandler and Conkling,
others simply wanted a haven for seeking office. Discontented
Republicans, discouraged Democrats, merged into an uneasy,
unhappy political organization that failed to nominate a leader
who could convey a common cause or carry them to victory. The
nomination of Horace Greeley as standard bearer almost destroyed the party at the start. A Radical Republican, high tariff
man, hater of Democrats, and opponent of any kind of foreign
relations made an unfortunate candidate.

As early as January 1872, *The New York Times* reported that
Wilson's friends did not hesitate to say that he was in the field
for the Vice Presidential nomination. They were confident of the
votes of Pennsylvania, Ohio, Illinois, Virginia, and Alabama,
and looked to New England for further support. Wilson busily
moved around the country filling speaking engagements. In one
week in February he spoke at Manchester, Nashua, Rochester,
Farmington, and Winchester in New Hampshire.[27] Two of his
set speeches were, "What The Republican Party Has Done for
the Laboring Man," and "Stand by the Republican Colors." In
the first, he declared that the Republicans had struck down
Southern aristocracy, made labor honorable, and favored small
farms over great plantations. He deplored a few men or a few
corporations accumulating large fortunes. In the second, he portrayed Democrats as men who were on the side of privilege,
caste, and degraded barbarism. Republicans stood for liberty,
justice, humanity, and Christian civilization. The administration
was not more corrupt than the Democrats; it simply did more to
expose thieving. "While we were trying Major Hodge, and sending him to the penitentiary at Albany for ten years, with the
approval of the entire Republican Party of the country, Boss
Tweed, the greatest thief in all the history of human frailty, the
boss thief of the world was sent to Albany, not to the penitentiary

but the State House as a State Senator by 12,000 Democratic majority."[28]

For the sake of appearance rather than modesty, Wilson declined to preside at the state convention at Worcester for the selection of delegates to the National Convention. The Republicans of Massachusetts refused to recognize any schism in the party when they met in April and scarcely mentioned Sumner. They recommended the renomination of Grant, and urged naming Wilson for Vice President.[29]

During the 1870 Congressional campaign Vice President Schuyler Colfax had announced that he would retire at the end of his term. It was probably done for affect, but no man capitalized on the statement more than Wilson. By January 1, 1872, Colfax had changed his mind and announced that he was in the running again. Wilson had probably never taken too much stock in Colfax' earlier announcement, but he now told a *New York Tribune* correspondent that he had assented to become a candidate for Vice President only after ascertaining that the Colfax decision had been final. "The revocation of the Vice President of his declination was to me a surprise. It placed me in an unpleasant position, and my first impulse was to withdraw from the contest, by the advice of some of the best Republicans of the land— East, West, and South—I leave the question to personal and political friends. Whatever may be the result I shall be content and I shall do what I can for the unity and success of the Republican party."[30]

Colfax considered himself fair game and never complained about Wilson's aggressiveness. Later he said that Wilson succeeded partly because of his declinatory letter, but more by his thorough and persistent electioneering. Nearly every evening, he claimed, Wilson held audiences with newspapermen and asked them to telegraph that he was gaining steadily. Still, as late as June, *The New York Times* stated that the Vice Presidential candidate would probably be Colfax. The Vice President presumably had 134 instructed votes, while Wilson had only 56.[31]

The anti-Colfax contingent argued that it was against usage to renominate a Vice President when the President had been renominated. It was also said that he came from the wrong geographical area. Wilson's friends, on the other hand, painted their man as well known in every part of the country, popular

in the West as well as New England, a vote getter among
Negroes, and possessed of irreproachable private and public
character. The canvassing at the National Convention held at the
Academy of Music in Philadelphia, was brisk, and Wilson picked
up unexpected strength in the West and South. Much of his
backing appeared to come from a disposition among Republicans
to reward the faithful colleague of the erratic Sumner.[32]

After the nominating speeches, including one by Geritt Smith,
the old time abolitionist, as a seconder for Wilson, the voting commenced. The contest between Wilson and Colfax was close, and
at the end of the first round no one had a majority. But before the
announcements of results, two states sought to switch their votes.
Virginia had cast twenty-two votes for their Governor, while
Tennessee had cast twenty-six for Horace Maynard. If the chair
had recognized Tennessee, Colfax would have been renominated,
but it turned to Virginia and assured Wilson's success. Since there
were reports that Grant requested the shift in running mates it
may only have appeared to be a tight race.[33] Always popular
with the press, some newspapermen also thought that they had
something to do with Wilson's nomination. But *The New York
Times* disagreed. "If the reporters at Phila. flatter themselves that
they had anything to do with the nomination of Henry Wilson,
they merely afford a fresh application of the fable in which the
fly on the wheel expressed prodigious astonishment at the dust
he is raising."[34]

Wilson received the news at his desk in the Senate where a
River and Harbor Bill was under discussion. Colfax, upon hearing the same report, went into the Chamber from the Vice
President's room, and was among the first to congratulate the
candidate. Senators Schurz, Trumbull, and Tipton also wished
Wilson well. At the close of business Wilson went to his hotel
room to receive friends.[35] It had been a long climb up in the
world, and now that he was so near the top, he had no close
family to share the joy. In his hour of triumph, crowded with
visitors and congratulations, his thoughts turned to old friends
like Edward Pierce.[36]

Pundits of the time looked upon Wilson as a help to Grant.
"He is a strong man and will assist the ticket," said *The New
York Times*.[37] Assuming a down to earth attitude, *The Nation*
believed that, all things considered, he was better than the

majority of public men with whom he had been associated for so long. "The only objection that we see urged against him are on the general ground that he is purely a politician, no statesman, and given to time serving, and on the special ground that he ought to be odious to the Germans. The Germans, however, probably know that Mr. Wilson was a Know Nothing for strictly personal reasons, and has not, and never had, any fiercer hatred of the foreign born citizen than was requisite for a struggling young politician with his way to make in the world." They were rather pleased, too, that he was still a poor man after twenty years of public service and many opportunities to enrich himself.[38] The *Atlantic Monthly* thought that Wilson would be an asset in the South and in the doubtful states of Pennsylvania, Connecticut, and New Hampshire. Comparing Wilson to Greeley they commented, "Mr. Greeley goes to the other extreme; he is of the people too much to hold their respect, even when he arouses their enthusiasm; there is nothing august about him, and he does not rise with the occasion as Lincoln did, and the moods of his mind, like the tones of his voice are more apt to provoke a smile than to compel attention and deference. In these regards he is not the equal of Senator Wilson, whom in many points he closely resembles, though a man of far wider reach and power of mind."[39]

Writers regarded the platform as an extraordinary production which matched comprehensiveness with vagueness. Supposedly it was the work of reformers George W. Curtis, Dr. G. B. Loring, Wendell Phillips, S. B. Cummings, and Henry Blackwell, the husband of Lucy Stone, the women's rights leader. "The dupes especially aimed at by the whole document are thirteen in number," remarked *The Nation,* and listed them as Man; Colored man; The Irishman; The German man; The Free Trader; The Protectionist; The States Rights man; The Centralizer; The Capitalist; The Laborer; The Moderate Drinker; Women; The Opponent of Female Suffrage."[40]

Wilson received official notification on June 10, 1872 in a little ceremony at the Capitol, appropriately held in the room of the Committee on Military Affairs. Modestly, and typically, he offered the hand of reconciliation to all and paid tribute to Colfax and his adherents. "We have been personal and political friends for nearly 20 years, and it is a source of profound satisfaction to me that our personal relations have not been disturbed by the recent contest."[41]

His letter of acceptance a few days later looked to a future of equality for all, and touched upon almost all elements of the platform. He proposed civil service reform, bounties to disabled soldiers and sailors, reduction of the national debt and interest rates, careful encouragement of voluntary immigration with zealous protection of the rights of adopted citizens, resumption of specie payments, encouragement of commerce, protection of the ballot box, abolition of franking privileges, adjustment of duties on imports to secure remunerative wages to labor, use of the public domain for homes for the people, a humane policy towards Indians, and enforcement of recent constitutional amendments. "To woman, too, and her new demands, it extends the hand of grateful recognition and proffers its most respectful inquiry. "He left no stone unturned. A Republican vote getter, he knew how to offer something for everyone. Foremost among the great social problems of the day was the labor question. "The Republican party accepts the duty of so shaping legislation as to secure a full protection and amplest field for capital, and for labor the creation of capital the largest opportunities and a just share of these two great servants of civilization."

Beyond this all encompassing recitation for the purpose of party formality, Wilson closed with an attempt to prevent future trouble over his Know Nothing connections by writing, "Having accepted for 36 years of my life the distinguishing doctrines of the Republican party of today; having, during years of that period, for their advancement subordinated all other issues, acting in and co-operating with political organizations with whose leading doctrines I sometimes had neither sympathy nor belief; having labored incessantly for many years to found and build up the Republican party, and during its existence taken an humble part in the grand work, I gratefully accept the nomination thus tendered, and shall endeavor, if it shall be ratified by the people, faithfully to perform the duties it imposes."[42]

But Wilson's new eminence did not bring joy to all of his longtime acquaintances in Massachusetts. John Palfrey accused him of using his old "truck and dicker" politics to get the nomination. James Russell Lowell regarded the Vice Presidential nominee as a more despicable demagogue than Grant. Richard

Henry Dana looked upon Grant as a lesser evil than Greeley, but "Henry Colbraith [*sic.*] makes me sick. Having discarded his trade as a shoemaker thirty years ago, he has tried to live as a gentleman, on politics, ever since." The narrow, aristocratic New England minds were not ready to forgive so crude a man as Henry Wilson, probably more so, because their bitterness blended with jealousy. With their background, education, connections, and talent it was incomprehensible to them how they could be overshadowed by this very common man.

One aristocrat, Robert Winthrop, expressed a kinder, although perplexed view of Wilson. During the campaign Wilson dropped strong hints to Winthrop, about a foreign mission for him, but Winthrop did not want to be drawn into endorsing the Grant administration. Nevertheless, Winthrop appreciated Wilson's thoughtfulness and felt that he meant well. He knew that no man had done more to halt his own Senatorial career twenty-two years ago than Wilson, and in the intervening years they had exchanged many hard knocks, "but in spite of all this I have acquired a sort of liking for him" and he thought it remarkable that Wilson could have attained his present position without any early advantages.[43]

Since Presidential candidates did not campaign in those days, Wilson led the stumping, a task for which no one was better suited. His Democratic-Liberal Republican counterpart, Governor B. Gratz Brown of Missouri, a man of some ability, proved to be a hindrance to his ticket when he made an indiscreet speech at a Yale banquet criticizing the East and getting drunk in the process. From that time on his candidacy was not treated seriously. At times the campaign became heated and bitter, but Wilson controlled himself well and never spoke unkindly of those who had broken away from their party.

A new campaign feature was the use of women speakers. Members of the Equal Rights Association had attended both national conventions to gain support for the women's movement and in some quarters they gained sympathy. Grant had appointed postmistresses, and Wilson always friendly to their cause, had introduced a bill early in the year to give women in the territories the right to vote and hold office. Wilson had known feminist Susan Anthony for many years, and it was said that he never passed through Philadelphia without taking tea with the lady orator, Anna Dickinson. The Equal Rights Association endorsed the Republicans, but despite his flirtation, Anna Dickinson turned down an offer from Wilson to campaign and accepted one from Whitelaw Reid for $10,000 to speak for Greeley. Sadly, however, she never collected her $10,000. Some leaders of the Equal Rights group received a small subsidy from the Republican National Committee and they conducted a number of mass meetings.[44]

Wilson made an effective campaigner, but the Liberal Republicans gave him some stormy days by tagging him as an ex-Know Nothing with lingering racial prejudices. One speech ascribed to Wilson presented him as a hate monger, but it was obviously a forgery and fell short of its mark. The speech slandered "Dutchmen" and Irishmen by calling them "brutal," "degraded," "villains," and "ruffians." Schuyler Colfax wrote to him that this exact speech had been attributed to him in 1868 by hostile newspapers all over the Union.[45] About two weeks later Wilson wrote confidentially to a friend, probably William Claflin, that this speech was "put on" John Wilson of Indiana in 1858, exposed by the *Tribune* in 1860, and "put on" Colfax in 1868. "Colfax writes me that it cost no votes to us in that year—it will harm no one now."[46] When Wilson returned to Natick he publicly revealed this story in a hometown address and added, "Now the *New York Tribune*, which denounced it as a forgery in 1860, says I wanted to deny I had any association with the Native American Party. Well, good God! I never thought of denying that."[47]

Prosperous times enabled the regular Republicans to take credit for steady payment of the national debt, good credit, the fall in gold premium, and an economical administration which reduced taxes. When the Liberal Republicans presented Greeley as pro-labor, the regulars countered with Henry Wilson who had supported the Eight Hour Labor Bill for workmen employed by the government, and he became known throughout the campaign as the "father of the eight hour law."[48]

Early in September the *New York Sun* published letters which appeared to implicate a number of Republicans in the Credit Mobilier scandal, but there were too many groundless charges in the air, and too few facts, which gave the appearance of nothing more than campaign propaganda. Serious exposures revealed after the election might have made a difference in the results if they had shown up sooner.[49] Wilson's old friend, Samuel Bowles, publisher of *The Springfield Republican,* may not have been totally unbiased or completely informed, but he held Oakes Ames, the leading force of Credit Mobilier, in low regard. "You know very well," he wrote Henry Dawes, "that if you and Wilson and Washburne could tell what you actually know about Oakes Ames' business and other business at both ends of the avenue at Washington, I should be justified in all I have said about them; not perhaps in supporting Greeley. . . . but in denouncing Ames as a briber and in opposing the re-election of Gen. Grant."[50]

The scandalous rumblings continued, but they did not prevent the election of Grant and Wilson. Railroad lobbies had operated in Washington for years, and they appeared to get their way much of the time in land grants directly from Congress or from Western states to which Congress granted the public domain for railroad subsidies. By 1871 direct and indirect land grants to railroads amounted to 160 million acres, conservatively valued at $335 million. The roads stubbornly, and often crudely, sought preferential treatment and it was discovered that Congressman Oakes Ames of Massachusetts had distributed shares in Credit Mobilier among Senators and Representatives, where, by his own admission, it would do him the most good. The impact of these revelations grew until they became the biggest story in Washington, and the economic crash of 1873 magnified the indiscretions. Accusations, investigations, and prosecutions persisted until the next Presidential election.

Credit Mobilier was the construction company for the Union Pacific Railroad, but actually they were one and the same organization. The men who directed one, directed the other, and the stockholders were identical. Credit Mobilier profits became Union Pacific profits. Oakes Ames, the leader, found that he had many defenders even after he was expelled from the House of Representatives. The company faced great hazards and obstacles in building the road across the country. Gangs of men worked day and night in all kinds of weather, and frequently fought Indians along the way. To prudent capitalists the venture was a wild waste of money.

Not infrequently darkness quickly follows the bright light of victory, and Wilson soon had to pay a price for his new glory. Mention of Wilson's connection with Credit Mobilier first appeared in a newspaper about the time he attended a large public meeting during the Presidential campaign. George Hoar later related that General James Hawley, one of the speakers on the platform, told Wilson that his name had been mentioned as one of the owners of Credit Mobilier stock. Wilson replied that he never owned any such stock, and Hawley, in his speech alluded to the subject and said that he was authorized by Wilson to say that he was not involved. More deliberately, in September 1872 Wilson authorized a dispatch to *The New York Times* which contradicted a statement that he owned any of the stock. It was true. Wilson did not own any such stock, but Mrs. Wilson did, and his omission and lack of frankness concerning this detail made his position more difficult. But the blow did not fall until after the election.

In a House investigation convened in December 1872 an Oakes Ames list of Congressional Union Pacific stockholders divulged the name of Wilson along with Blaine, Colfax, Dawes, Boutwell, and others. There were some extenuating circumstances about the Wilson ownership which softened the public criticism. Still, the association hurt him severely. Wilson was not naive, and, at best, his connection with Credit Mobilier showed a serious lapse of judgment.

The money for the stock purchase had come from a happy occasion when the Wilsons celebrated their twenty-fifth wedding anniversary late in 1865 with the help of about fifteen hundred friends and neighbors. Natick had never seen anything like it. Many moguls were on hand including Hannibal Hamlin, Oakes Ames, and Charles Sumner. The couple received a number of gifts, one was a silver service set, another, an envelope designated especially for Mrs. Wilson which contained $3810 contributed by a number of friends. It was a lot of money, probably the most cash that the Wilsons had ever possessed at a single time, but the custom of receiving such a gift was not unusual then and *The Natick Times* proudly reported the affair.[51]

But the trouble came when Mrs. Wilson consulted a Mr. McMurtrie about investing it. McMurtrie, a counsel for Oakes Ames, read a statement on direct testimony that, "I recommended twenty shares of the (Union Pacific) stock for $2000 and the money was paid some months afterward; she objected to the investment, and I felt bound from what had occurred to take it off her hands and return the money, which I did."[52]

The testimony had a ring of truth and was generally accepted since the records bore out the return of the money. But the episode damaged Wilson's reputation even though the Senate investigating Committee let him off easily. They declared, "The committee does not believe that Sen. W. is affected by the transaction with Ames. But they feel constrained to advert, in this connection to the fact that on the 15th of Sept. last, Mr. W. authorized to be sent to the public press of N.Y. a dispatch which, in effect, is regarded as an unqualified denial that he ever obtained from Oakes Ames or any other person, the slightest interest in the C.M., and to remark that the dispatch was calculated to convey to the public an erroneous impression."[53]

The Credit Mobilier stir prevented Wilson from resigning his seat as quickly as he had anticipated. Upon the advice of older Senators he decided to remain in the Senate until the close of the session so that he would not give the impression that he was trying to escape Washington while the Senate investigation took place. So he did not officially give up his duties as Senator from Massachusetts until March 3, 1873.[54]

Barely missing ruin, the Wilson inaugural ceremony went off as scheduled. Grant's friends had intended that his second inauguration would be more impressive than the first, but severe cold and grey skies cut down the crowds and festivities. Nevertheless, the galleries filled with richly dressed ladies, diplomats in court dress, and military and naval officers in full, gold-trimmed uniforms. At 11:45 A.M. Wilson entered the Senate Chamber and sat at the right of the Vice President's desk. Immediately following him were feeble Chief Justice Chase, and other Justices of the Supreme Court. At three minutes to twelve, President Grant, cabinet members, and senatorial escorts entered to witness Wilson take the oath of office.[55]

As the new Vice President, Wilson used his influence to unify the Republican Party. He helped to restore Sumner to the party fellowship, and prepared the way for the re-election of his old colleague to the Senate. According to Thurlow Weed, Wilson also appealed to Grant to strengthen and elevate the administration by associating with Secretary of State Hamilton Fish and other men of talent, experience, and integrity, but he was ignored.[56] Perhaps in an effort to build a better public image for himself, Wilson also refused to accept back pay voted by the previous Congress and requested that the Secretary of the Treasury devote his share to payment of the public debt. The gesture was not lost when the press picked up the story. The *New York Times* called it an "honest act."[57]

Trouble still followed Wilson. Less than three months after he took office, he suffered a stroke. The attack, which distorted his face, was kept from the public. In strictest confidence he wrote to the ailing Sumner, "I am conquered and must submit."[58] Mrs. Claflin cared for Wilson and early in June reported to Sumner that he was improving. Sumner replied, "I wish I could help him; he must help himself by abnegation. I have often trembled for him, knowing his constitutional tendency, especially since his superadded literary labor. His work on that book was very much that of a horse in a street-car, one constant pull."[59]

Reports about Wilson's illness appeared in the newspapers in June, but they were either vague or attempted to make things look better than they were.[60] During the summer Wilson went to the Massachusetts seashore, and by late July confirmation appeared in the press that he had been seriously ill and that there was a question whether or not he would return to office. Extremely sensitive about his condition, Wilson did as much as he could to allay fears. In August he appeared in Boston and told everyone that he was improving rapidly. By October he was sufficiently well to correspond on political matters, but in December he turned down an invitation from Susan Anthony because his physician forbade public speaking at the risk of death. Nevertheless, when Congress convened in the same month Wilson attended the first day to pointedly greet Sumner in the hope of harmonizing discordant factions. Sumner, no less ill than Wilson, thought that his own case was less menacing. "Wilson's work on his book," he worriedly told Francis Bird, "will bring death or worse." Still, Sumner was the first to die.[61]

In January Wilson showed up at the National Woman Suffrage Convention at Washington and could not resist saying a few words. "I wish to simply say that I am under imperative orders to make no speeches on any subject. I will add, however, that twenty years ago I came to the conclusion that my wife, my mother, and my sisters were as much entitled to the right of suffrage as myself, and I have not changed my mind since." To the delighted ladies in the audience Mrs. Anthony announced that, "Vice President Wilson is the first Vice President we have ever had who was in favor of woman suffrage."[62]

Early in 1874, Charles Sumner passed away. Wilson was very conscious that his fellow participants in the antislavery battle were falling by the wayside. Stevens, Wilmot, Giddings, Lovejoy, Seward, Chase, and Hale were all gone. Still, the genuine loss of his old partner did not blind him to human failings. At a memorial service at Faneuil Hall, Robert Winthrop felt a sense of the ludicrous when he found himself wedged in between William Lloyd Garrison and Henry Wilson who were by no means indisposed to qualify their admiration for the departed. Since Winthrop was one of the pall bearers, he, unfortunately, did not think it becoming to repeat what they said.[63] A few days earlier Wilson had met James Fields at a charity fete at Mrs. Claflin's. The last time they had been at the Claflin's, Sumner had been with them. Wilson said that it was strange that Sumner was so often a failure. His style of writing was overlaid with quotations, often incorrect, his judgment was poor, and he knew little about people. Once, after he had made a critical speech about Grant, Sumner told Wilson that he had destroyed the President's chances of election and that there would not be three states that would vote for him. Wilson replied that there would be thirty states for Grant, and there were thirty. "But the wonder of it all," Wilson told Fields, "was to see how having made up his mind on a few subjects as to their right and wrong, his moral strength was such that he held his position through all odds—That was his greatness —no man can be more than one thing; that was his part of strength."[64]

In July Wilson sent John Palfrey a copy of his newly published second volume of the *Rise and Fall*. Palfrey noted that it was "a specimen of high courtesy." Wilson hated the intolerance and exclusiveness of the aristocratic New England mind and he was under no illusion about their opinion of him. But the Vice President could afford to be broad minded about the cultivated New Englander who was more than happy to have finally landed a job as Boston Postmaster. Palfrey's dear friend, Charles Francis Adams, must have gnashed his teeth, too, when he read public remarks that Wilson would be gratified to see the statesman take his seat in the Senate. The gratification never seemed to take the form of anything more helpful to Adams than a few general remarks for public consumption.[65]

The publication of Wilson's second volume was a great relief. The first had appeared in 1872. The two works, consisting of one hundred chapters, traced slavery from its introduction in 1620 to the opening of the Civil War, and there was little left out. "Of the living and the dead I have written as though I was to meet them in the presence of Him whose judgments are ever sure," he wrote in his preface. The third volume, planned for publication in 1875, was to describe the series of measures which extinguished the Slave Power, and reconstructed the Union on the basis of freedom and citizenship with civil and political rights for all. The books received good reviews, and in his sales promotion Wilson was able to quote some heady endorsements from such people as William Lloyd Garrison, John C. Whittier, and Lydia Maria Child. Aside from looking up references to themselves, it is questionable that many read the books from cover to cover.

Rumors persisted that Wilson would resign because of ill health. Morbidly sensitive, he continually scanned newspapers to see what they had to say about his condition. References to his health annoyed him, and he assured everyone that he never felt better in his life. He kept battling to regain his powers and made considerable progress. He did his best to be careful and by the end of the year he was sure that he did not feel any bad effects from his labors. He moved up and down the East Coast, Boston, New York, and Washington, occasionally making informal talks which included some remarks that sounded to some like veiled slights of the President. Wilson convinced himself that Grant was destroying the Republican Party and suspected that Grant was serious about a third term in the White House. He told James Garfield that Grant was more unpopular than Andrew Johnson was in his darkest days, that he was struggling for a third term, "in short that he is a millstone around the neck of our party that would sink it."[66]

The party organization bothered Wilson. The break with the Liberal Republicans had been a great blunder and he believed that they held the balance of power that would decide the election in 1876. He had no desire to inflict penalties upon the prodigal Republicans or on Southerners. Instead, he favored inviting the defected Republicans back into the party, and promoting liberal policies in the South. The "White League" activities in the South and the indifference of the Northerners alarmed him, however, and he asked Garrison to give the country a new warning. He wanted antislavery men to speak out again, but he met with little response.[67] Generally, however, he believed the success of the Republican Party required "broad, wise, and magnanimous policies" and was sure the country was against a third term for any man. He told John Alley that the Republicans would be out of power soon if they did not do something to change public sentiment.[68]

Wilson was now working about three hours a day and looked forward to increasing it to six hours soon. A trip to Europe appealed to him, but he finally decided not to set a precedent by being the first Vice President to leave the country. Still, he had an urge to keep on the move; travel became a necessity. His legs and speech still somewhat impaired, he climbed three flights of stairs at the New York Times office to talk to Alexander McClure about some public question he thought was important.[69]

The major piece of official business that he transacted was to cast the deciding vote in the Senate for the Equalization of Bounties Bill which Grant in turn vetoed. Even his best friend, William Claflin, thought Wilson's heart was right, but his head was wrong on this measure. Hamilton Fish regarded the bill as a dangerous piece of political buncombe. It was meant to increase bounties for the three year recruits who had enlisted early in the war and saw heavy fighting. Later recruits had been given $300 bounties, which was $200 more than the men who had joined up early received. Estimates to remedy the injustice varied between $59 million and $100 million. Opponents argued that no such sum was due since payments of $60 million, considered final, had already been made. Also, the Treasury Department, with reduced receipts, could not bear the burden. Even if it was only a vote getting maneuver, Wilson's vote was not out of keeping with his career. Whenever he had to decide between men and money, he chose men.[70]

In the spring Wilson made a six weeks tour of the South and West, allegedly for his health. But he attended twelve dinners, twenty-three receptions, and made twenty-nine speeches which

he found invigorating. When accused of playing politics, he vehemently claimed that the trip was for his health, and that he
had not made any political speeches. He talked on law and
order, peace, industry, natural development, temperance, and
justice to the black man. He conversed for a few moments in the
streets of Memphis with Mrs. Jefferson Davis, and visited the
sick bed of the dissident Democrat John Breckinridge. But this
only made his critics more suspicious. The "wandering Vice President" was "too unanimous," he was the "victim of Presidential
aspirations." Not too convincingly, he replied that he had neither
money, patronage, nor press to back him in such an ambition. At
the same time he denied lack of respect for the President. "My
opposition to the third term folly has been construed, too, into
opposition to the President." He felt newspapers were trying to
start a quarrel between Grant and himself. He did not see anything in the Constitution or the traditions of the people that
forbid a Vice President to entreat or advise political associates
to heed lessons of experience. He reminded his critics that eighteen
months ago he had warned his fellow Republicans of impending
peril in the Congressional elections. They called him an alarmist
and told him not to play the part of a prophet, but disaster came
on election day. Wilson may have been sincere in his disclaimers
of Presidential aspirations, but Thurlow Weed thought Wilson's
last years were spoiled by his unreasonable and unquenchable
desire to reach the White House. "For the last year or two his
ambition got the better of his judgment. Like most men spoken
of for the Presidency, the thought came to possess him. It was
his misfortune, not an offense."[71]

Wilson may not have fooled himself about his health or ambitions, but it was his nature not to give up, to keep fighting until
the end. He confided to Mrs. Claflin that he would try to fight
the battle of life even though he did so with a "heavy heart and
brain." In a rare philosophical mood, he advised a group of young
men that life was not a brilliant parade or holiday warfare. "It is
a stern, continuous never ceasing conflict. . . . Before you the
embattled hosts of ambition, of avarice, and of adverse and
mighty interests will contest and dispute every step of your advance. . . . Wearied with the never ceasing conflicts, by disappointments and losses, the harmonies of your feelings will be
rudely jarred, and your natures grow sterner and harsher. The

confident hopes and high raised expectations that now make the
smiling future gleam and glitter before you, may lead to perplexing doubts and chilling distrusts. Even the greatest of earth's
losses, a believing heart, may pass away from you." But, whatever their fate, he pleaded that they strive to keep the heart hopeful and trustful, and to respond to the appeal of want and the cry
of pain. "Then, when the possessions of earth are vanishing, the
passing soul will see the heavenly mansion in the Father's house
prepared by him who will say 'In as much as ye have done it unto
one of the least of these my brethren, ye have done it unto me.'"
It did not sound like the message of a Presidential candidate. Still,
he kept on going, and wherever he went he preached unity.[72]

Wilson arrived in Washington on November 10 in a weakened
condition. He had suffered an acute pain in the back for some
days and while in New York during the week had hot irons applied without affect. Thinking that a warm bath might give
relief, he went to the Capitol baths on the morning of the eleventh.
After the bath he went to the barber shop and while in the chair
he rolled his head in a convulsive manner. Attendants immediately
applied cold water to his head and rubbed his limbs with whiskey
and salt. Dr. Baxter, an army man, summoned at Wilson's request,
found nothing to indicate brain lesions or paralysis. Taken to his
own room at the Capitol, Wilson rested on a plain oak bed, and
there he remained during his last sickness tended by officers of
the Senate. Over his head hung the celebrated portrait of Washington by Rembrandt Peale, but it was a cheerless scene, and there
were no women about to nurse him.

When Wilson's condition worsened he received a morphine
injection under the shoulder, but it did no good. The pains in his
back remained and his extremities were cold. He was well rubbed,
and after a hypodermic injection of a half dram of whiskey his
pulse became stronger. Postmaster General Jewell remained with
him the first night. The next few days and nights were restless
ones. Once, at least, he got out of bed and paced the room for
two or three minutes, and at other times seemed comfortable. He
slept with the aid of "bromide of potassia and morphis, followed
by hyoscyamus." President Grant visited for about ten minutes.
Other callers were Associate Justice Clifford, James Garfield,
Senator Morrill of Vermont, and George Bancroft. At times
Wilson conversed easily, read newspapers, and enjoyed the com-

pany of friends more than doctors. He drank beef tea and chicken broth, and ate scraped raw beef, and made plans to return to Natick. On the sixteenth he had a bad night and Dr. Baxter complained that he received too many letters which he insisted upon reading. He requested that friends refrain from writing because it caused too much excitement, but bouquets and letters flowed in from all parts of the country. Reports claimed that he was gaining, but he lost thirty pounds, and suffered from nervous depression. On the eighteenth he wanted to go out, but the doctors restrained him. On the twenty-second he passed away.[73]

NOTES

[1] *Natick Times,* Feb. 9, 1869.

[2] Wilson to William Claflin, March 1, 1869, Claflin MSS, RBH; Wilson to unknown person, March 20, 1869, Claflin MSS, RBH.

[3] Elias Nason to Wilson, June 10, 1870, Huntington Library; *Natick Bulletin,* June 4, 1870.

[4] Wilson to Mrs. Claflin, Feb. 3, 1869, Claflin MSS, RBH.

[5] *NYT,* Feb. 7, 1870.

[6] *NYT,* Feb. 26, 1870; McClure, *Recollections,* p. 253.

[7] *Cong. Globe,* 40 Cong., 3 Sess., p. 1627.

[8] *Ibid.,* 41 Cong., 2 Sess., p. 5161; *NYT,* Feb. 19, 1869.

[9] *Ibid.,* 42 Cong., 2 Sess., p. 4040.

[10] *Ibid.,* p. 553.

[11] Irwin Unger, *The Greenback Era. A Social and Political History of American Finance, 1865-1879* (Princeton: Princeton University Press, 1964), p. 66.

[12] *Cong. Globe,* 40 Cong., 3 Sess., p. 1434.

[13] *Ibid.,* 41 Cong., 2 Sess., p. 2835.

[14] *Ibid.,* 41 Cong., 1 Sess., p. 545.

[15] *Ibid.,* p. 672.

[16] Wilson to James Parton, July 26, 1869, Misc. Microfilm, HL.

[17] Wilson to William Lloyd Garrison, Aug. 19, 1869, Aug. 29, 1870, Rare Book Dept., Boston Public Library; Wilson to Eli Thayer, Oct. 18, 28, 1869, Brown University Library; Wilson to William Seward, May 23, 1870, University of Rochester; Wilson to Theodore Weld, June 11, 1870, Misc. Microfilm HL; Wilson to Gerrit Smith, July 23, 1869, Sept. 19, 1870, Oct. 14, Nov. 4, 1871, Syracuse University Library; Wilson to Cassius Clay, March 21, Nov. 6, 1871, Lincoln Memorial University.

[18] Wilson to William Claflin, July 20, 1871, Claflin MSS, RBH; Wilson to Clara Barton, Aug. 5, 1871, Smith College Library.

[19] Mary B. Claflin, *Under the Old Elms* (Boston: Thomas A. Crowell, 1895), pp. 30-33.

[20] Samuel Hunt to "My dear babies," March 2, 1870, Brown University Library; *First Congregational Church, Natick, Mass.,* 1877, pp. 68, 69.

[21] *Cong. Globe,* 41 Cong., 3 Sess., p. 670.

[22] Wilson to Hamilton Fish, Oct. 31, 1870, Hamilton Fish MSS, LC.

[23] Charles Sumner to unknown person, n.d., Sumner Misc. Personal Papers, LC; Pierce, *Memoir and Letters,* IV, 454, 497.

[24] *Cong. Globe,* 42 Cong., 1 Sess., pp. 34, 42, 52.

[25] E. D. Ross, *The Liberal Republican Movement* (New York: Henry Holt & Co., 1919), pp. 1-44; McClure, *Recollections,* pp. 290, 291.

[26] Pierce, *Memoir and Letters,* IV, 521, 531.

[27] *NYT,* Jan. 24, 26; Feb. 17, 1872.

[28] *NYT,* Feb. 24, 29, March 30, 1872; *The Nation,* April 25, 1872.

[29] *NYT,* April 11, 1872.

[30] Willard H. Smith, *Schuyler Colfax* (Indianapolis: Indiana Historical Bureau, 1952), pp. 324-347.

[31] *NYT,* June 2, 3, 1872; Smith, *Colfax,* pp. 357, 358.

[32] *NYT,* June 4, 6, 1872; *The Nation,* June 13, 1872.

[33] George D. Seilhamer, *Leslie's History of the Republican Party* (4 vols., New York: L. A. Williams Publishing, 1899), I, 303; Ross, *Liberal Republican,* p. 117; Curtis, *Republican Party,* II, 27, 28.

[34] *NYT,* June 7, 1872.

[35] *Ibid.*

[36] Wilson to E. L. Pierce, June 11, 1972, Misc. Wilson Letters, HL.

[37] *NYT,* June 7, 1872.

[38] *The Nation,* June 13, 1872, pp. 381, 387.

[39] *Atlantic Monthly,* August 1872, pp. 255, 256.

[40] *The Nation,* June 13, 1872, pp. 381, 387.

[41] *Proceedings—Republican National Union Convention, 1872.* Convened at Academy of Music, Philadelphia, June 5, 1872.

[42] *Ibid.*

[43] Robert C. Winthrop, Jr., *A Memoir of Robert G. Winthrop* (Boston: Little, Brown & Co., 1897), p. 281; Samuel Shapiro, *Dana,* p. 294; Denis T. Lynch, *The Wild Seventies* (New York: D. Appleton-Century Co., 1941), p. 175.

[44] *NYT,* Jan. 19, 1872; Katherine Anthony, *Susan B. Anthony: Her Personal History and Her Era* (New York: Doubleday & Co., 1954), pp. 273, 275.

[45] Schuyler Colfax to Wilson, Aug. 19, 1872, Huntington Library; *NYT,* Aug. 1, 1872.

[46] Wilson to unknown person, Sept. 3, 1872, Claflin MSS, RBH.

[47] *NYT,* Sept. 7, 10, 1872.

[48] *Cong. Globe,* 40 Cong., 1 Sess., p. 413; 40 Cong., 2 Sess., p. 3426; Montgomery, *Beyond Equality,* p. 373.

[49] Ross, *Liberal Republican,* pp. 150-190.

[50] Samuel Bowles to Henry Dawes, Sept. 20, 1872, Henry Dawes MSS, LC.

[51] *Natick Times,* Nov. 4, 1865; *NYT,* Feb. 16, 1872; Hoar, *Autobiography,* I, 318, 319.

[52] *NYT,* March 5, 1873; James C. Blaine, *Twenty Years of Congress* (2 vols., Norwich, Conn. H. Bill Publishing Co., 1884-86), II, 537.

[53] Smith, *Colfax,* 405n. Cites U. S. Senate Reports, 42 Congress, 3 Session, IV.

[54] H. L. Dawes MMS, LC, Wilson to Dawes, February 6, 1873; J. B. Crawford, *The Credit Mobilier of America* (Boston: C. W. Calkins & Co., 1880).

[55] *NYT,* March 5, 1873; Blaine, *Twenty Years of Congress,* II, 537.

[56] William P. Phillips to Wilson, Feb. 12, 19, 1873, telegram Feb. 21, 1873, Misc. Wilson Letters, HL; McClure, *Recollections,* 290; Thurlow Weed, *Life of Thurlow Weed* (2 vols., Boston, New York: Houghton Mifflin & Co., 1883, 1884), II, 520.

[57] *Barre Gazette,* April 4, 1873; *NYT,* April 3, 1873.

[58] Pierce, *Memoir and Letters,* IV, 562, 563.

[59] *Ibid.*

[60] *NYT,* June 23, 1873.

[61] Wilson to Mrs. Anthony, Dec. 9, 1873, Huntington Library; Charles Sumner to Francis Bird, Dec. 26, 1873, Bird MSS, HL; *NYT*, July 16, 29, Aug. 6, 11, 1873; Pierce, *Memoir and Letters*, IV, 564.

[62] *NYT*, Jan. 17, 1874.

[63] Winthrop, *Memoir*, p. 286.

[64] James Fields, *Diary*, March 1874, MHS.

[65] Wilson to John G. Palfrey, July 8, 1874, Palfrey MSS, HL; *NYT*, April 28, 1874.

[66] *NYT*, Jan. 18, 1875; Theodore C. Smith, *The Life and Letters of James Abram Garfield 1831-1877* (2 vols., New Haven: Yale University Press, 1925), I, 519.

[67] Wilson to William Lloyd Garrison, Dec. 17, 1874, Rare Book Dept., Boston Public Library.

[68] J. B. Alley to Henry Dawes, Jan. 31, 1875, Henry Dawes MSS, LC; William B. Hesseltine, *Ulysses S. Grant, Politician* (New York: F. Ungar, 1957), p. 373.

[69] Wilson to Mrs. Claflin, Jan. 17, 1875, Claflin MSS, RBH; NYT, April 10, 1875.

[70] William Claflin to Edward Pierce, April 1, 1875, E. L. Pierce Misc. Letters, HL; *NYT*, March 16, 1875; Nevins, *Hamilton Fish*, p. 760.

[71] Wilson to Mrs. Claflin, June 10, 1875, Claflin MSS, RBH; *NYT*, June 6, 25, Nov. 11, 1875; *NYDT*, Nov. 24, 1875.

[72] Wilson to Mrs. Claflin, August 5, 1875, Claflin MSS, RBH; *NYT*, January 26, 1875.

[73] *NYT*, Nov. 11, 12, 13, 14, 15, 17, 23, 1875.

11

Conclusion

Tributes flowed in from everywhere, but at least one aristocrat, Richard Henry Dana, bitter to the end, privately summed up Wilson's career for his son, "not cognizant of honor; given to maneuver, excessively ambitious of public posts. . . . He always tried to keep out of public life in Massachusetts highly educated and high minded men who might interfere with his views for himself."[1] Lack of understanding between the two sons of New England was complete. Notwithstanding his detractors, Henry Wilson led a full political life, a sad personal life, and an unsuccessful financial life. His entire estate was valued at $6,000.[2] Thurlow Weed, a man who understood the workings of government, made an unavoidable comparison with the other Senator from Massachusetts. "The country will always overestimate Sumner, I think, though I dislike to say it. Wilson was more useful than Sumner, though not so cultured."[3]

The early experiences of the "bound out" boy, son of a neer-do-well father, must have developed a strong psychological motivation to get ahead in the world.[4] The dreams of youth turned into real ambitions. The years of servitude must have had something to do, too, with his deep and genuine conviction that there should be equal rights for everyone. The young days were hard, but there were also friends along the way who saw a spark of fire in his make up and lent a helping hand. It was probably

243

his boundless energy that they quickly recognized. There was the kindly lady in Farmington, the Congregational minister at Natick, and even such an austere person as Charles Francis Adams in the early forties.

From his first days at the State House at Boston, and at the Constitutional Convention, Wilson used his place as a seat of action, and in the process, he learned how to become a lawmaker. He was not afraid to become embroiled in a battle, and he withstood all the criticism that came his way. The art of getting a group of men to move together for any cause requires skill, and the possession of a combination of personal qualities that can be respected by his fellow workers. Wilson's open personality was appreciated by those with whom he worked. He was hearty, generous, and optimistic under the most trying circumstances, and he never stopped working. They liked him, and when he tried to connive, as he sometimes did, his ulterior motives were immediately transparent. Wilson was no respecter of political parties, but he would have remained with the Whig Party throughout his life if it had taken a strong antislavery position. The party was nothing more than an instrument to work for freeing the slave. But in the transformation of parties in Massachusetts and in the nation, Wilson was a valuable man to help with the work of organization.

Henry Wilson is an obscure figure today. Not one person in ten thousand knows the name. Occasionally he serves as an example of a Radical Republican, and until very recently such reference was considered derogatory, but there is rarely an indication of his faults, virtues, or achievements. The battle for a great cause, the personal skirmishes, the bitter jealousies, and the forceful ambition have left scarcely a trace. So why bother with Henry Wilson?

Perhaps the answer lies in the belief that history is made up of more than great men and great events, or the special brand of rediscovery that categorizes people into classes and customs, but leaves individuals to anonymity. History is a record of life which is neither broad classifications of eras nor narrow actions of a few stars. There are lesser roles which are still significant in any period.

Henry Wilson was not a great man, but he was an unusual one. If his talents were modest he, at least, had an abundance of energy and used his powers to their utmost without despair over lack of greater abilities. He found a cause early in life and the cause elevated him. It gave him the strength and reason to enter circles that otherwise might have been forbidden. In defeat and success he remained true to a single purpose.

It was said that Wilson was a self-seeker, and he was. He sought office avidly. He liked the glory, but he also used the authority that the office possessed to get things done. The title was never an end in itself. His severest critics were other self-seekers whose ambitions were hindered by his success. Henry Wilson was not in the image of Charles Francis Adams, John Palfrey, Samuel Gridley Howe, or Richard Henry Dana. Each, in his own way, could have accepted Wilson with a certain amount of forced understanding if he had only kept his place. They could have been generous about his shortcomings, restrained their condescension, and restricted their patronizing airs for the sake of the antislavery cause. He was a useful, energetic lieutenant who should have been a loyal supporter, not a difficult competitor. But Henry Wilson had something that his early aristocratic companions lacked. He had a toughness of fiber and resourcefulness that enabled him to enter the fray, scramble through each encounter, risk disaster, and still survive. He did things they did not even know how to do. He could mingle with "the boys" and enjoy it while they could only show resentment. He once told Charles Sumner that he did not want the endorsement of the "best society" in Boston until he was dead, and then he knew he would gain their support because "it endorses everything that is dead."[5] Perhaps he lacked their scruples, but their scruples do not always stand up under close scrutiny. It was easier for them to scorn his dynamic vulgarity than it was to admit a jealousy that blinds fair appraisal. It was easier for them to stand on principle than to fight the battle in the center of the grasping, scheming, cynical world of state and national politics.

There are many misconceptions about the antislavery cause. Sometimes forgotten are the wheels within wheels, the factional scraps, the disorganization. Slavery was attacked on many fronts by all kinds of people, writers, clergymen, teachers, lawyers, lecturers. Some were saints and some were sinners. Each fought according to his light and all. were needed. But the final battles for equal rights took place in the political parties and in Congress. Success required politicians who had the courage to face able opponents in the day to day business of government. Henry Wilson was one of those politicians and he deserves recognition for his contribution to the life of the country. He knew how to work, he knew how to work with people, and he looked for real accomplishments. He did not think a problem was solved with a speech. He was a practical Radical.

NOTES

1 Shapiro, *Dana,* p. 314. Quotes letter of RHD Jr. to RHD III, Nov. 22, 1875.
2 *Natick Bulletin,* Dec. 3, 10, 1875.
3 *NYDT,* Nov. 24, 1875.
4 *Natick Bulletin,* Jan. 28, 1876. Rev. Samuel Hunt, in a memorial address delivered in Natick on Jan. 16, 1876, said, "If the story be true that his attentions to his master's daughter were repelled because of his family and social position, is there wonder that treatment so unjust and senseless should have bred a mutiny in the young man's soul, and given birth to resolves that never lost their force until he died? . . . Thus enlightened and conscious of his superiority over the very people who were looking down upon him because of his plebian birth and poverty there is nothing strange that his whole nature revolted, and that he assumed an attitude of antagonism and defiance that never fully disappeared."
5 Wilson to Sumner, Sept. 1, 1853, Sumner MSS, HL.

Bibliographical Note

The Henry Wilson papers in the Library of Congress are few in number and not very helpful in studying his life, but to the best of my knowledge they are the only collection in existence. Other diaries and letters are far more helpful. The Charles Francis Adams Diary in the Massachusetts Historical Society is a valuable source concerning Wilson's activities from 1845 to 1855 and indicate the diarist's change in attitude as Wilson became increasingly powerful in the state. Other collections at the same location that lend insight are the John A. Andrew papers and the Edward Everett Diary. Everett clearly shows the snobbery and upper class feeling that Wilson faced, and the Andrew letters give a glimpse of the relationship between two conscientious men in key state and federal positions during wartime. The voluminous Charles Sumner papers at the Houghton Library at Harvard occasionally shed some light but they become scarce after Wilson joined Sumner in the Senate. The William Claflin papers at the Rutherford B. Hayes Library in Fremont, Ohio contain the best, although tantalizingly few, references to Wilson's personal life. The rest of the letters, personal or political, are scattered in libraries and historical societies throughout the country.

Among public documents the *Congressional Globe* is invaluable for Wilson's entire career as United States Senator and especially for the Reconstruction period.

Oddly enough, the *New York Daily Tribune, New York*

Times, and *New York Herald* are of greater assistance than the Boston papers. "Oliver," apparently Samuel Bowles, the Boston correspondent for the *New York Daily Tribune,* is a good source for information in the fifties.

Autobiographies and memoirs by contemporaries give some attention to Wilson. Among the more helpful are George S. Boutwell, *Reminiscences of Sixty Years in Public Affairs* (1902), George F. Hoar, *Autobiography of Seventy Years* (1903), Edward L. Pierce, *Memoirs and Letters of Charles Sumner* (1878-93), Mrs. William S. Robinson (ed.), *"Warrington" Pen Portraits* (1877), and Charles Sumner, *The Works of Charles Sumner* (1870-1883).

In recent years there have been a number of excellent biographies of contemporaries of Wilson which give important information about the times and offer different viewpoints. Among them are Irving Bartlett's well written *Wendell Phillips* (1961), David Donald, *Charles Sumner and the Coming of the Civil War* (1960), Martin B. Duberman, *Charles Francis Adams* (1961), Tilden G. Edelstein, *Strange Enthusiasm, A Life of Thomas Wentworth Higginson* (1968), Frank Otto Gatell, *John Gorham Palfrey and the New England Conscience* (1963), Samuel Shapiro, *Richard Henry Dana* (1961), and Benjamin P. Thomas and Harold M. Hyman, *Stanton: The Life and Times of Lincoln's Secretary of War* (1962). Somewhat earlier was the fine study of Nathaniel Banks by Fred Harrington, *Fighting Politician* (1948). To a surprising degree the lives of abolitionists and antislavery workers have become a battleground for today's radical, liberal, and conservative historians. This seems unfortunate, but I suppose it adds spice to the historiography of the times.

The important works of LaWanda and John H. Cox, *Politics, Principle and Prejudice 1865-66* (1963), and Eric McKittrick, *Andrew Johnson and Reconstruction* (1960), are especially helpful for developing an understanding of the period. David Montgomery has specialized in a phase of politics relating to Wilson in *Beyond Equality—Labor and the Radical Republicans 1862-1872* (1967). An excellent study written many years ago by E. D. Ross, *The Liberal Republican Movement* (1919) gives worthwhile background for the national campaign of 1872.

Bibliography

I. Source Materials

A. MANUSCRIPTS

Adams Family Papers, Massachusetts Historical Society.
Andrew, John A. Papers, Massachusetts Historical Society.
Bancroft, George. Papers, Massachusetts Historical Society.
Barton, Clara. Papers, Smith College Library.
Bird, Francis W. Papers, Harvard Library.
Chase, Salmon P. Papers, Historical Society of Pennsylvania.
Chase, Salmon P. Papers, Library of Congress.
Claflin, William Papers, Rutherford B. Hayes Library. Fremont, Ohio.
Dawes, Henry L. Papers, Library of Congress.
Everett, Edward. Papers, Massachusetts Historical Society.
Fish, Hamilton. Papers, Library of Congress.
Johnson, Andrew. Papers, Library of Congress.
Julian, George—Giddings, Joshua. Papers, Library of Congress.
Lawrence, Amos A. Papers, Massachusetts Historical Society.
Lincoln, Robert T. Papers, Library of Congress.
Mann, Horace. Papers, Massachusetts Historical Society.
Morgan, Edwin D. Papers, New York State Library.
Palfrey, John G. Papers, Harvard Library.
Pierce, Edward L. Papers, Harvard Library.
Robinson, Charles. Papers, Kansas State Historical Society.

249

Schouler, William. Papers, Massachusetts Historical Society.
Seward, William A. Papers, University of Rochester.
Stanton, Edwin M. Papers, Library of Congress.
Sumner, Charles. Papers, Harvard Library.
Webster, Daniel. Papers, Dartmouth College.
Wilson, Henry. Papers, Library of Congress.

B. GOVERNMENT PUBLICATIONS

Congressional Globe, 33-42 Congresses, 1855-1872.
Massachusetts General Court Legislator Documents—1842. House Report No. 22.
Massachusetts General Court Legislator Documents—1844. Senate Report No. 28.
Massachusetts General Court Legislator Documents—1846. House Report No. 89.

C. NEWSPAPERS AND PERIODICALS

1. The Daily and Political Press.
    American Bee
    Barre Gazette
    Boston Atlas
    Boston Commonwealth
    Boston Daily Whig
    Boston Journal
    Boston Morning Post
    Boston Republican
    The Liberator
    Natick Bulletin
    Natick Times
    National Anti-Slavery Standard
    New York Daily Tribune
    New York Evening Post
    New York Herald
    New York Times
    Salem Gazette
2. Journals of General Opinion.
    Atlantic Monthly
    The Nation

D. PROCEEDINGS

Massachusetts Constitutional Convention. Official Report of the Debates and Proceedings. Boston, 1853.

Republican National Union Convention Proceedings. Philadelphia, June 5, 1872.

E. PAMPHLETS, PRINTED SPEECHES

Massachusetts Anti-Slavery Society, 18th Annual Report. January 23, 1850.

Wilson, Henry. "Lecture on American Slavery" n.d. (1855?).

Wilson, Henry. "How Ought Workingmen to Vote in the Coming Election?" East Boston, October 15, 1860.

Wilson, Henry. "On Bill to Abolish Slavery in D. C." March 27, 1862.

Wilson, Henry. "Prohibition," April 15, 1867.

F. AUTOBIOGRAPHIES, MEMOIRS, AND COLLECTIONS OF PRINTED LETTERS

Adams, Henry. *The Education of Henry Adams*. New York: The Modern Library, 1931.

Bennett, Edwin C. *Musket and Sword—The Army of the Potomac*. Boston: Coburn Publishing Co., 1900.

Blaine, James G. *Twenty Years of Congress*. Norwich, Conn.: H. Bill Publishing Co., 1884-1886.

Boutwell, George S. *Reminiscences of Sixty Years in Public Affairs*. New York: McClure, Phillips & Co., 1902.

Child, Lydia Maria. *Letters*. Boston: Houghton Mifflin & Co., 1882.

Claflin, Mary B. *Under the Old Elms*. Boston: Thomas Y. Cromell, 1895.

Congdon, Charles T. *Reminiscences of a Journalist*. Boston: James R. Osgood & Co., 1880.

Hoar, George F. *Autobiography of Seventy Years*. New York: Charles Scribner's Sons, 1903.

McClure, Alexander. *Recollections of Half a Century*. Salem, Mass.: The Salem Press Co., 1902.

Pierce, Edward L. *Memoirs and Letters of Charles Sumner.* Boston: Roberts Brothers, 1878-93.

Richards, Laura E. (ed.). *Letters and Journal of Samuel Gridley Howe.* Boston: Dana Estes & Co., 1909.

Robinson, Mrs. William S. (ed.). *"Warrington" Pen Portraits.* Boston: Published by Mrs. W. S. Robinson, 1877.

Smith, Theodore. *The Life and Letters of James Abram Garfield 1831-1877.* New Haven: Yale University Press, 1925.

Sumner, Charles. *The Works of Charles Sumner.* Boston: Lee & Shepherd, 1870-1883.

Villard, Henry. *Memoirs of Henry Villard—Journalist and Financier.* Boston: Houghton Mifflin Co., 1904.

Weiss, John. *Life and Correspondence of Theodore Parker.* New York: D. Appleton Co., 1864.

Welles, Gideon. *The Diary of Gideon Welles.* Boston: Houghton Mifflin Co., 1911.

Winthrop, Robert C. Jr. *A Memoir of Robert C. Winthrop.* Boston: Little, Brown & Co., 1897.

G. BOOKS AND ARTICLES BY CONTEMPORARIES

Greenhow, Rose. *My Imprisonment.* London: Richard Bentley, 1863.

Mann, Jonathan B. "Henry Wilson's Boyhood." *The Historical Collections* of the Historical, Natural History and Library Society. South Natick, Mass. 1910.

Mann, Jonathan B. *The Life of Henry Wilson.* Boston: James R. Osgood & Co., 1872.

Nason, Elias and Russell, Thomas. *The Life and Public Service of Henry Wilson.* Boston: B. B. Russell, 1876.

Owen, Robert Dale. "Political Results from the Varioloid," *Atlantic Monthly,* XXXV, June 1875.

Parker, John L. and Carter, Robert C. *Henry Wilson's Regiment.* History of the Twenty-Second Massachusetts Infantry—The Second Company Sharpshooters and the Third Light Battery in the War of the Rebellion. Boston: The Regimental Association, 1887.

Schouler, James. "The Massachusetts Convention of 1853." *Proceedings* of the Massachusetts Historical Society, Nov. 1903.

H. MISCELLANEOUS PRIMARY

United States Senate Military Affairs Committee Record Book, 1861. National Archives.

Letters attributed to Henry Wilson and allegedly written to Rose Greenhow, 1861. National Archives.

Letters received by the War Department, 1861, 1862. National Archives.

II. SECONDARY MATERIALS

A. BOOKS: GENERAL HISTORIES, SPECIAL STUDIES, MONOGRAPHS.

Barnes, William H. *History of the 39th Congress of the United States,* New York: Harper & Bros., 1861.

Bentley, George R. *A History of the Freedmen's Bureau.* Philadelphia: University of Pennsylvania Press, 1955.

Bowers, Claude. *The Tragic Era.* New York: Halcyon House, 1929.

Curtis, Francis. *The Republican Party.* New York: G. P. Putnam's Sons, 1904.

Coulter, E. Merton. *The South During Reconstruction, 1865-1877.* Baton Rouge: Louisiana State University Press, 1947.

Cox, La Wanda and Cox, John H. *Politics, Principle and Prejudice 1865-66.* New York: Glencoe Free Press, 1963.

Duberman, Martin (ed.). *The Antislavery Vanguard: New Essays on the Abolitionists.* Princeton: Princeton University Press, 1965.

Fite, Emerson. *The Presidential Campaign of 1860.* New York: The Macmillan Co., 1911.

Gunderson, Robert G. *The Log Cabin Campaign.* Louisville: University of Kentucky Press, 1957.

Handlin, Oscar. *Boston's Immigrants—1790-1865.* Cambridge: Harvard University Press, 1941.

Hazard, Blanche Evans. *Organization of the Boot and Shoe Industry in Massachusetts Before 1875.* Cambridge: Harvard University Press, 1921.

Hesseltine, William B. *Lincoln and the War Governors.* New York: A. A. Knopf, 1948.

Huidekoper, Frederic L. *The Military Unpreparedness of the United States.* The Macmillan Co., 1915.

Kraditor, Aileen S. *Means and Ends in American Abolitionism.* New York: Pantheon Books, 1969.

Leech, Margaret. *Reveille in Washington 1860-1865.* New York: Harper & Bros., 1954.

Lynch, Denis T. *The Wild Seventies.* New York: D. Appleton Century Co., 1941.

McKittrick, Eric. *Andrew Johnson and Reconstruction.* Chicago: University of Chicago Press, 1960.

Meneely, A. Howard. *The War Department, 1861.* New York: Columbia University Press, 1928.

Montgomery, David. *Beyond Equality—Labor and the Radical Republicans—1862-1872.* New York: Alfred A. Knopf, 1967.

Nevins, Allan. *The Emergence of Lincoln.* New York: Charles Scribner's Sons, 1951.

Nye, Russel B. *Fettered Freedom.* East Lansing: Michigan State College Press, 1949.

Overdyke, W. D. *The Know Nothing Party in the South.* Baton Rouge: Louisiana State University Press, 1950.

Ross, E. D. *The Liberal Republican Movement.* New York: Henry Holt & Co., 1919.

Sefton, James E. *The United States Army and Reconstruction—1865-1877.* Baton Rouge: Louisiana State University Press, 1967.

Seilhamer, George D. *Leslie's History of the Republican Party.* New York: L. A. Williams Publishing, 1899.

Shannon, Fred A. *Organization and Administration of the Union Army.* Cleveland. Arthur Clark Co., 1928.

Unger, Irwin. *The Greenback Era, A Social and Political History of American Finance, 1865-1879.* Princeton: Princeton University Press, 1964.

Williams, Kenneth. *Lincoln Finds A General.* New York: The Macmillan Co., 1949.

Wilson, Henry. *History of the Anti-Slavery Measures of the 37th and 38th Congresses.* Boston: Walker, Fuller & Co., 1865.

Wilson, Henry. *History of the Reconstruction Measures of the 39th and 40th Congresses—1865-68.* Hartford: Hartford Publishing Co., 1868.

Wilson, Henry. *History of the Rise and Fall of the Slave Power in America.* Boston: James R. Osgood & Co., 1875-1877.

B. BOOKS: BIOGRAPHIES

Anthony, Katherine. *Susan B. Anthony: Her Personal History and Her Era.* New York: Doubleday & Co., 1954.

Barnes, T. W. *Life of Thurlow Weed.* Boston: Houghton Mifflin Co., 1884.

Bartlett, Irving. *Wendell Phillips, Brahmin Radical.* Boston: Beacon Press, 1961.

"By his children." *Francis William Bird—A Biographical Sketch.* Boston: Privately printed, 1897.

Crandall, A. W. *The Early History of the Republican Party.* Boston: R. G. Badger, 1930.

Donald, David. *Charles Sumner and the Coming of the Civil War.* New York: Alfred Knopf, 1960.

Duberman, Martin B. *Charles Francis Adams.* Boston: Houghton Mifflin Co., 1961.

Edelstein, Tilden G. *Strange Enthusiasm. A Life of Thomas Wentworth Higginson.* New Haven: Yale University Press, 1968.

Fuess, Claude M. *The Life of Caleb Cushing.* New York: Harcourt, Brace & Co., 1923.

Gatell, Frank Otto. *John Gorham Palfrey and the New England Conscience.* Cambridge: Harvard University Press, 1963.

Hamilton, Holman. *Zachary Taylor—Soldier in the White House.* New York: The Bobbs Merrill Co., Inc., 1951.

Hamlin, Charles E. *The Life and Times of Hannibal Hamlin.* Cambridge: The Riverside Press, 1899.

Harper, Ida. *Life and Work of Susan B. Anthony.* Indianapolis: The Hollenbeck Press, 1948.

Harrington, Fred H. *Fighting Politician.* Philadelphia: University of Pennsylvania Press, 1948.

Hesseltine, William B. *Ulysses S. Grant, Politician.* New York: F. Ungar, 1957.

Kamm, Samuel H. *The Civil War Career of Thomas A. Scott.* Philadelphia: University of Pennsylvania Press, 1940.

Kirwan, Albert D. *John J. Crittenden.* Louisville: University of Kentucky Press, 1962.

Korngold, Ralph. *Thaddeus Stevens*. New York: Harcourt, Brace & Co., 1955.

Lawrence, William. *Life of Amos A. Lawrence*. Boston: Houghton Mifflin Co., 1888.

Merriam, George. *Life and Times of Samuel Bowles*. New York: The Century Co., 1885.

Mordell, Albert. *Quaker Militant*. Boston: Houghton Mifflin Co., 1933.

Nevins, Allan. *Hamilton Fish—The Inner History of the Grant Administration*. New York: Dodd, Mead & Co., 1936.

Nevins, Allan. *Fremont-Pathmarker of the West*. New York: D. Appleton-Century Co., 1939.

Nicolay, John G. and Hay, John. *Abraham Lincoln—A History*. New York: The Century Co., 1914.

Pearson, Henry G. *The Life of John A. Andrew*. Boston: Houghton Mifflin Co., 1904.

Ross, Ishbel. *First Lady of the South*. New York: Harper & Bros., 1958.

Seward, Frederick W. *William Henry Seward*. New York: Derby & Miller, 1891.

Shapiro, Samuel. *Richard Henry Dana*. East Lansing: Michigan State College Press, 1961.

Sherwin, Oscar. *Prophet of Liberty*. New York: Bookman Associates, 1958.

Smith, Willard H. *Schuyler Colfax*. Indianapolis: Indiana Historical Bureau, 1952.

Thomas, Benjamin P. *Abraham Lincoln*. New York: Alfred A. Knopf, 1954.

Thomas, Benjamin P. and Hyman, Harold M. *Stanton: The Life and Times of Lincoln's Secretary of War*. New York: Alfred A. Knopf, 1962.

Van Deusen, Glyndon. *The Life of Henry Clay*. Boston: Little Brown & Co., 1937.

Van Deusen, Glyndon. *William Henry Seward*. New York: Oxford University Press.

Weigley, Russell F. *Quartermaster General of the Union Army*. New York: Columbia University Press, 1959.

Weisenberger, Francis P. *The Life of John McLean*. Columbus: The Ohio University Press, 1937.

C. ARTICLES

Carman, Harry J. and Luthin, Richard H. "Some Aspects of the Know Nothing Movement Reconsidered." *The South Atlantic Quarterly,* XXXIX, April 1940.

Mirak, Robert. "John Quincy Adams, Jr. and the Reconstruction Crisis," *The New England Quarterly,* XXXV, June 1962.

Shapiro, Samuel. "The Conservative Dilemma: The Massachusetts Constitutional Convention of 1853." *The New England Quarterly,* XXXIII, June 1960.

Sigaud, Louis A. "Mrs. Greenhow and the Rebel Spy Ring," *Maryland Historical Society Magazine,* XLI, Sept. 1946.

D. UNPUBLISHED DOCTORAL DISSERTATION

Bean, William G. *"The Transformation of Parties in Massachusetts . . . from 1848 to 1860."* Harvard University, 1922.

E. MISCELLANEOUS SECONDARY

Johnson, Allen, and Malone, Dumas (eds.), *Dictionary of American Biography.* New York: Charles Scribner's Sons, 1928 ff.

Index

258